Pilgrims and Popes

Pilgrims and Popes

A Concise History of Pre-Reformation Christianity in the West

TOBIAS BRANDNER

Forewords by
HENRY S. WILSON
and LIMUEL R. EQUINA

CASCADE *Books* • Eugene, Oregon

PILGRIMS AND POPES
A Concise History of Pre-Reformation Christianity in the West

Copyright © 2019 Tobias Brandner. All rights reserved. Except for brief quotations in critical publications or reviews, no part of this book may be reproduced in any manner without prior written permission from the publisher. Write: Permissions, Wipf and Stock Publishers, 199 W. 8th Ave., Suite 3, Eugene, OR 97401.

Cascade Books
An Imprint of Wipf and Stock Publishers
199 W. 8th Ave., Suite 3
Eugene, OR 97401

www.wipfandstock.com

PAPERBACK ISBN: 978-1-5326-6214-0
HARDCOVER ISBN: 978-1-5326-6215-7
EBOOK ISBN: 978-1-5326-6216-4

Cataloguing-in-Publication data:

Names: Brandner, Tobias, author. | Wilson, Henry S., foreword. | Equina, Limuel R., foreword.

Title: Pilgrims and popes : a concise history of pre-reformation Christianity in the west / Tobias Brandner ; with forewords by Henry S. Wilson and Limuel R. Equina.

Description: Eugene, OR: Cascade Books, 2019 | Includes bibliographical references and index.

Identifiers: ISBN 978-1-5326-6214-0 (paperback) | ISBN 978-1-5326-6215-7 (hardcover) | ISBN 978-1-5326-6216-4 (ebook)

Subjects: LCSH: Church history—Primitive and early church, ca. 30–600.| Church history—Middle Ages, 600–1500. | Church history.

Classification: BR142 .B736 2019 (paperback) | BR142 .B736 (ebook)

Manufactured in the U.S.A.   10/28/19

Contents

List of Figures | vii
Foreword by Henry S. Wilson | ix
Foreword by Limuel R. Equina | xi
Abbreviations | xiii
Introduction | xv

Part I: The History of the Early Church | 1

CHAPTER 1
Christianity in the First and Early Second Century | 3

CHAPTER 2
Christianity and Politics: Persecution
and Growth in the First Three Centuries | 23

CHAPTER 3
Challenges to the Christian Movement
and Trends toward a Unified Faith | 42

CHAPTER 4
Christianity and Culture: The Encounter with Hellenist Philosophy | 62

CHAPTER 5
Christianity Becomes the Religion of the Empire | 82

CHAPTER 6
Theological and Ecclesial Controversies in the Fourth Century | 100

CHAPTER 7
Theology and Christological Debates in the Fifth Century | 116

Part II: The History of the Medieval Church | 141

CHAPTER 8
Mission History: The Extension of the Catholic Church and Its Inculturation in New Contexts | 143

CHAPTER 9
Papal History: The Growth of Papal Power | 166

CHAPTER 10
The History of a Growing Division: The Churches in East and West Go Separate Ways | 188

CHAPTER 11
The History of "the Other Church": Revivals, Reform, and Alternative Faith Expressions in Medieval Times | 205

CHAPTER 12
Outward Militancy and Inward Divisions in High and Late Medieval Times | 226

CHAPTER 13
Theological Developments during the Medieval Time | 242

Epilogue: Faith, God-Talk, and Historical Studies | 261

Bibliography | 277
Index | 285

Figures

Fig. 1.1: Summary: From Jesus to Christianity in the first century | 7
Fig. 1.2: From Judaism to Gentile Christianity | 8
Fig. 1.3: Different religious groups at the time of Jesus and the earliest church | 9
Fig. 1.4: Missionary strategies in early Christianity | 11
Fig. 1.5: Seven stages in the spread of early Christianity, according to Acts | 13
Fig. 1.6: Jewish Christianity: A conflict of loyalty | 14
Fig. 1.7: Survival and disappearance of different religious groups after the First Jewish-Roman War (66–73 CE) | 15
Fig. 1.8: Problematic antagonisms of supersessionist theology | 16
Fig. 2.1: The early Christians' conflicts with various groups | 26
Fig. 2.2: Waves of persecution in the first three centuries | 30
Fig. 3.1: The diversity of early Christian groups and their development | 45
Fig. 3.2: From diversity to unity | 45
Fig. 3.3: Graphic description of the Gnostic salvation story | 49
Fig. 3.4: Christian responses to doctrinal challenges in the second century | 59
Fig. 4.1: Image of Plato's Allegory of the Cave | 65
Fig. 4.2: Neo-Platonism's hierarchy of being | 67
Fig. 4.3: Important theologians of the first four centuries | 70
Fig. 4.4: Early Trinitarian models | 79
Fig. 5.1: Map of the Roman Empire before Constantine at the end of the third century | 83
Fig. 6.1: Summary comparison between Arianism and Orthodoxy | 111

Fig. 7.1: Five centuries of Trinitarian and christological debates under different names | 118

Fig. 7.2: Conflicting positions in the christological debates of the fifth century: Part I | 120

Fig. 7.3: Comparison between Nestorianism and Orthodoxy | 121

Fig. 7.4: Conflicting positions in the christological debates of the fifth century: part II | 123

Fig. 7.5: Comparison between Eutychianism and Orthodoxy | 124

Fig. 7.6: Topics in Augustine's theology and its influence on later Western theology | 130

Main events and developments in early Christianity before Constantine | 139

Fig. 8.1: Map of invasions of the Roman Empire | 145

Fig. 8.2: The expansion of the Islamic Empire during the first 130 years | 152

Fig. 8.3: Europe at the end of Charlemagne's reign (814) | 155

Fig. 9.1: Different leadership models: Episcopalism vs. papalism | 169

Fig. 9.2: Summary: Seven steps in the development of papal power | 185

Fig. 10.1: Seven steps in the conflict between Roman Catholicism and Eastern Orthodoxy | 196

Fig. 11.1: The basic pattern of development of the other church in medieval Catholicism | 207

Fig. 11.2: The dual governance structure of the Catholic Church | 220

Fig. 12.1: The first Crusades | 232

Fig. 12.2: The targets of the Crusades and the Inquisition | 236

Fig. 13.1: Medieval concepts of faith and reason | 247

Fig. 13.2: Four periods of medieval theological development | 248

Fig. 13.3: Different positions in the controversy about the universals | 254

Fig. 13.4: An overview of medieval movements of theology and philosophy | 258

Core dialectics in Christianity's historical movement | 271
Basic views of historical development | 276

Foreword
Henry S. Wilson

FROM THE EIGHTEENTH CENTURY onward, the Christianity that was established in South Asia and beyond by European and North American churches and mission boards was strongly shaped by theologies and ecclesial models of Euro-North America. The Western Christianity of that time, though maintaining its autonomy, was predominantly steeped in the prevailing worldviews and values, generally known as Western Christendom. The recipient Asian Christians had little choice other than to accept the theologies and ecclesial practices handed to them. Eventually, as these Asian Christians began to reflect on Christian faith and practices in the Asian context, they could do so only bilingually. That is, they needed both a familiarity with the history of inherited Western Christian theologies and ecclesiologies, *and* knowledge about Asian religious, cultural, and spiritual traditions in order to discern the appropriate contextual theologies and ecclesiologies for Asia.

With the many changes that have taken place the world over, one of the realities of the twenty-first century is the demographical shift in global Christianity, with the bulk of followers now in the majority world (Africa, Asia, Latin America, the Caribbean, and the Pacific). With a number of these Christians migrating to Europe and North America, the Western Christendom ethos is forced to embrace the reality of World Christianity or, better, worldwide Christianities. This calls for a fresh look into inherited theologies and ecclesial practices in order to discern the best practices of the Christian faith for the present. That mandates that even Euro-North Americans must be bilingual. That is, besides being familiar with their inherited Christianity, they also need to understand and accept the gifts of Christianities from the majority world, some of whom now reside in their neighborhoods.

Tobias Brandner, having taught for many years at the Divinity School of the Chung Chi College of the Chinese University of Hong Kong, demonstrates just such a consciousness—he is truly a Western Christian who is a bilingual theological educator in Asia. In this book, Brandner presents the history of Western Christianity over its first fifteen hundred years—its "formative" years, as he says, from a perspective that is helpful to his Asian students and to others interested in the history of Christianity. He diligently unfolds how the movement started by Jesus was incorporated in the Western world and led to the formation of a type of Christianity that eventually evolved into a foundation for Western civilization.

In an epilogue, after his critical engagement with the past in the body of the textbook, Brandner highlights the dialectic nature of Christianity as it continues to engage in its witnessing in the contemporary world. He articulates this as "constant tension between hegemony and emancipation, between institutionalization and protest, between petrification and renewal."

The book is enriched with charts and maps, and it comes with an electronic learning tool to help those who would like to deepen their learning by reading some texts from the history of Christianity and by testing their knowledge.

I am sure that this book, besides providing a fresh look at the history of Christianity, will also provide needed insight to further the Christian movement in Asia for individuals and communities witnessing in their particular contexts.

Henry S. Wilson
Executive Director
Foundation for Theological Education in Southeast Asia
Philadelphia, PA, USA

Foreword
Limuel R. Equina

"WHAT IS THE HISTORY of Christianity . . . and whose history is it?" Tobias Brandner raises these questions in his *Pilgrims and Popes: A Concise History of Pre-Reformation Christianity in the West*. Those questions echo the concerns of many Asian church historians, who acknowledge the fact that the available resources on the history of Christianity have been written largely by Western authors. As such, Asian church historians deem it expedient to read critically—through Asian lenses—the stories of the church. Otherwise, Asians find it less interesting to relate the history of Christianity to their own contexts.

Brandner's book is a welcome response to the above concerns. His long years of engagement in academia, the church and community ministry in Asia make his work a unique hybrid of Western and Asian perspectives in understanding the development of Western Christianity during its first fifteen hundred years. Intended for Asian readers, Brandner's book addresses the multilayered issues surrounding the emergence and progress of the Jesus movement through the doctrinal and political struggles of the first centuries, the medieval extension through mission and conquest, and the medieval reform and revival movements up to the eve of the Reformation. Many of the issues raised resonate strongly with present-day Asian readers—for instance, Brandner's description of how Jesus revived the notion of communal solidarity to counter exploitation and marginalization of disenfranchised groups like widows and the poor. This issue has a strong bearing on the church's religio-moral accountability in a society of unequals. Similarly, Asian readers will be inspired by the discussion of growth factors in the history of early Christianity, as they will naturally discover parallels to their present contexts. Brandner notes that current mission perspectives and strategies are likewise reminiscent of the early church's experience. The book's discussions of the nature of the early Christian community as countercultural provide a context for interpreting the experiences of the first believers. Their unwavering devotion to their newfound faith, and their commitment to an ideal lifestyle and a rejection of cultic worship, explain why they were persecuted by the powers that be. Critical readers will also appreciate Brandner's highlighting of the invaluable contribution of women martyrs to the rise of the Christian movement.

Brandner argues that whether Christianity is in a situation of persecution or peace, it has always remained dynamic. His discussions on theology and faith in the history of Christianity, following different dialectical movements, are fascinating. These "dialectic tensions" provide the impetus for the church to be creative and critical in seeking relevance to the complex challenges of each emerging context.

Each chapter of the book concludes with suggested activities for pedagogical purposes—for the classroom, small-group discussions, or individual reflection—helping readers engage with the text. The questions for discussion and reflection help readers focus on core aspects of past history, stimulate them to consider parallels between the past and the present, and encourage them to discover the relevance of the past for the present Asian context. Indeed, this book is a welcome resource and a helpful guide to Asian church historians and students of the history of Christianity.

Limuel R. Equina
Executive Director
Association for Theological Education in Southeast Asia

Abbreviations

ANF   *The Ante-Nicene Fathers: Translations of the Writings of the Fathers Down to A.D. 325.* Edited by Alexander Roberts and James Donaldson. 10 vols. 1885–87. Reprint, Buffalo, NY: Christian Literature Company, 1886.

NPNF 1   *A Select Library of Nicene and Post-Nicene Fathers of the Christian Church.* First series. Edited by Philip Schaff and Henry Wace. 14 vols. 1886–89. Reprint, Buffalo, NY: Christian Literature Company, 1886–1890.

NPNF 2   *A Select Library of Nicene and Post-Nicene Fathers of the Christian Church.* Second series. Edited by Philip Schaff and Henry Wace. 14 vols. 1886–89. Reprint, New York: Christian Literature Company, 1890–1900.

Introduction

WELCOME TO THE STUDY of the history of Christianity. This book will lead you through the first fifteen hundred years of that history. The decisions taken in the first few centuries about how to understand the events surrounding the person of Jesus of Nazareth have fundamentally shaped the journey of the Christian faith movement. The exploration of this story will lead through historical peaks and valleys, breakthroughs and disappointments, moments of joy and pain. As you enter this book and begin to learn about the history of Christianity, it is helpful to take note about how to use it.

This book addresses all those who have little knowledge of Western Christianity and who want or need to learn about its history. More specifically, it is meant for three kinds of readers: first, students of theology for whom the history of Christianity is part of their curriculum; second, ordinary Christian believers who want to expand upon the church's mainly Bible-based teaching by learning about how this teaching developed through history; third, people who want to understand one of the core ingredients of Western culture and who, through studying the history of the Christian movement, want to deepen their understanding of what made the West. While it may be read by any interested person, it is particularly aimed at people, Christian or not, in Asia and, more generally, in the Global South. This is indeed one of the reasons for the writing of this book. Many excellent books on the history of early and medieval Western Christianity are already available, and I am truly indebted to many of them. A particularity of *this* book is that it addresses readers unfamiliar with the Western context, presenting them a story from an alien context in an understandable form and in a way that shows its ongoing relevance for people living in a different place and time. Aware of the significant distance of readers in the Global South to the events described, it focuses on learning, discussing, and building bridges to the present.

To be clear, this book is about the history of *Western* Christianity, i.e., Christianity in western Europe. The Western church is not and has never been the only church in the world—from its earliest beginnings, Christianity equally spread to Africa and Asia. Still, developments in the West are historically important because of the way they have influenced Christianity worldwide. The Christian faith is a pillar of Western society and a root of its culture. As such, it has also had an impact on global developments. That is why this book may be interesting also for those who want to understand more about Western culture in general. The book tries to present historical and theological events, developments, and ideas as simply as possible, while trying not to ignore the complexity of the issues at stake.

Since many important decisions regarding the Christian faith were taken during the first few centuries, the book may equally be used to learn about Christianity and Christian theology as a whole. The reader will find core topics of theological teaching laid out in a historical narrative, for instance: How did the belief develop that Jesus of Nazareth was more than a specially anointed prophet, i.e., that he was God? Why and how did the belief in the one God existing in three persons emerge? How did the understanding of humanity's radical corruption develop?

Other questions are more related to the interface between faith and society, or between faith and culture: How did a faith movement of poor people turn into a powerful religion that was able to shape politics? How did Christianity absorb elements of non-Christian cultures and philosophies? What were the strengths and weaknesses of these syntheses?

HOW TO USE THIS BOOK

This book is a textbook that helps users grasp the rich and complex history of Christianity in the Western context. Its thirteen chapters are designed to roughly fit the academic term of a seminary or university course. They are divided into two parts. The first part, seven chapters on the early church, covers the period from Jesus to the christological debates of the fifth century. The second part, six chapters on the medieval church, covers the period from the fall of Rome in the fifth century to the eve of the Reformation in the fifteenth century. Because of the length of this period, the chapters are arranged in thematic order and systematically present several topics, from mission history through political history to a theological history of the medieval time. The separation of early and medieval history is for the reader's convenience—the narrative does not always fit, with some stories and persons overlapping. An epilogue offers thoughts about the relationship between faith and theology, about the place of historical studies within theology, and about what drives church history. This epilogue helps explain the author's view of the history of Christianity as basically dialectic. The Christian faith movement stands in constant tension between hegemony and emancipation, between institutionalization and protest, between petrification and renewal. Something of this dialectic is reflected in the title. Popes and pilgrims represent two opposing faith movements: the church as a community that establishes itself within the context of human society and interacts with it; and the church as a community that is never at home and will never find an abiding city. It corresponds with what the famous missiologist Andrew Walls called the *indigenizing principle* and the *pilgrim principle*.[1] The epilogue may actually best be read with the introduction, but it has been placed at the end of the book to avoid sidetracking the reader.

Obviously, there is not *one* history of the Christian movement to be told, but many. Of the many possible stories, this book chooses a few and connects them into a narrative, while leaving out other possible stories that may be similarly important and equally worthy of being told. A diligent reader will easily discover that particularly the first part of the book chooses to emphasize the history of theological development over other possible historical accounts while neglecting topics such as the worship practices, faith, and social life of early Christians. It is hoped that this book inspires readers to engage in further studies, reading these important stories and filling these gaps.

Each chapter is structured in the same way. A short introduction presents basic questions and themes to be dealt with and provides an overview of the most important developments. It allows readers to gain a quick understanding of the whole period. The body of the chapter provides a step-by-step description of the most important events of the period. Summarizing charts and maps in the text may appeal to those who prefer a more visual approach. Suggestions for further reading direct interested readers to further paths of learning.

Finally, the end of each chapter contains three kinds of review questions for individual or group study: (*a*) questions to recall important historical facts, (*b*) questions for deeper understanding, and (*c*) questions that offer starting points for group discussions that relate the past to the present. These review questions respond to the necessity of *remembering*, *understanding*, and *applying* as three parts of cognitive learning. Regarding the first, I am well aware that memorization is not popular and smacks of rote learning. This is one reason why so many people are afraid of studying

---

1. Walls, *Missionary Movement in Christian History*, 7.

history: they are scared of foreign names and find it hard to remember dates and places. This book does try to keep the memorization of historical data to a minimum. But memorizing some important facts is helpful and makes our communication easier, and so the book tries to support readers in this effort. Learning history is partly like learning a foreign language—you cannot avoid memorizing unfamiliar words or sentences if you want to communicate. By repeatedly reviewing the short, factual questions, students can gain a quick grasp of the keywords of a period and will more easily be able to remember what they signify and how they relate to various topics. Yet, to be clear, studying history is not about memorizing names and years but about getting to know our (in this case) spiritual ancestors, about widening our relational networks, and ultimately about extending our understanding to those who have gone before us. History is further about engaging critically with the past—for example, by identifying similarities and differences, by asking what we would have done in similar situations, and by imagining alternative courses of history. Even though such mental exercises cannot change the past, they help us build bridges of understanding, establish relationships, and strengthen our empathy for people in a past that is our own past. Gaining this wider understanding of the past may help us grow in wisdom and prepare us for future moments where we need to take decisions in the semidarkness of the present.

This book is accompanied by an electronic learning tool, a website with further material that can be accessed without the book but closely interacts with it (http://www.crs.cuhk.edu.hk/historyofchristianity/). Here you will find both primary sources—with short introductory comments to familiarize you with the material from which the writing of history comes—and a good number of multiple-choice questions to test your understanding. Footnotes have been kept to a minimum, used only for direct quotes or where crucial to point out the origin of a specific thought or information. When the reference material is already listed under the reading list at the end of each chapter, only the short title is given.

WHAT CHRISTIANS CAN LEARN FROM STUDYING HISTORY

Having taught church history for many years, I am aware that many students, both of theology and of religious studies, struggle with it. For Christians, the popularity of studying the history of their faith lags far behind the study of the Bible. The Bible is, so they emphasize, the source of our knowledge of Jesus Christ. This is particularly the case for Protestants, whose initial intention was to lead the church back to its biblical roots and to overcome the decay that, according to them, history had brought. This view is still held today. Many Christians regard history as a story of continuous decline, of deviation from an original that needs to be constantly recovered. Many also find it discouraging to be confronted with the dark chapters of their own faith's history. An additional obstacle for the study of history in the Asian context (where this book was written) is that students are understandably more interested in Asian church history.

Yet, the programmatic "Back to the Bible," popular in Protestantism and beyond, is not possible without knowing how history and tradition have shaped our reading and understanding of the Bible. We should also be aware how present-day conflicts—both religious and secular ones—are commonly carried out on the field of history. We may look at the ongoing debate about colonialism and its legacy, or competing interpretations of the events during the Second World War, during the formative years of the Chinese Communist Party, or during China's more recent history. A debate over the past allows us to move on in the present. Besides, it is my deep conviction that the study of the history of Christianity will ultimately deepen our faith and theological thought and may eventually have a therapeutic effect, healing our community's divisions. I will elaborate in the epilogue how the study of history contributes to spiritual formation.

WHY THE GLOBAL SOUTH NEEDS THE HISTORY OF WESTERN CHRISTIANITY

Although people in the Asian or African context may be more interested in historical developments closer to home, the historical study of Western Christianity is meaningful for several reasons. First and most simply, the forms of Christianity that came to Asia and Africa and still exist today—be they Roman Catholic or Protestant—first emerged in the West. An understanding of how they developed is thus part of the history of the church in the Asian and African context. Second, the situation of Christianity in some parts of the Global South, maybe most clearly in China, in many ways mirrors that of the church in the first centuries. The most obvious parallel is the growth pattern of early Christianity and present-day Chinese Christianity, with the latter probably even surpassing the former. We may, based on various estimations of the present number of Christians in the Chinese context, assume a growth rate of *10 percent per year* over the past thirty years.[2] This compares to an average growth rate of *40 percent per decade*,

2. Based on research by scholars at Baylor University (2007) or by the Pew Research

according to some estimations, in the first three centuries of Christianity (see more about this in ch. 2). A second parallel is the high percentage and the important role of women in the church then and now. Observers assume that 70 to 80 percent of today's Chinese Christians are female.[3] In early Christianity, women (many of higher social status) also played a major role.[4] A third parallel is the reaction of political authorities, then and now, to the growth of Christianity, partly trying to contain it by promoting indigenous philosophies and beliefs, but partly trying to integrate it into their own political visions. Fourth, Chinese political authorities are interested, as was the Roman Empire, in religion *not* being a source of social conflict. This was, and still is, achieved through supporting officially sanctioned religiosity and suppressing nonofficial religious expressions or even labeling them heretical. An interesting intellectual parallel is Christianity's encounter with the spiritual and intellectual world of Hellenism then and Chinese philosophy now. Patristic theology interpreted Christ as revelation of the Logos, as known already in Greek philosophy; similarly, Chinese Christian intellectuals have identified the *Logos*, Christ, with the *Dao* of Chinese philosophy. Although such parallels should not be overstretched, it is clear that reading the history of early Christianity is more than an intellectual pastime. Rather, comparisons with the past allow today's Christians to receive inspiration and lessons from history for present-day challenges.

Finally, a question frequently discussed in the Asian context is this: How did Western countries come to dominate the world in the past few centuries even though China was, up to the fifteenth century, more affluent and more advanced in terms of technology? And are we today witnessing an end to this Western dominance? This book does not answer these questions. But it is interesting to note that answers given by historical scholars[5] do point out the important role that Christianity played in the progress of Western science and technology, and in the development of political and social institutions. The discussion of the important, even necessary ingredients for a

---

Center's Forum on Religion & Public Life (December 2011), both assuming a number of around 60 to 70 million Christians.

3. A 2010 report by the Chinese Academy of Social Sciences, posted on a now-defunct website of the China Christian Council, assumed 69.9 percent female Christians. My estimation, based on random head counts when visiting Chinese churches, would be even higher.

4. See overall Stark, *Rise of Christianity*, ch. 5.

5. See for instance Ferguson, *Civilization*, or Stark, *The Victory of Reason*. Both books are problematic in their triumphalism about Western achievements, in their generalizations, and in their "big story" approach to history, but they provide stimulating food for thought.

society's development—be they political, economic, or in the broadest sense cultural and social—thus directly touches on the role of religion in the West.

This book is a product of many years spent teaching church history at the Divinity School of Chung Chi College, Chinese University of Hong Kong. My gratitude goes to all my former students, whose responses to my teaching helped me improve and clarify various points. I would also like to thank several people who played a crucial role in the writing of this book. Most important was Luke DeKoster, who helped me improve the original English manuscript. His stimulating comments inspired me to clarify various issues. Mok Kieman accompanied me through several courses as teaching assistant and gave me substantial support. Gary Ling helped me in designing the maps and the charts. I relied on Patrick Cheng's advice, support, and ideas when creating the electronic learning tool. This book was first published in Chinese (under the title *fen jiu bi he, he jiu bi fen: cong yesu shidai dao gaige qian xi de xifang jidujiao pipan shi*, translated by Mok Kieman). The critical feedback I have received to the Chinese edition helped me improve for this publication several points that had led to misunderstandings. I am grateful for all these comments received. This textbook was made possible by the generous financial support of a Teaching Development Grant from the Chinese University of Hong Kong, to whom I am very grateful. I would also like to thank the Faculty of Arts, Chinese University of Hong Kong, for financially supporting the editorial process.

Tobias Brandner
Hong Kong, July 2019

PART I

The History of the Early Church

Chapter 1

Christianity in the First and Early Second Century

THE STORY OF CHRISTIANITY begins with a small group of rural people at the fringes of the great Roman Empire, a reform movement within Judaism led by Galilean farmers, fishermen, and other disenfranchised groups. Within only a few decades, the movement found new followers in urban areas as it transcended geographical, religious, cultural, and social boundaries. From its Palestinian origins, it spread around the Mediterranean and reached to the ends of the Roman Empire. From its Jewish origins, it became a movement that attracted non-Jewish followers, split with Judaism and gained official status under the Roman Empire.

This chapter will address the following questions:

- What is the relationship of Jesus to Christianity?
- What was Paul's role in the spread of early Christianity?
- Why did a Jewish reform movement spread to Gentiles (non-Jewish people)?
- Why was this Jesus movement more successful among Gentiles than were other reform movements?
- Why was this movement successful in the Hellenistic world and among Gentiles, but less so in Palestine and among Jews?
- How did a Jewish sect become a religion that attracted followers throughout the Roman Empire?

- How did a reform movement led by countryside peasants become a faith community that attracted city dwellers?
- Why did the Jesus movement, which started as a reform movement within Judaism, eventually separate from Judaism?

This first chapter traces the events and the decisions that set the early Christian movement on a track of continuous growth to reach new people groups. Our knowledge of the important decisions and events from this time is based mainly on the stories of the Bible—the Gospels, Acts, the epistles of Paul, and other letters—and to a lesser degree on some clues from historians like Josephus and Tacitus. Additionally, recent archeological findings have offered new evidence and insights into the social history of the Roman Empire.

FROM JESUS TO THE EARLIEST CHURCH IN JERUSALEM

Jesus did not intend to found a new religion. With his public ministry lasting only two or three years, he had neither the time nor the desire to establish a new religious community. Accordingly, Jesus did not lay down many rules for community life. His expectation of an imminent radical change in history and the coming kingdom of God made the establishment of an organized form of religion irrelevant. Rather, his intention was to *restore* Israel's traditional covenantal relationship with God and to *revive* communal solidarity, responding to the exploitation and marginalization of disenfranchised people at the periphery of a large empire. The stories of the New Testament offer a rare glimpse of the hopes and dreams of those who have found themselves at the bottom of civilization. Jesus' calling of the Twelve revitalized, in counterculturalform, the glory of old Israel and its twelve tribes. Jesus' Galilean peasant protest movement was not solely aimed at individuals but served as a way of transforming wider community life, and it assumed a national dimension with Jesus' journey to Jerusalem. Jesus thus must be seen as launching a reform movement within Judaism, but one that in its criticism of established religious life already carried the seed of a potential break with Judaism.

The Earliest Reference to Jesus outside of Christianity

The text below from the *Antiquities* of Josephus is the earliest reference to Jesus in non-Christian literature. It is assumed that the words describing him as the Christ are Christian interpolations: there is no indication that Josephus had accepted the Christian claim that Jesus was the Messiah the Jews were expecting.

> *Now, there was about this time Jesus, a wise man, if it be lawful to call him a man, for he was a doer of wonderful works, a teacher of such men as receive the truth with pleasure. He drew over to him both many of the Jews, and many of the Gentiles. He was (the) Christ. And when Pilate, at the suggestion of the principal men amongst us, had condemned him to the cross, those that loved him at the first did not forsake him; for he appeared to them alive again the third day; as the divine prophets had foretold these and ten thousand other wonderful things concerning him. And the tribe of Christians, so named from him, are not extinct at this day.*

Source: Flavius Josephus, *Antiquities of the Jews* XVIII, 3:3, in Purinton, *Christianity and Its Judaic Heritage*, 185.

The earliest church in Jerusalem remained within the framework of Jesus' relationship to Judaism. The followers of the Jesus movement gathering in Jerusalem saw themselves as belonging to the Jewish community that, naturally, observed the Mosaic law. There is evidence that this group stressed its Jewish character even more than during Jesus' lifetime, as it expanded from a community of Galileans to include Jews from Jerusalem. They saw themselves as a group of specially elected people waiting together for the second coming of Christ as king at the end of time. How exactly the earliest church in Jerusalem lived—did it really practice a form of primitive communism or is this simply an idealization?—remains a subject of scholarly debate. It is known that other radical Jewish groups like the Essenes did donate all their individual wealth and personal possessions to a communal treasury, so it may well be possible that the Jesus movement did the same.

FIRST STEPS BEYOND TRADITIONAL JUDAISM

Very soon, something crucial led the church on a course that increasingly steered it beyond its origins in Judaism: *foreign-born* Jews (in contrast to local Jews), who maintained a separate communal identity in Judaism, joined the community in Jerusalem.

> We can find a similar difference between *traditional* local churches (in cities of the Global South or elsewhere), which tend to be homogeneous and use the vernacular, and *English-speaking* local churches that appeal to local people who have returned from overseas and thus have mixed, international congregations.

Living together in this earliest church in Jerusalem were two groups, both Jewish and both observing the law: so-called Hebrews, Aramaic-speaking Jews of the Jesus movement who were more traditionalist; and so-called Hellenists, Greek-speaking Jews who were more shaped by Greek culture and may have been more open to change. These cultural differences soon led to tensions between the two groups. We can find hints of this in Acts 6—8:3, a story about the Hellenists feeling marginalized in the affairs of the church; as a consequence, seven deacons were appointed to feed the "neglected" Hellenists. However, it turned out that one of the Seven, Stephen, was more interested in preaching, and his powerful sermon brought him into conflict with the authorities.

Interestingly, the subsequent persecution by Jewish authorities was directed not against all followers of the Jesus movement, but only against the Hellenists who, as a consequence, spread the Christian faith beyond the boundaries of Israel and set up the first Christian community, consisting of both Jews and Gentiles, in Antioch. The Hellenist Jews served as the first bridge to the non-Jewish world because they were more willing to include Gentiles in the new community. Antioch then became the second and alternative (to Jerusalem) center of Christianity.

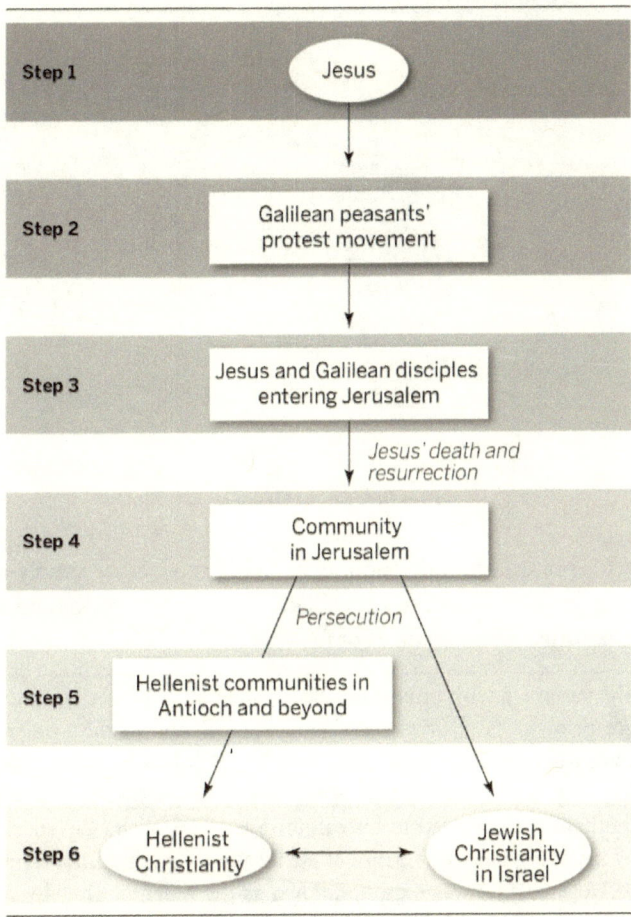

Fig. 1.1: *Summary: From Jesus to Christianity in the first century*

Now, a second crucial development occurred. Whenever the Hellenist Jews went to a place to spread the vision of a new community as inspired by Jesus, they naturally did so in the synagogue, where the Jews gathered. Among those listening, a strong response came from a group of people called "God-fearers" (in Greek, *theosebeis*), devout non-Jewish sympathizers of Judaism who had never formally converted to Judaism because they found it too daunting to undergo circumcision and observe all the purity laws. They were thus attracted by the teaching that Christians did not need to be circumcised or follow all the Mosaic law. These God-fearers can be described as a second bridge to the Gentile world. We can thus describe the spread of the gospel to the Gentiles as follows:

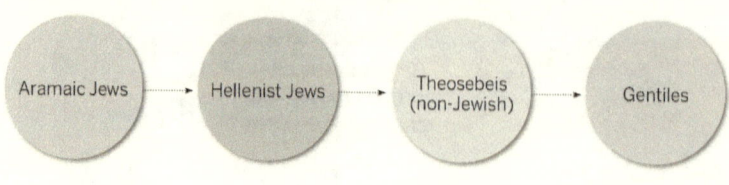

Fig. 1.2: *From Judaism to Gentile Christianity*

At this point, this early community was perceived as simply another of the many Jewish sects, all of which had unique social visions and some of which established an alternative community.

> The various Jewish groups can be mapped on two axes (see figure below)—as *different social groups* in relation to the Roman colonizers and their local allies, the Herodian family, and as different in their *sociocultural perspectives*. The followers of John the Baptist responded to his call for a renewal of the Covenant by baptizing people as a sign of purification. Another important sect of the time was a group known as the Essenes. They lived a strict community life, separating from the world and partly withdrawing into the desert. Whether the group known from Qumran is in fact the Essenes is still debated. Another notable group, the Zealots, played a more activist role in trying to overthrow the Roman colonizers and Herodian family. The Pharisees' common belief was that a return to the Mosaic law would bring about redemption. They were not as homogenous as they appear in the Gospels but instead followed various important teachers of the Mosaic law, like Hillel or Shammai. Some mystical groups suggested redemption through a Spirit-led reunion with God. Various apocalyptic groups similarly expected an imminent end to the present time and rule. All these groups had in common a deep criticism of the ruling elite, but they offered different strategies about how to cope with the oppressive network of military, political-institutional, economic, cultural, and religious power.

On the other side of the spectrum stand the Sadducees, who benefited from the Herodian support of the temple, through which they attempted to show their national and religious credentials.

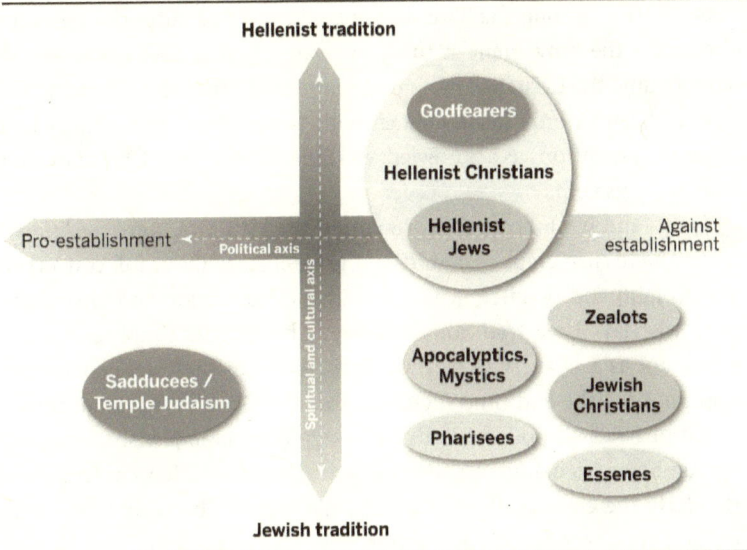

Fig. 1.3: *Different religious groups at the time of Jesus and the earliest church*

THE JERUSALEM COUNCIL AND COMPETING MISSIONARY STRATEGIES IN THE FIRST TWENTY YEARS OF CHRISTIANITY

In this early period we witness a conflict over strategies for the development of the new community initiated by Jesus. Our knowledge of this tension comes from the description (in Acts 15 and in Galatians 2) of what is usually called the Jerusalem Council, a gathering of several leaders of the community to discuss burning issues. At that time, the community of Jesus followers still had no uniform leadership structure. One form of leadership was that of James, the "brother of the Lord," who from around 44 CE until his martyrdom in 62 CE had some authority based on his blood relation with Jesus. Another form of leadership, that of Paul, was partly based on his supernatural experience on the road to Damascus, and partly on his authority as a powerful missionary. He was a Hellenist Jew from Tarsus, outside the land of Israel, and was well trained in the Mosaic law. Although he was not the first apostle to preach to the Gentiles and did not found most of the Gentile churches, he became famous for spreading the Jesus movement to the Gentiles. We could call this authority based on experience and charisma. The third leader was Peter, whose authority was based on his special position among the Twelve. We could call this authority based on tradition. As the movement at this time was still very heterogeneous, we should assume the existence of a good number of other local leaders, who may have been in only loose contact with James, Peter and John, whom Galatians 2:9 mentions as acknowledged leaders of the early Christian community in Jerusalem.

James and his followers, representing the Hebrews, were *traditionalists*. They were suspicious of admitting the Gentiles without full conversion to Jewish faith and practice, which included circumcision and observance of the Jewish law. Their traditionalism should be seen not simply as narrow-minded, but as a strategy in its own right. As far as they were concerned, the prophecy of the end time suggested that the Gentiles would all turn to the God of Israel—in other words, they would become Jewish. James and his group hoped to maintain good relationships with the Jews in Jerusalem, particularly the conservatives. They did not want to be seen as apostates from God's law because this perception would become a stumbling block to the dissemination of their message among the Jews. Maintaining the validity of the law of Moses seemed necessary for the peace of the church.

In contrast, Paul, Barnabas, and the Hellenist Christians had a view that we may describe as *more progressive* and that was particularly attractive to the God-fearers. Their position was that, in the new Israel, conversion to Judaism and full observation of the law were no longer necessary. Such an interpretation of the Christian community antagonized the Jews, who saw it as—using terms that would come into use only later—"cheap grace" and as "sheep-stealing."

Between these two positions stood Peter, who at first apparently supported the mission to the Hellenists and their unconditional admission to the Christian community without observation of the law but then, possibly under pressure from James, adjusted his position and returned to Jewish Christianity (Gal 2:12). He reportedly clashed with Paul over the question of the requirements for Gentiles (Gal 2:11–21) and eventually assumed a middle position. Acts, however, portrays Peter slightly differently, with his vision of the sheet and his report to the church establishing him as a proponent of the mission to the Gentiles.

These three positions can be found at the Jerusalem Council (48 or 49 CE). The core question was whether the Gentiles, in order to be saved, needed to be circumcised and observe the Mosaic law. This implies a deeper question: how could community members know that someone who accepted the apostles' preaching and who joined the early Christian community was not simply responding to a feeling? In other words, how could converts distinguish themselves from their old selves? How could a conversion be validated?

The conflict in Jerusalem was between a more Spirit-driven Christian movement and a more tradition-based movement, and the Jerusalem Council may be seen as the first moment when a growing movement needed to find theological coherence. The conclusion of those present was that there should be two missions, one to the Jews and the other to the Gentiles. The oneness and the solidarity between the two groups should be made visible by a contribution to the poor in Jerusalem (Gal 2:10). Besides this, the uncircumcised Gentile Christians were required to observe only four basic laws of abstinence (Acts 15:20): from the pollution of idols, from sexual immorality, from what is strangled, and from blood. The effect of the Council was that the Gentile Christian community gained solid principles from which to develop.

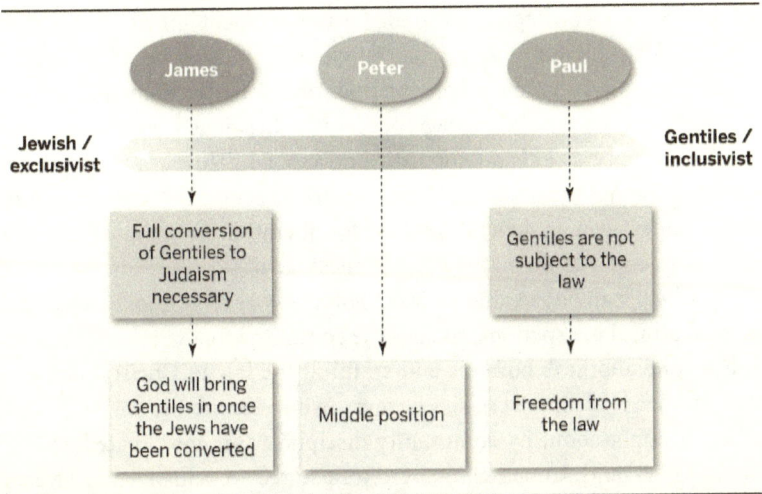

Fig. 1.4: Missionary strategies in early Christianity

CHRISTIANITY SPREADS INTO THE GENTILE WORLD

The Hellenist Jews and God-fearers played a crucial role in the spread of Christianity among the non-Jewish people in the Mediterranean world.

Various spiritual, cultural, religious, social, and economic factors attracted this group to the Jesus movement.

First, the God-fearers had already been attracted to Jewish monotheism and the underlying social ideals of the Mosaic law; they were even more attracted by the Jesus movement as a Jewish reform movement, which broke down the tight connection between faith and ethnic identity. The God-fearers initially considered the Jesus movement a fully Jewish faith group, though one that extended (or even universalized) the essence of Judaism. The Jesus movement also allowed them to fully participate in an admired and precious heritage without being subject to the ceremonial laws that reflected a specific Palestinian cultural context.

Second, joining the Jesus movement allowed Hellenist followers to make their Jewish faith more universal. They adopted a more liberal approach to the Torah by maintaining the moral aspects of the Mosaic law and relinquishing the ceremonial ones and those linked to the temple, which were irrelevant in the Diaspora; they also emphasized principles of love and of equality in Christ. This allowed their faith to be successfully inculturated in different contexts of the Mediterranean world. The Hellenist Christians and God-fearers who began to join the Jesus movement linked universalism with the particularism of a very old religious faith. This would remain an important factor in the spread of Christianity. Third, due to their fluency in the widely spoken Greek language, Hellenist Christians were able to communicate across cultural and linguistic barriers. Fourth, many hard-pressed peasants, whether uprooted and living in urban centers or suffering under Roman imperialism in general, yearned for liberation from the yoke of economic hardship. For them, the twofold message of renewal—of covenantal community life and of an alternative kingdom—was truly good news. Paul's practical ethical instructions, such as the command for Galatian Christians "to bear one another's burdens and so fulfill the law of Christ" (Gal 6:2), fitted the needs of impoverished farmers, whose economic survival could be best brought about by community discipline and coordinated action.[1] Finally, Greek and Roman cities were well-suited to actualize the ideas of equality, love, and reconciliation because these urban societies had more mobility and were not bound by the traditionally legitimized social stratification of rural Palestine.[2]

The earliest history of Christianity can be summarized in these seven steps:

---

1. Horsley and Silberman, *Message and the Kingdom*, 151.
2. Theissen, *Sociology of Early Palestinian Christianity*, 118.

1. **Before Pentecost (Acts 1:1-26)**
   Remaining in Jerusalem; expectation of Kingdom of God as restoration of Israel; reestablishing of the Twelve.

2. **Pentecost (Acts 2-5)**
   Eschatological fulfillment; outreach to international Jewish community in Jerusalem; community still bound by the Mosaic Law.

3. **Stephen and the Hellenists (Acts 6:1-8:3)**
   Outreach to Hellenistic Jews; scattering of the church (except Apostles!) through persecution.

4. **The ministry of Philip – beyond Judaism (Acts 8:4-40)**
   First outreach beyond Judaism – to half-Jews (Samaritans) and people at the margins; not yet formal opening to the gentiles.

5. **Conversion of the missionaries and beginning of mission to the gentiles (Acts 9:1-11:18)**
   Conversion of Paul (Acts 9); conversion of Peter (Acts 10) from mission focusing on Israel to mission to the gentiles; household of Cornelius as first public conversion of gentiles.

6. **Church in Antioch: the church's first encounter with the gentile world (Acts 11:19-30)**
   The church in the gentile world of Antioch; inclusive preaching and contextualization in the language of the Hellenistic cults; Christians appear with separate identity (v26).

7. **Mission to the gentiles (Acts 12-28)**
   Steadily expanding mission to the gentiles; ambiguous continuity between the mission to the Jews and the mission to the gentiles.

Fig. 1.5 : Seven stages in the spread of early Christianity, according to Acts (based on Bevans and Schroeder, "Constants in Context")

THE DISAPPEARANCE OF JEWISH CHRISTIANITY

Let us now return to the Jewish Christian community in Jerusalem, led by James and other apostles. Despite the compromise at the Jerusalem Council, we may assume that the previous tensions between Gentile and Jewish Christians did not disappear instantaneously. In the eyes of Jewish Christians, the Gentile Christians' failure to fully observe the Torah disqualified or at least devalued them. In the eyes of Gentile Christians, the Jewish Christians' insistence on Jewish credentials represented a lack of faith and a disregard for the radical new era that had begun with Jesus.

However, the more serious challenge for Jewish Christians came from their Jewish compatriots, who questioned their loyalty to their land at a time when the Jews found themselves already under intense political pressure. In fact, the Pauline letters repeatedly point to a Jewish counter-mission challenging the young Gentile communities. The Jewish Christians were thus torn between their ethno-religious group and their faith group. It seems that the affinity between Jewish Christians and Jews was stronger than that between Jewish Christians and Gentile Christians; to the neutral observer, Jewish Christians would have appeared closer to mainstream Judaism than to non-Jewish Christianity.

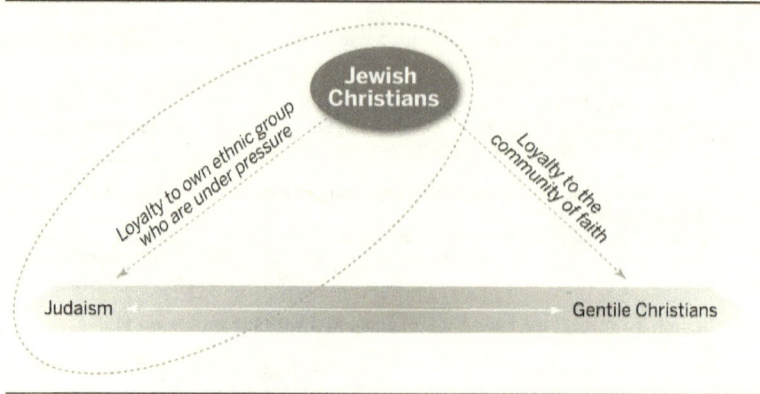

Fig. 1.6: Jewish Christianity: A conflict of loyalty

The years between 66 and 73 CE brought a deep crisis to Judaism. What had been occasional attacks by Zealots against the Roman colonizers and their local representatives and collaborators turned into a full-scale war, the First Jewish-Roman War. The Roman army was used to armed resistance, even at its remote borders, and reacted quickly. It punished not only the Zealots but also the whole Jewish community, expelling the Jews and destroying Jerusalem and the symbols of cultural and religious identity. The temple complex was burned down and never restored. What is today known as the Wailing Wall or Western Wall is the last remaining wall of what was once the Second Temple. The Jesus followers—that is, the Jewish Christians in Jerusalem—were likewise expelled. They moved to the upper Jordan Valley, where they survived in small sects like the Ebionites that were later regarded as heretical. The loss of their spiritual center was the beginning of the end. They had already been hard-pressed before the war to prove their loyalty to the Jewish tradition. Now, amidst the wreckage, Judaism took a course that left no room for the ambiguity of Jewish Christianity, as we will see in the next section. The biblical tradition retains no document that is assuredly from the Jewish Christian tradition; what may come closest is the Letter of James.

THE CHRISTIAN COMMUNITY SEPARATES FROM THE JEWISH COMMUNITY

The short but brutal war had yet another result: the disappearance of most Jewish groups that had existed at the time of Jesus. The Essenes were eliminated when their hideout at Qumran was destroyed in 68 CE. The Sadducees lost their relevance and the basis of their economic and cultural power when the temple ceased to exist. The Zealots collectively committed suicide in 73 CE as their last outpost, Masada, a fortification in the Judean desert, was about to be raided by the Roman army. The only surviving factions were small groups of apocalyptic believers who lacked organizational coherence and, more importantly, the Pharisees, who, with the loss of the temple, became the only authoritative representatives of the Jewish faith.

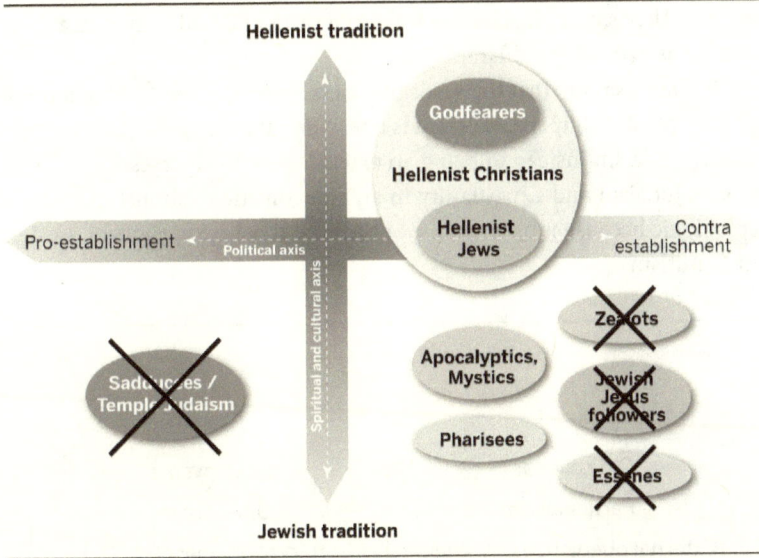

Fig. 1.7: Survival and disappearance of different religious groups after the First Jewish-Roman War (66–73 CE)

Having lost its religious center, the temple, Judaism was left only with the Torah. A new center, a rabbinic school at Yavneh, was founded. It represented so-called rabbinic Judaism, a Jewish doctrine and faith that had been developed independently from the temple theology and that emphasized the ethnic, religious, and cultural identity of Judaism. Certainly, the hope for a restoration of the temple remained alive, as the Jewish apocalyptic writers IV Ezra and II Baruch show, their names reminiscent of the era of the first temple, destroyed by the Babylonian army some centuries earlier.

But now, as the temple was again lost, both the synagogue—as a local assembly hall—and believers' homes became centers of worship where the knowledge of the Torah was handed down. The priestly rituals of the temple were replaced by prayers and rituals conducted in the home.

With only the Pharisees and Gentile Christianity left to claim the heritage of the Jewish tradition, growing hostility between the two emerged, and with Jewish Christianity gone, no bridge between the two sides remained. As Christianity became more a movement of Gentiles, it lost its popularity among the Jews. The Gospels' description of Jesus' struggles with the Pharisees may reflect the situation after 70 CE rather than the situation during the lifetime of Jesus. The Pharisees regarded Christians as a threat, undermining the cohesion of the Jewish community and despising the Jewish tradition and law. The Christians interpreted the destruction of the temple and of Jerusalem as punishment for the Jewish persecution of Jesus and his disciples. They saw themselves as truly inheriting the tradition of Israel, not anymore as *extending* old Israel.

It is at this point that the seeds of supersessionist or replacement theology were planted. Supersessionism is a teaching that regards Christianity as *replacing* Judaism instead of being an extension of it. Supersessionist theology sees Judaism and Christianity in an antagonistic relationship, a fateful step of logic because it became one of the core theological roots of Western anti-Semitism.

Supersessionism is a teaching that regards the church as **replacing** instead of **extending** Judaism.

Israel	Church
Old covenant	New covenant
Particularism	Universalism
External obedience to the law	Internal obedience to God

Fig. 1.8: Problematic antagonisms of supersessionist theology

It was in this climate of antagonism (around 90 CE) that the Jews introduced a condemnation of the Christians in their Prayer of 18 Benedictions that they recited three times a day:

> For the renegades let there be no hope, and may the arrogant kingdom soon be rooted out in our days, and the Nazarenes and the *minim* perish as in a moment and be blotted out from the

book of life and with the righteous may they not be inscribed. Blessed art thou, O Lord, who humblest the arrogant.[3]

The Gospel of John, which most biblical scholars agree was written around the end of the first century, reflects this situation in reporting that Christians were cast out from the synagogue (John 9:22; 12:42; 16:2). This caused serious hardship among Christians who lived in a dominantly Jewish environment, as this exclusion from the synagogue also extended to their becoming targets of an economic boycott. The strong condemnation of the Jews in the Gospel of John, later tragically misused to legitimate anti-Semitism, is assumed to have grown out of this context of hardship of minority Christians. The negative portrayal of Jews in John and in other parts of the Bible thus grew out of the experience of Christians at the margins of society who were facing the regionally hegemonic power of rabbinic Judaism.

The Growing Animosity between Christians and Jews

The Epistle of Barnabas reflects a growing animosity between Christians and Jews. The letter claims that the covenant belongs to the Christians, not to the Jews, because even the practice of circumcision was pointing towards Jesus.

The authorship of the text is debated, but its ascription to Barnabas, Paul's coworker, has little support. It is usually assumed to have been written sometime between 70 and 130, to Gentile Christians.

> Ch. 9. . . . 3 But also circumcision, in which they trusted, has been abrogated. He declared that circumcision was not of the flesh; but they transgressed because an evil angel deluded them. . . . 6 Learn, then, my beloved children, concerning all things richly, that Abraham, the first who enjoined circumcision, looking forward in spirit to Jesus, circumcised, the teaching of the three letters having been received. 7 For the Scripture saith: "Abraham circumcised eighteen and three hundred men of his household." What, then, was the knowledge given to him in this? Learn that he says the eighteen first and then, making a space, the three hundred. The eighteen are the Iota, ten, and the Eta, eight; and you have here the name of Jesus. And because the cross was to express the grace in the letter Tau, he says also, three hundred. He discloses therefore Jesus in the two letters, and the cross in one. He knows this who has put within us the engrafted gift of his teaching. 8 No one has learned from me a more excellent piece of knowledge, but I know that ye are worthy.

Source: Epistle of Barnabas, ch. 9 (excerpt), in Ayer, *A Source Book for Ancient Church History*, 15–16.

---

3. Barrett, *New Testament Background*, 211.

The separation of Christianity from its Jewish roots was a gradual process in which the First Jewish-Roman War played an important role. However, the process did not end there. The complete break came with the Second Jewish-Roman War (132–35), in which another Jewish leader, Bar Kochba, claimed to be the Messiah and led his followers into rebellion against the Romans.

Gradually, Christians took over the Jewish heritage: they appropriated the Jewish scriptures as the Old Testament and preserved and transcribed non-rabbinic Jewish texts like Jewish apocalyptic literature. In their church administration they introduced patterns taken from the organization of the synagogues. Increasingly, the Roman authorities perceived the two groups as different and separate religions.

In his book *The Partings of the Way*, James Dunn describes how Rabbinic Judaism saw Christianity increasingly move away from four central theological pillars of Judaism:[4]

(a) The belief in the one God, Yahweh: While the Jesus followers' faith in their leader as the Messiah was already difficult for traditional Jews to accept, the christological development that led to Jesus being described as *kyrios* and as *incarnate logos* was unthinkable within the context of Judaism.

(b) The belief in being God's people and the belief in the election of Israel: The Christians' self-understanding—that they were the new Israel superseding the old Israel, and that the covenant was not linked to ethnicity—challenged the covenantal self-understanding of the Jews.

(c) The belief in the Torah as normative revelation of God: The criticism of traditional Torah-centered belief (by Jesus and Paul, in particular), the refusal to restrict God's revelation to the words of the Torah, and the relativizing of the Torah's ultimate authority went deeply against traditional Jewish understanding.

(d) The belief in the relevance of the temple: The Christian rejection of a temple-centered faith stood in opposition to traditional Jewish faith that regarded the temple as a guarantee of the presence of God. However, with the destruction of the temple, rabbinic Judaism equally organized itself around the Torah rather than around the temple. The conflict between Rabbinic Judaism and Christianity was thus between belief in the Torah and belief in Christ as the new temple of God.

---

4. Dunn, *Partings of the Ways*, 318–38.

THEOLOGICAL SHIFTS THROUGH THE FIRST CENTURY

The earliest Jewish Christian community saw their faith not as a denial of Judaism but as an affirmation that the long-awaited messianic age had begun. The distinctive message was that Jesus of Nazareth, despite his death on the cross, was the eschatological Messiah; that his death on the cross was the fulfillment of Jewish scripture (Luke 24:45-47); and that his messianic identity was confirmed by his resurrection from the dead (Acts 2:1-36). When the followers of the Jesus movement gathered after the resurrection, they did so in joyful expectation of Jesus' imminent return to restore Israel. Their mission, then, was to prepare Israel in the short intervening period that remained before the second coming of Jesus, when he would judge the world and gather the nations as an eschatological sign. They had no interest in establishing special and lasting rules for community life. Rather, they were waiting in a festive mood, celebrating the imminent Kingdom and remembering Jesus' martyrdom. They continued to participate in synagogue worship and held gatherings for prayer and meals at each other's homes, thus continuing the eucharistic community of Jesus. A typical form of their earliest creed can be found in 1 Cor 15:3-7.

As the Jesus movement was extended to Gentile believers, it turned more and more into a movement centered on Christ. It was in Antioch that the followers of the movement were first called Christians. This christological shift is particularly visible in Paul's writings addressing Hellenistic Christians, where we find less reference to the events in the life of Jesus of Nazareth. The emphasis on Jesus' divinity built an important bridge to the Gentile world, de-emphasizing Jesus' cultural and ethnic particularity and emphasizing his universal significance. An example of this contextualization in the non-Jewish context is the title *kyrios* (Lord) used beside the title *christos* (Messiah). For Paul, the death of Christ both relativized and fulfilled the Jewish law. The socially and politically radical character of Jesus' message gave room for a more spiritual interpretation and a waning expectation of Christ's imminent return, that is, moving from the proclamation of the kingdom of God to the proclamation of Christ. Yet, the belief in Christ as universal ruler remained a continuous challenge to imperial claims of bringing salvation to the people.[5]

The practice of sharing goods and money remained a crucial element of early Christian communities, as we see in the early house churches. Often, the young church benefited from the hospitality of affluent supporters.

---

5. Horsley and Silberman, *Message and the Kingdom*, 156.

On the other hand, dependence on the hospitality of wealthier Christians could, as in the Corinthian church, be problematic when the hosts' patronage led them to claim higher social status.

After the First Jewish-Roman War, from the 70s CE on, a theological debate arose, as the Christians and the Pharisees made competing claims about who was rightfully the inheritor of Jewish tradition. Against the Jewish emphasis on the Mosaic law, Christians maintained that in Christ a new law had begun. Against the Pharisees' criticism that they had given up their belief in the one God, they developed a Christology aimed at showing how belief in Christ was consistent with the belief in one God. In worship and prayer, these Christians started to rely on fixed prayers and liturgical elements, such as the Lord's Prayer or the Eucharistic Prayer,[6] and on doctrinal formulations that were widely recognized by the community. At the same time, they relied on an edited collection of highly respected writings: the letters of Paul (which had a high degree of authority), the Gospels, and apocryphal accounts of the apostles. The leadership developed as well, moving from the earlier charismatic form—apostles, with prophets, teachers, and preachers simply anointed by the Spirit—to a more orderly structure with bishops, presbyters, and deacons. We will see later (ch. 3) how this development was accelerated by external threats to the Christian community.

For Further Reading

Brown, Schuyler. *The Origins of Christianity: A Historical Introduction to the New Testament.* Rev. ed. Oxford: Oxford University Press, 1984.

Dunn, James. *The Partings of the Ways: Between Christianity and Judaism and Their Significance for the Character of Christianity.* 2nd ed. London: SCM, 2006.

Horsley, Richard A., editor. *Christian Origins.* People's History of Christianity 1. Minneapolis: Fortress, 2005.

Horsley, Richard A., and Neil Asher Silberman. *The Message and the Kingdom: How Jesus and Paul Ignited a Revolution and Transformed the Ancient World.* Minneapolis: Fortress, 1997.

Theissen, Gerd. *Social Reality and the Early Christians: Theology, Ethics, and the World of the New Testament.* Translated by Margaret Kohl. Minneapolis: Fortress, 1992.

———. *Sociology of Early Palestinian Christianity.* Translated by John Bowden. Minneapolis: Fortress, 1982. (= *The First Followers of Jesus.* London: SCM, 1978.)

Learning Activities

1) Describe the characteristics of each of the following groups:

---

6. *The Didache*, chs. 9 and 10, in Niederwimmer, *Commentary*, 144–72.

- Pharisees
- Sadducees
- Essenes
- Zealots
- Apocalyptics and Mystics
- Hellenistic Jews
- God-fearers
- Jewish Christians
- Hellenistic Christians

2) Events and persons to be remembered: describe them and locate them historically
    - Jerusalem Council
    - First Jewish-Roman War
    - Bar Kochba Rebellion
    - Stephen

3) Probe your understanding by discussing the following questions:
    - Trace the history of conflicts within the church of the first century: what are the conflicts about? How were these conflicts resolved?
    - What are the factors that led to the spread of the early Christian faith? Try to distinguish sociological, demographic, geographical, political, economic, theological and other factors.
    - Why did Jewish Christians gradually disappear from the church?
    - Why did Judaism and Christianity separate? Do you think it was a necessary development?
    - What was the early message (*kerygma*) of the followers of Jesus?
    - How did early Christians relate to the surrounding culture?

4) To deepen the significance of what we have learned about this period, discuss the following questions in small groups:
    - As the saying goes, "Jesus came proclaiming the Kingdom, and what arrived was the Church" (French theologian Alfred Loisy). What do you think about this sentence? What does it mean for us?
    - Is the link between persecution and mission a necessary one?

- There is a gradual shift from Jesus' proclamation of God's Kingdom to Paul's and later Christians' proclamation of Jesus Christ. What is this shift about? What does this mean for our proclamation?
- How do you see the relationship between Christianity and Judaism?

Chapter 2

Christianity and Politics
Persecution and Growth in the First Three Centuries

WHAT CHARACTERIZED THE EARLY Christian movement from its very beginning was its countercultural character—its rejection of the dominant currents of society and of what was taken for granted in cultural and religious life. This critical opposition was most visibly expressed in the Christian refusal to participate in emperor worship or the worship of other communal gods. The early Christians' vision of an alternative community and its separation from the political, economic, and social powers fundamentally upset the Roman Empire and those who cooperated with it. This kind of challenge to the political, economic, cultural, and religious elite was what had caused the death of Jesus. Many faithful followers of his movement continued to challenge the elite in the same way and met the same end.

The imperial government played a crucial role in the waves of persecution that accompanied the history of early Christianity during its first three centuries. Yet, other social groups equally and for various reasons loathed the Christians, even where they remained low-key and managed to assimilate.

This chapter describes the conflicts between Christianity and society (including the state and various social groups) during that time and the reactions that the emerging Christian movement provoked. It then shows how Christians dealt with the rejection they encountered and how Christianity grew continuously despite opposition and persecution. Finally, it describes the conflicts that emerged within Christianity between those who persevered despite suffering for their faith and those who forsook their faith under pressure.

This chapter will address the following questions:

- What were the reasons that some Christians were heavily persecuted in the first three centuries?
- How were the different waves of persecutions similar? How were they different?
- What was the situation of Christians during periods of relative political calm?
- What motives did the martyrs have?
- What were some of the factors that made Christianity grow despite the opposition it encountered?
- How did the martyrs shape Christianity?
- How should Christians treat those who give in to the pressure of persecution?

CONFLICTS AND PERSECUTION: WHY?

Christians experienced rejection from various quarters: sometimes simply from spontaneous crowds, sometimes from local or regional authorities, and sometimes, most severely, from the highest levels of the Roman Empire. The reasons for these conflicts were partly specific and local, but partly also due to the general perception of Christians. A good example of a local conflict is found in Acts 16:16–24: Paul casting out a demon from a slave girl who had the gift of fortune-telling. Her owners were understandably upset about losing a good source of income and reacted angrily, but clearly the context is limited to one specific city. A different kind of conflict, one of a more basic nature, is the conflict with Jewish groups. They perceived the Christians' challenge to and diversion from fundamental elements of the Jewish faith as a dangerous division among their already hard-pressed group. They feared that tolerating what they regarded as clear heresy would bring God's wrath upon them. Conflicts between Christians and Jews occurred in different areas but were geographically always limited to areas where Jews comprised the majority of the population and where the small minority of Christians was thus socially and economically excluded. The biblical reflections on this hardship (as in the Gospel of John), however, had a lasting and tragic impact on the later history of Jewish-Christian relations (see previous chapter).

The most significant conflict was with the authorities of the Roman Empire. While Jews, due to their long and respected history, were exempted from emperor worship, Christians were required to participate, as they were more and more perceived as a separate faith group. The Christian opposition to emperor worship was a clear denial of the emperor's supreme authority and political legitimacy. It was seen as undermining social cohesion and failing to give due respect to the symbol of the superior unity of the state. This opposition was modeled on that of Jesus, who, together with his peasant movement, had challenged the city-based aristocracy in Jerusalem and thus had angered the Jewish and Roman authorities. Just as Jesus had contradicted the empire and made a mockery of political power displays—for instance, when riding in mock triumph on a donkey into Jerusalem—later Christians' central terms seemed to plagiarize or stand in open contradiction to imperial language. For instance, the term *good news* was originally used to describe the Emperor Augustus' birthday; *parousia* originally meant the emperor's arrival in a city.[1] The Christians' fundamental opposition to the empire prevailed even where they increasingly accommodated themselves to political power and became more "spiritual," with limited interest for political matters. Regarding the empire as part of the present age and bound to vanish anyway, they denied its ultimate authority.

Interestingly, the Roman government's allegation against the Christians was that they were practicing atheism, not that they were worshiping another god. Atheism here refers not to the philosophical position that there is no god but to the actual practice of worshiping no Roman god. This was not a spurious accusation: Christians did refuse to participate in the cult of the patron god of a city;[2] even more strange and suspicious, having no images, no altar, no temple, and no sacrifice, they lacked all the ingredients of common religious life. For the Romans, both subjects and rulers alike, atheism was not only a religious problem but also a social and political one (a distinction, it should be noted, the Romans would not have made). Worshiping the gods had the purpose of securing the well-being and prosperity of the state or city. The Christians' separation from the community's religious life was interpreted as a social separation and an unwillingness to contribute to the common good.[3]

---

1. See Young, "Prelude," 14–15, for these and many more examples of how early Christians used language from the ruler-cult tradition to describe Christ.
2. Justin Martyr, *First Apology*, chs. 5 and 6.
3. *Epistle to Diognetus* 5.1–17.

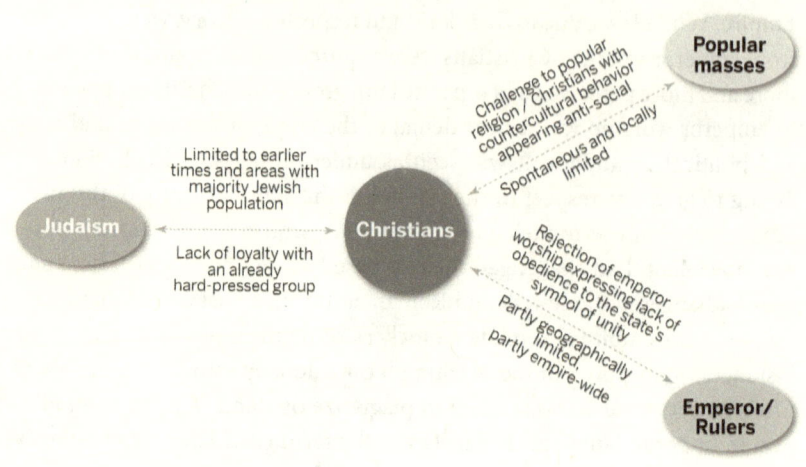

Fig. 2.1: The early Christians' conflicts with various groups

Another common reason Christians were persecuted was that they were an ideal group to blame, thus deflecting popular discontent from the real reasons for people's misery. The tactic of blaming less powerful minority groups for tragic but mysterious events and existing social injustices has throughout history been used to pacify the majority. Not always was the government the source of such scapegoating. Often, other social groups held Christians responsible for any problem or disaster that could not be explained. The second-century theologian Tertullian described this common experience: "If the Tiber has overflowed its banks, if the Nile has remained in its bed . . . , your cry immediately is, 'This is the fault of the Christians!'"[4] Tragically, Christians themselves in later years actively used such blaming strategies to persecute "witches," Jews, and other social minority groups.

Indeed, Christians were a relatively easy target for scapegoating, as their strict lifestyle and separation from common social activities seemed disruptive to mainstream society. They did not participate in military service, less due to their pacifism than to the fact that military service commonly included attendance at ceremonies including sacrifices to other gods. Similarly, their separation from much of public life was necessary because public life was inextricably linked to popular religion. Christians did not go to the public theater, the public bath, or the circus, nor did they join popular festivals. All these were important centers of social life, and thus Christians appeared unsociable, stubborn, and intolerant. Equally, their strict ethical

---

4. Tertullian, *Ad Nationes* I.9 (ANF 3:117).

standards regarding sex, divorce, abortion and infanticide made them clearly distinct from the majority. Social class was another dimension of Christians appearing to be a strange community. Their egalitarianism and their link to poor social groups alienated them from leading social groups. Sometimes, their evangelization caused conflict within a family—when, for example, the women or slaves of a house were converted to Christianity but not the patriarchal head of the family.

Hostility was also aroused by Christians' separation from other social and religious groups. Encountering such hostility, they responded with exclusivism, which contrasted with the generally tolerant religious context. As the Christians became a more significant social group, they were increasingly perceived as condescending toward other groups. The Christian description of nonbelievers as pagans (Latin *pagani*, meaning "country people") that emerged from the third century on reflected something of this negative attitude.

Also, the Christians' secretiveness easily led to *misunderstandings*. A common rumor was that Christians engaged in cannibalism, as they gathered in privately held eucharistic celebrations where they were said to "eat the flesh and drink the blood" of their savior. Similarly, the love meals where men and women ate together, and where people from various social groups were in unusually close association, were sometimes perceived as orgiastic and promiscuous feasts. Only toward the end of the second century did such misunderstandings abate.

An Apologist's Defense of Christianity

In this text, Justin counters allegations of Christian godlessness by pointing out the irrationality of popular beliefs and by reminding his readers that Socrates, a hero of the Greek tradition, similarly became a victim of this irrationality.

Chapter 5: Christians charged with atheism

Why, then, should this be? In our case, who pledge ourselves to do nothing wicked, nor to hold these godless opinions, you do not investigate the charges made against us; but, giving in to unreasoning passion, and the instigation of evil demons, you punish us without trial or consideration. For the truth shall be told; since of old these evil demons manifested themselves, both defiled women and corrupted boys, and showed terrifying sights to people, that those who did not use their reason in judging the acts that were done, were filled with terror; and being taken captive by fear, and not knowing that these were demons, they called them gods, and gave to each the name which each of the demons chose for himself. And when Socrates tried, by true reasoning

> *and definite evidence, to bring these things to light, and deliver people from the demons, then the demons themselves, by means of people who rejoiced in wickedness, compassed his death, as an atheist and impious person, on the charge of introducing new divinities; and in our case they show a similar activity. For not only among the Greeks through Socrates were these things revealed by reason [logos], but also among the Barbarians were they revealed by logos personally, when He had taken shape, and become man, and was called Jesus Christ; and in obedience to Him, we not only deny that they who did such things as these are gods, but state that they are wicked and impious demons, whose actions will not bear comparison with those even of people who long after virtue.*
>
> *Chapter 6: Charge of atheism refuted*
>
> *Hence we are called atheists. And we confess that we are atheists with reference to gods such as these, but not with reference to the most true God, the Father of righteousness and temperance and the other virtues, who is unmixed with evil. But we worship and adore both Him and the Son who came from Him and taught us these things, and the army of the other good angels, who follow Him and are made like Him, and the prophetic Spirit, giving honor [to Him] in reason and truth; and to everyone who wishes to learn handing over without grudging, what we have been taught.*

Source: St. Justin Martyr, *First Apology*, chs. 5 and 6, in *The First and Second Apologies*, 25–26.

SIX WAVES OF PERSECUTION AND THE CHRISTIANS' PRECARIOUS LEGAL STATUS

Throughout the first three centuries, Christians experienced six important waves of persecution. In between these waves of persecution, they were able to live relatively normal lives, though always on precarious legal ground. At least during the first two centuries, the Christians were numerically too insignificant to be of serious concern to the Roman authorities. This changed in the third century when Christians started to turn into an increasingly substantial minority.

The first persecution happened almost accidentally—and not on any fundamental point of principle—under the Emperor Nero in the year 64 CE. In order to counter the rumors that blamed him for a disastrous fire that had caused the death of thousands of Romans, Nero blamed the Christians for having caused the blaze. He could argue that their faith was based on the teaching of a convicted Jewish criminal who had prophesied the destruction of the world, and that they themselves had often enough alluded to biblical passages about vengeance and fire, such as Isaiah 66:15.

The church historian Eusebius wrote vividly about this period:

> Once Nero's power was firmly established, he plunged into nefarious vices and took up arms against the God of the universe. To describe his depravity is not part of the present work. ... With various sorts of deaths, he did away with his mother, brothers, and wife, as well as countless other near relatives, as if they were strangers and enemies. Despite all this, one crime still had to be added to his catalogue: he was the first of the emperors to be the declared enemy of the Deity. ... So it happened that this man, the first to be announced publicly as a fighter against God, was led on to slaughter the apostles. It is related that in his reign Paul was beheaded in Rome itself and that Peter was also crucified, and the cemeteries there still called by the names of Peter and Paul confirm the record.[5]

Nero's accusation against the Christians was supported by the fact that the areas where they lived were less affected by the fire. However, his attempt to sway public opinion met with limited success. Nero was widely seen as the one setting the fire so that he could expand his palace and proceed with his plans of a new and glorious Rome. Sixty years later, the non-Christian historian Tacitus, writing about the fire, even expressed some sympathy toward the Christians.[6]

This first wave of persecution by the emperor, then, was not yet due to any sense of deep ideological conflict between Christians and the state, and it was geographically limited to Rome. However, it became a precedent for magistrates to condemn Christians simply because they were Christians, without any other charges made. Being a Christian alone risked capital punishment. According to church tradition, Peter and Paul were killed during this persecution. The event also showed how the government was starting to distinguish between Christianity and Judaism and thus deal with them differently.

---

5. Eusebius, *Church History* II, 25, 74–75.
6. Tacitus, *Annals*, bk. 15, ch. 44, in *Annals of Tacitus*, 304–5.

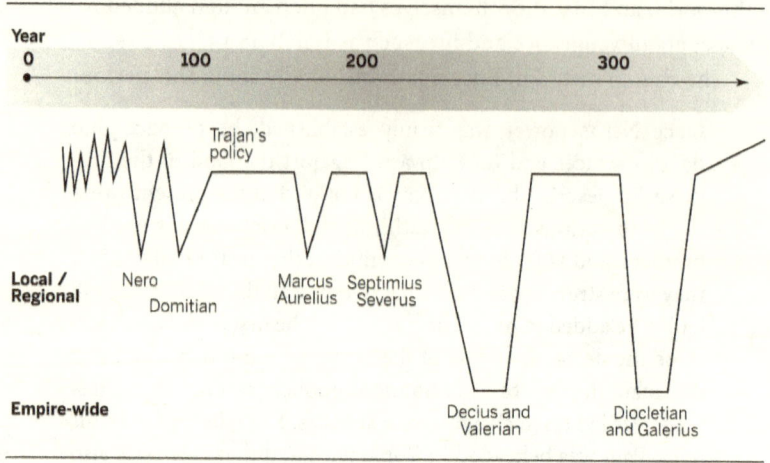

Fig. 2.2: Waves of persecution in the first three centuries

A second wave of persecution happened under the Emperor Domitian (81–96 CE), who styled himself as "master and god" and demanded to be worshiped as a god. In contrast to earlier emperors, who had discouraged overenthusiastic veneration and the offering of divine honors, Domitian made the oath to the emperor compulsory. His persecution may stand in the context of an attempt to restore Roman traditions, and it was felt mainly around Rome and in Asia Minor. It is assumed that it formed the background to the book of Revelation.

The Emperor Trajan (98–117 CE) did not like the cult of the emperor being made a compulsory loyalty-test, and the wave of persecution passed. Trajan was the first to spell out a policy of how to deal with Christianity, which brought Christians a period of relative safety and peace. The policy formulation was triggered in 112 CE by Pliny the Younger, governor of Bithynia in Asia Minor, who asked the emperor how to deal with Christians. Pliny could not find any obvious crime in what Christians were doing, except that because of their evangelization many pagan temples had been deserted and those who were engaged in businesses related to traditional faith practices faced economic hardship because nobody wanted to buy sacrificial animals anymore.[7] In response, Trajan advised Pliny not to actively prosecute Christians and only to intervene when someone was brought to court by a responsible individual. Anonymous accusations should not be accepted. The goal of the government's intervention was not to punish or

---

7. The exchange of letters can be found in Pliny the Younger, *Complete Letters*, 278–79.

kill Christians, but to give them a chance to offer their prayers to the gods. If through such an action they would show that they were not Christians, they should be pardoned. This pragmatic response of Trajan sidestepped the principal question—the actual nature of the crime—but it became common practice during most of the second century and thus brought a period of relative peace and safety for Christians. Trajan's policy was reaffirmed by his successor, Emperor Hadrian (117–38). Christians continued to experience martyrdom under Trajan, but they were not actively and systematically persecuted.

This period of relative stability was interrupted by a third wave of persecution during the reign of Emperor Marcus Aurelius (161–80). Marcus Aurelius was not only a politician but also a famous philosopher and a highly educated statesman. It is thus quite a surprise that such a man turned to persecuting Christians. Once more, Christians were used as scapegoats for bad harvests, epidemics, invasions, and other disasters. The most affected areas were in the Rhone Valley in France, in Asia Minor, and around Rome. One of the most famous martyrs during this period was the apologist Justin the Martyr, who was killed around 165.

After the persecutions during the reign of Marcus Aurelius, the situation for Christians was again relatively calm until a new wave began during the reign of Septimius Severus (193–211). Seeking to unite the people through the worship of the god *Sol Invictus* (the unconquered Sun), he issued an edict prohibiting conversions to Christianity. Yet, these first four periods of persecutions could not stop the church from gradually growing. Identifying themselves as citizens of another world, Christians led lives separate from political involvement and tried to stay away from the government.

Only in the third century, when Christianity had already grown to an estimated 3 to 5 percent of the overall population,[8] did the church experience more large-scale persecution. The persecutions under Decius (249–51) and Valerian (253–60) were the first applied to the whole empire and they were clearly the most serious that any Christians had experienced. Several reasons can be found for this oppression. Decius hoped to restore Rome's ancient glory by reviving traditional religion and eradicating what he perceived as a foreign and non-Roman faith. By reviving the ancestral religion, he tried to counter both the growing internal decay that had resulted from a domestic economic crisis and the external threat of increasing attacks by migrating people groups from the East. The imperial government felt

---

8. This is based on an assumption of around 8 to 10 percent Christians by the year 300. It may be expected that the number was significantly lower half a century earlier. See Stark, *Rise of Christianity*, 6 and 13; Bevans and Schroeder, *Constants in Context*, 83.

increasingly challenged by a Christian minority who built a "state within the state."

The persecution unfolded through several edicts of increasing severity. An initial edict in 250 CE declared it mandatory for everyone, including children, to participate in pagan sacrifice. A second edict some years later was aimed particularly at Christian clerics, who were threatened with exile if they refused to participate in pagan worship. The pressure was further increased by a third edict that threatened clerics with an immediate death sentence, wealthy Christians with confiscation of their wealth and deprivation of their aristocratic titles, and ordinary people with forced labor and confiscation of personal goods unless they denied their faith. Decius and Valerian knew that martyring Christians would actually promote the cause. Their strategy thus aimed more at damaging the church financially, at coercing Christians to abandon their faith, and at hurting the Christian community by dividing it. Those who maintained their faith while suffering such coercion (but without actually dying for their faith) were called confessors. A famous victim of persecution under Decius was the theologian Origen of Alexandria.

A final wave of persecution in the history of Western Christianity (i.e., before Christianity became the official state religion), known as the Great Persecution, was initiated by Emperor Diocletian (284–305) and happened with an unprecedented ferocity. Initially rather indifferent to Christianity, Diocletian increasingly perceived the Christians as an obstacle to his attempt of reunifying the empire under the traditional Roman gods. Once more Christians were perceived as subverting the harmony and coherence of the empire and its institutions. This final wave of persecution began in 302 and reached its peak under the rulers of the eastern part of the Roman Empire, Galerius and Maximinus, in the years 305 to 311. It ended with the victory of Constantine in the battle of the Milvian Bridge near Rome (see ch. 5).

The Growth of Christianity

The peak of persecution came toward the end of Diocletian's rule in 303 CE and under Galerius, the next emperor. The persecution happened much more in the eastern part of the empire, where Diocletian and Galerius ruled, than in the western part under Maximian and Constantius Chlorus, the father of Constantine.

In the following excerpt, Eusebius criticizes the growing arrogance fostered by the growth of Christianity; thus, he interprets what he called the "Great Persecution" as divine judgment. The text also shows that at this time many Christians could already be found in senior government positions.

Chapter 1—The Growth of Christianity

Before the persecution of my day, the message given through Christ to the world of reverence to God was accorded honor and freedom by all men, Greeks and non-Greeks alike. Rulers granted our people favors and even permitted them to govern provinces, while freeing them from the agonizing issue of [pagan] sacrifice. In the imperial palaces, emperors allowed members of their own households—wives, children, and servants—to practice the faith openly, according men like the loyal Dorotheus and the celebrated Gorgonius higher favor than their fellow servants or even officers. All governors honored the church leaders, mass meetings gathered in every city, and congregations worshiped in new, spacious churches that replaced the old. This all progressed day by day, the divine hand protecting its people from jealousy or plot so long as they were worthy.

But greater freedom brought with it arrogance and sloth. We began envying and attacking one another, making war on ourselves with weapons formed from words. Church leaders attacked church leaders and laymen formed factions against laymen, while unspeakable hypocrisy and pretense reached their evil limit. Finally, while the assemblies were still crowded, divine judgment, with its accustomed mercy, gradually started to intervene, and the persecution began with our brothers in the army. In our blindness, however, we made no effort to propitiate the Deity but, like atheists, assumed that our affairs went unnoticed, and we went from one wickedness to another. Those who were supposed to be pastors, unrestrained by the fear of God, quarreled bitterly with one another and only added to the strife, threats, jealousy, and hate, frantically claiming the tyrannical power they craved. Then it was that the Lord in his anger humiliated his daughter Zion, in the words of Jeremiah, and threw down from heaven the glory of Israel [Lam. 2:1-2]. And, as foretold in the Psalms, he renounced the covenant with his servant and profaned to the ground his sanctuary—through the destruction of churches—exalting the right hand of his servant's enemies, not assisting him in battle, and covering him with shame.

Source: Eusebius, *The Church History*, bk. VIII, ch. 1, 259-60.

THEOLOGY AND SPIRITUALITY OF CHRISTIAN MARTYRDOM

The different waves of persecution brought suffering and death to many Christians. However, though persecution did shape the life of early Christianity, the overall number of victims was rather small—probably a few thousand for the whole period until Constantine.[9] Usually, it was aimed at Christian leaders or prominent Christians rather than ordinary believers. Many martyrs' accounts tell how people were able to interact with those facing martyrdom, apparently without attracting punishment. They were allowed to listen to the impending martyrs' preaching, visit them in prison, and feed and clothe them.

A good number of the victims are still remembered as martyrs, witnesses with an unshakable faith. Our knowledge about these martyrs comes mainly from a collection of stories, the *Acts of the Martyrs*. Eusebius of Caesarea in the fourth century (see ch. 5) was probably the first to produce such a collection of stories about martyrs.[10] These accounts of suffering were collected and used in churches even from the earliest times. Some were based directly on trial records; others appear more legendary.

One of the most famous early martyrs, besides those recorded in the Bible, is Ignatius of Antioch, the third bishop of Antioch and, according to legend, the little child to whom Jesus referred in Mark 9:36. He probably died in Rome sometime between 110 and 117. His martyrdom is documented through several letters that he wrote to his congregation while on his way to Rome. Other famous martyrs include Polycarp, bishop of Smyrna in Asia Minor; Justin Martyr; and Origen of Alexandria. One particularly popular and well-documented story is that of Perpetua and Felicitas in the early third century. Perpetua came from an affluent family and accepted martyrdom despite nursing an infant child. Felicitas was pregnant at the time of her arrest and gave birth while waiting for her execution. Even children were said to have become martyrs, such as the fifteen-year-old Ponticus. According to early accounts, he was one of the martyrs of Lyon who died in 177, together with a young female martyr, Blandina.

---

9. W. H. C. Frend, whose research on martyrdom and persecution in the early church is regarded as authoritative, gives such an estimation for the Decian-Valerian persecution: "Deaths over the whole Empire may probably be numbered in hundreds rather than thousands..." Referring to the Diocletian persecution, he assumes a grand total of three thousand to thirty-five thousand. See Frend, *Martyrdom and Persecution*, 308 and 394.

10. "Acts of the Martyrs," in Cross, *Oxford Dictionary of the Christian Church*, 14; Musurillo, *Acts of the Christian Martyrs*.

It is important to understand that martyrdom was not simply something tragically imposed by a cruel Roman government and passively suffered by innocent Christian victims. Rather it was an ideal, a spiritual journey, which some believers actively sought; it was an active form of Christian witness—molded by existing theological and spiritual patterns. Martyrdom was a conscious and powerful witness and an active form of Christian existence. Several aspects should be noted:

- The idea of martyrdom was inspired by elements of Jewish tradition, particularly the prophets Isaiah and Daniel. Important motives were the idea of the vicarious suffering of the servant of God and the idea of martyrdom as a propitiating sacrifice for the sins of the community.

- The Christian community found a pattern for martyrdom in the death of Jesus. It understood martyrdom as imitation of and participation in the suffering of Jesus Christ and as an opportunity to give public witness. As a result of this public witness through martyrdom, persecution in the first centuries actually contributed to the spread of Christianity.

- The ultimate theological rationale for martyrdom reflected the same upside-down pattern as the crucifixion and resurrection of Jesus Christ: through the martyr's death the persecuting authorities apparently triumphed but were in fact defeated.

- Martyrs accepted their suffering not only because of the promise of an eternal reward but also because of the recognition they received from the Christian community while still alive.[11]

- Martyrdom had an egalitarian dimension in the early church. Anyone, independent of education and social standing, could become a martyr. Several famous martyrs were women who, through their martyrdom, attracted popular veneration.

- Martyrs in the early church were an alternative source of authority and challenged a church that was increasingly governed by hierarchical and patriarchal church leaders. The martyrs' authority stood in tension with the institutional church. They can be seen as part of the "other" church, an alternative community (more about this in ch. 11). The challenge to institutional authority was one of the factors in the conflict between Cyprian and Novatian (see below).

---

11. Stark, *Rise of Christianity*, 180–84.

In the first centuries, the theology of martyrdom became part of popular Christian literature, and the stories of heroic martyrs turned into an important source of Christian communication. Martyrdom was not simply an act of a heroic individual—it also played a role in the Christian community's framework of belief. Christians believed in the special powers of martyrs and in their ability to distribute favors to the community. From an early time, the Christian community venerated martyrs as saints and commemorated them on special days and through special liturgies.

IMPACTS OF THE PERSECUTIONS: THE PROBLEM OF THE LAPSED

The first consequence of persecution, of course, was the physical suffering that it caused. Another impact, however, was the question of how to react: Was it worth sticking to one's faith if it meant losing one's life? Should a church leader accept martyrdom or, rather, hide or escape in order to continue to serve the community?

It is obvious that these questions belong not only to the past. From a modern perspective, however, it is difficult to fully understand the relatively widespread willingness of early Christians to accept martyrdom.

Possibly even more divisive was the question of how to deal with those who had yielded to the pressure of persecution. Not surprisingly, under threat of punishment, some Christians gave up their faith and participated in sacrifices to pagan gods. Others compromised their faith by buying certificates from the Roman authorities attesting to their participation, though in fact they had not participated. The question was thus compounded by these different ways of yielding to the government's threats.

So, then, how should the community deal with those who had denied their faith? And who had the authority to answer this question?

Underneath these administrative or disciplinary questions lay more fundamental questions about the self-understanding of the church. What are the characteristics (or the marks) of the true church? How far should forgiveness be extended toward those who had denied their faith? Is the church foremost an exclusive and morally strict community or an inclusive and forgiving one?

These questions were so divisive that the church experienced its first schism: the Novatian Schism.

> Church terminology usually distinguishes between *schisms* and *heresies*: While a schism is a split in the community based on

> questions of right authority without actual division over matters of doctrine, heresy is a division over the right doctrine. In reality, the two cannot be strictly separated because underneath a division regarding the authority of the church, there are doctrinal or political divisions. Furthermore, people who use the terms "heretic" and "schismatic" see themselves as orthodox; they express the view of a victorious party in a conflict. The defeated party in turn likewise regards the opposite party as schismatic or heretical. The perception of the opposition as schismatic or heretical is thus mostly mutual.

During the persecutions by Decius and Valerian, two responses stood against each other. Cyprian, bishop of Carthage (c. 200–258), called for a readmission (after a period of penance) of those who had lapsed; he emphasized that the Christian community should first be one of forgiveness, love, and unity.

What undermined his position in the eyes of his opponents, however, was that Cyprian himself had gone into hiding during the persecution by Decius and Valerian, from where he maintained contact with his congregation through written correspondence. Still, his later death as a martyr (in 258) showed that he had hid not so much out of fear as out of a desire to continue serving his community.

Novatian, on the other side, criticized Cyprian and denied his authority to decide the question. Novatian said only the so-called confessors, those who had maintained their faith even under torture and imprisonment, had the authority to decide on the restoration of the lapsed. Novatian saw the church first as a pure and morally strict community.

The majority of the Christian representatives at a synod in Carthage (251) supported the position of Cyprian and reaffirmed this decision some years later. Yet the followers of Novatian continued to spread across the empire and existed until around the seventh century. As in later cases, the controversy was deepened by the different parties receiving backing from different social groups. Similar schisms, the Donatist schism and the Meletian schism, arose again in the fourth century (see ch. 6).

THE SPREAD OF CHRISTIANITY IN THE FIRST THREE CENTURIES

Geographically, the Christian church extended gradually throughout all parts of the empire and beyond the Roman Empire. It is a mistake to assume that Christianity spread mainly from Jerusalem toward the West. In fact, during the first centuries Christianity spread much more in the eastern part of the Roman Empire than in Italy, Spain, Gaul (present-day France), or Britain. Moving from Palestine eastward and beyond the Roman Empire, Christianity established important centers in Edessa, in the Persian kingdom of Adiabene, in Armenia, and probably even in India.[12]

Socially, Christians were until the middle of the third century more likely to be found among the lower class and in urban communities, where Christianity was a small but vibrant and significant minority. Based on the number of churches, it is estimated that Christians in Rome around 250 CE comprised 3 to 5 percent of the city's population. As Christianity had grown more in urban contexts, the demographic percentage of Christians was smaller in the rest of the Roman Empire than in Rome. However, Christianity began to increasingly attract intellectuals and members of the economic and political elite; even some emperors were said to be sympathetic to the Christian faith, among them Severus Alexander (222–35), whose mother was at one time a disciple of Origen, and Philipp the Arabian (244–49), who was even rumored to be a Christian. On the other hand, the Christian faith seldom attracted members of the army, where the dominant cult was the cult of Mithras, which originated in Persia.

Culturally, the church was dominated more by Hellenistic culture than by Roman culture. Until the middle of the third century, Greek was the official language of the church, even in Rome. The church increasingly built important links within the vast empire to pass on values, learning, and culture. As such, the church became a significant part of civil society. The leaders of the church acquired authority over many aspects of civil life because church discipline and penance gave the church effective sanctioning instruments and the power to exclude people from the civil community. The church thus became a part of civil society that linked the whole of the vast empire.

What Factors Attracted People to the Christian Faith?

The continuous growth of Christianity despite several waves of persecution shows evidence of an amazing tenacity of this faith movement. The factors mentioned above (ch. 1, "Christianity Spreads into the Gentile World") continued to draw people from various social groups to the Christian community: the community's inclusive faith, its power to transform people, and the value it gave to the lives of alienated people lacking upper-class privileges was convincing. In other words, *Christianity was attractive not*

12. Moffett, *History of Christianity in Asia*, vol. 1, chs. 2 and 3.

because it won philosophical arguments but because it worked, as the following examples show.

Hospitality was a primary Christian virtue that was not only extolled by biblical texts and early Christian writings but was also commonly practiced. Worship celebrations in private houses were linked to the sharing of food and to providing accommodation for itinerant preachers. As the institutional church became increasingly patriarchal, house churches and the service of hospitality turned into an alternative venue for women to engage in Christian ministry.

Hospitality was also practiced toward the sick and the dying. During a severe second-century epidemic in Rome, the Antonine Plague (165–80), Christians did not flee the city but stayed behind to take care of the sick and dying. Christians were not afraid of losing their lives and were therefore willing to risk showing mercy to the suffering. With ancient Rome's lack of basic hygiene, even simple acts of care effectively reduced mortality during epidemics. This gave Christianity a positive image. In addition, people who had survived these epidemics were now immune and could expose themselves to the epidemic without falling ill again. They were thus able to pass on the care they had received. These acts of mercy and love stood in contrast to the values of both Roman pagan religions and moral philosophy.

Christianity was particularly attractive to women, many of them of higher social status.[13] Within the Christian church, women were able to assume leadership positions, as shown by the greetings in Paul's epistles to various female Christian leaders. Christian sanctification of the marital bond, condemnation of promiscuity, a relatively symmetrical understanding of marital relationships, and respect for widows were other factors in Christianity's appeal to women.

Christians were known to share generously because they cultivated a critical attitude to private property. Many of the earliest hermits (see ch. 5) sold all their goods and gave the proceeds to the poor. Biblical teaching—and the Christian preaching that flowed from it—saw the poor in a positive light, while wealth was frowned upon.

It was this overall critical distance to the world and its values, combined with the provision of care and hospitality for those in need, that contributed to the steady growth of Christianity.

However, Christianity grew not only through conversion but also through a different population development, in particular the higher fertility rate of the Christian community, which was linked to Christians' different morals. Christians rejected abortion and female infanticide, both widely

---

13. See overall on this Stark, *Rise of Christianity*, ch. 5.

practiced in the Roman context; this led to lower mortality among women and a higher number of marriageable Christian women. Many of them subsequently led their husbands to convert.

By the early fourth century, it is estimated that about 10 percent of the roughly fifty million people of the Roman Empire were Christians.[14]

For Further Reading

Bevans, Stephen B., and Roger P. Schroeder. *Constants in Context: A Theology of Mission for Today*, Maryknoll, NY: Orbis, 2004, 74–98 (a summary of Moffett's more detailed account).

Frend, William H. C. "Persecutions: Genesis and Legacy." In *The Cambridge History of Christianity*, vol. 1, *Origins to Constantine*, edited by Margaret M. Mitchell and Frances M. Young, 503–23. Cambridge: Cambridge University Press, 2006.

———. *The Rise of Christianity*. Philadelphia: Fortress, 1984.

Moffett Samuel Hugh. *A History of Christianity in Asia*. Vol. 1, *Beginnings to 1500*. Maryknoll, NY: Orbis, 1998.

Stark, Rodney. *The Rise of Christianity: A Sociologist Reconsiders History*. Princeton: Princeton University Press, 1996.

Young, Robin Darling. "Martyrdom as Exaltation." In *Late Ancient Christianity*, edited by Virginia Burrus, 70–94. Minneapolis: Fortress, 2005.

Learning Activities

1) Review key elements of this chapter by completing the following exercises:
   - Name two examples of persecution in the New Testament and list the factors causing the persecution.
   - Describe the role and political interests of the following persons:
     - Nero
     - Domitian
     - Tacitus
     - Decius
     - Diocletian
   - Review the following events, persons, and terms, describe what they stand for, and locate them historically
     - Cyprian
     - Confessors

14. Bevans and Schroeder, *Constants in Context*, 83. See also Stark, *Rise of Christianity*, 69–70.

- Trajan
  - Name three early Christian martyrs and describe the circumstances of their martyrdom.

2) Probe your understanding by discussing the following questions:
   - Why were Christians persecuted? Give both external (societal) and internal (faith) reasons, and notice where the two types overlap.
   - What were the Roman government's policies toward Christians during this period?
   - What were important motives in the theology of martyrs?
   - What was the Novatian Schism about? How did the church resolve it?
   - What motives and beliefs encouraged Christians to accept martyrdom?
   - What factors were causes for the continuous growth of Christianity in the first centuries?

3) To deepen the significance of what we have learned about this period, discuss the following questions:
   - Think of the church under persecution and ask yourself: Ethically, how should Christians respond to persecution?
   - How should the church respond to the lapsed? Discuss the debate between Cyprian and Novatian and compare it to modern-day situations. What is the significance of the debate?
   - Discuss similarities and differences (in the church and its theology) between the time before Constantine and present-day China.
   - Can you find modern parallels to the Roman emperor's requirement for Christians to participate in emperor worship?
   - What are differences and similarities between some modern states' requirement for religious groups to submit to the authority of the state and the Roman Empire's requirement to do so?
   - Decius and Valerian tried to overcome social problems by reviving traditional Roman religion. Can you find modern parallels?

Chapter 3

Challenges to the Christian Movement and Trends toward a Unified Faith

As the Christian movement grew—in numbers, in age, in geographical, social, and cultural extension—it was not surprising that it began to develop a more unified organization and a more coherent doctrine. This trend is a natural process for any reform movement. In the history of Christianity, it is usually described as the emergence of a "catholic" church. *Catholic* refers here not to the specific Roman Catholic Church but to a doctrine and a structure that is comprehensive and universal and that has validity beyond one narrow context. The trend toward a more comprehensive and universal structure and doctrine developed gradually from the first century and can already be seen in the Pastoral Letters of the New Testament. Yet, in the middle of the second century, this trend gained momentum when the Christian movement encountered some fundamental challenges to its doctrine.

This chapter discusses the three most important doctrinal challenges to the church in the second century: the Gnostic movement, the teaching of Marcion, and Montanism. These alternative interpretations of the significance of Jesus Christ triggered a veritable faith crisis in the still-young movement because each doctrinal challenge asked fundamental and reasonable questions that the Christian movement had to resolve.

The Gnostics asked, how does God relate to the created world?

Marcion asked, how does the Christian tradition relate to its Jewish heritage?

The Montanist movement asked, what about the expectation of the imminent end of time?

We will see how the Christian movement responded, attempting to clarify its own position in light of the challenges from these three alternative faith movements. These responses led the church toward increasing unification of organizational structure and gradual homogenization of doctrine.

This chapter will address the following questions:

- What was the pre-catholic church like? How was the church organized before the more catholic structure emerged?
- What is Gnosis? Why did the Gnostic faith movement become so dangerous to the Christian faith?
- What was the teaching of Marcion, and in what way did it challenge Christian teaching?
- What was the teaching of Montanus, and what was the appeal of the Montanist movement?
- What elements of catholicism developed under the faith crisis of the second century?
- Finally, how should we interpret the outcome of this process of clarification and homogenization of faith? What did the church lose or gain through this process?

FAITH CRISIS AND CONTEXTUALIZATION: A QUESTION OF COMPATIBILITY

The context into which the Christian movement came was not like a blank sheet of paper. Rather, new converts influenced Christianity with elements from their own cultural or religious backgrounds and, likewise, Christianity used elements of local cultures to make itself contextually understood. In this process, the diverse Christian traditions needed to clarify how contextualization should happen and how compatible elements of non-Jewish cultures were with the Christian message. At the same time, they had to reject elements of recipient cultures that stood in opposition to the Christian faith and could not be reconciled with the message of Jesus Christ.

On the other hand, upon its entry into a new context, the Christian movement had to reassess the significance of its own background (the Jewish tradition) that had shaped it previously. This is the question that Marcion raised. In the challenges to the Christian faith in the second century, we can thus see a basic pattern of contextualization, asking about how Christian faith should relate to a new context and how relevant the context of origin is.

THE PRE-CATHOLIC CHURCH BEFORE THE FAITH CRISIS OF THE SECOND CENTURY

Until the middle of the second century, the church was a loose movement, with scattered congregations in different places following their own traditions and developing distinct habits. Different forms of leadership coexisted, although a tendency toward bishops (as heads of congregations), presbyters, and deacons can already be seen in the first century (see above, ch. 1, "Theological Shifts through the First Century"). Most importantly, there was no common and universal church authority but instead different centers of limited authority. To be sure, Jerusalem was a traditional center, but it had little spiritual authority over Gentile churches after 70 CE. Other centers of limited and regional authority were Antioch, Rome, and later Alexandria, major cities of the Roman Empire where a significant number of Christians lived. Thus Gentile churches developed their theologies and practices individually and independently. The theological diversity that already existed in the various christological views of the New Testament simply continued.

From a systematic rather than geographic perspective, we can distinguish four major early theological traditions:

1. *Jewish Christianity*: after the First Jewish-Roman War the remaining Jewish Christian groups dispersed into the upper Jordan Valley. Known as Ebionites, they maintained their own tradition for some time until eventually disappearing.

2. *Hellenistic Christianity*: as the Christian movement entered Hellenistic culture, it absorbed significant elements of it. The Gnostic movement can be understood as a radical consequence of the Hellenization of Christianity.

3. *Apocalyptic Christianity*: the Jewish apocalyptic expectation that had shaped early Christianity gradually lost its influence when the eschatological hope faded. It was revived in the Montanist movement.

4. *Early Catholicism*: responding to the fading expectation of an imminent second coming of Christ, the church developed institutionalized forms to put down roots in a world that seemed, for the time being, to be somewhat permanent. The establishment of orderly church structures and offices of leadership, as well as the consolidation of faith into set forms, can already be seen in the later writings of the New Testament (e.g., the Pastoral Letters).

Challenges to the Christian Movement and Trends toward a Unified Faith 45

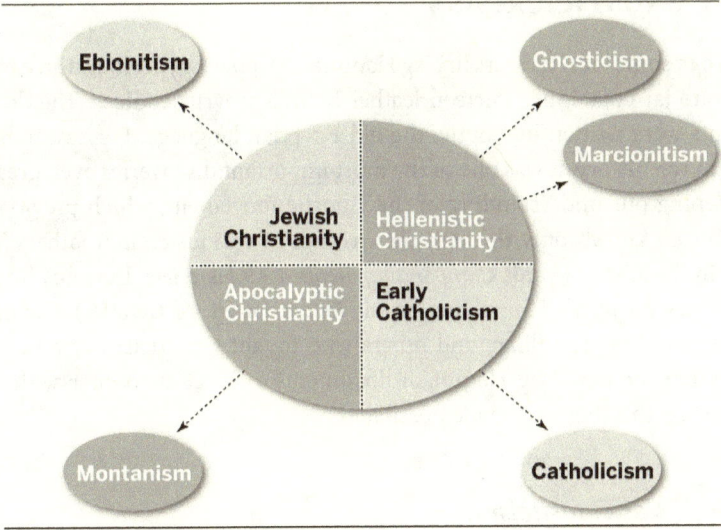

Fig. 3.1: The diversity of early Christian groups and their development[1]

The development toward growing unity can be summarized in the following chart:

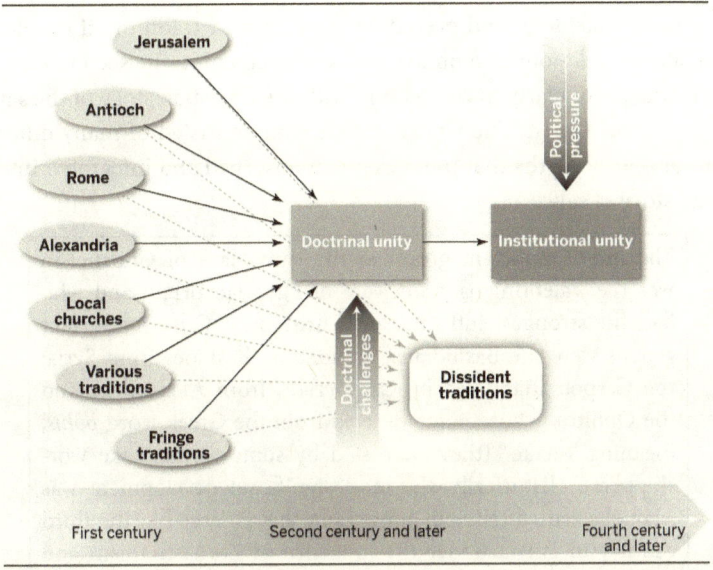

Fig. 3.2: From diversity to unity

1. Based on Dunn, *Unity and Diversity*, 235–366.

THE GNOSTIC CRISIS

In 1945 some local farmers in Nag Hammadi (Upper Egypt) found an earthenware jar containing thirteen leather-bound papyrus codices. The documents were written in Coptic, the old Egyptian language. For researchers of church history, it was one of the most important discoveries ever, greatly widening our understanding of the Gnostic movement, which previously had been known only through the writings of various church fathers like Justin the Martyr (in his *Compendium against All Heresies*), Irenaeus (in his *Adversus haereses*), Hippolytus (in his *Refutation of All Heresies*), Clement of Alexandria, Tertullian, and others who fought Gnosticism as a heresy. Through the new Nag Hammadi documents a direct encounter with the Gnostics' theology was made possible.

What Was Gnosticism?

Gnosticism was a strongly dualistic and syncretistic faith movement that integrated elements of mystery religions, oriental pagan religions, Jewish faith, and Hellenistic philosophy. *Gnosis* means knowledge and, indeed, the gnostic faith movement regarded knowledge (namely, knowledge about one's origins) as the key to salvation. Although Gnosticism drew from various sources outside of and preceding the Christian tradition, it developed as a coherent religious and philosophical movement in the second century, flourishing particularly in connection with the Christian story of the savior figure of Jesus Christ. The Gnostic movement consisted of many different forms and local myths that the movement absorbed and integrated into its overall story of salvation.

> The most important group in the early days of Gnosticism was the Valentinians, who were of Egyptian origin and who had the strongest influence on Christianity. Other important groups were the Basilidians, founded by Basilides from Syria; the Carpocratians, led by Carpocrates from Alexandria; and the Ophites, whose name derived from the Greek word *ophis*, meaning "snake" (they were said by some to be snake worshippers). Historically, the most significant development was Manichaeism, a religious movement that emerged in the third century in Persia under the influence of Zoroastrianism and combined that religion with Jewish-Christian asceticism and a Gnostic cosmology.[2] Manichaeism spread to North Africa

---

2. Moffett, *History of Christianity in Asia*, 1:106–12.

> and influenced the theology of Augustine and, through him, significant parts of Western Christianity. There is evidence that Manichaeism even reached China.[3]

Gnosticism was influenced by various sources—dualist and apocalyptic Jewish groups, Platonism, and, most importantly, Persian Zoroastrianism, with its strict dualism of good and evil. The Hellenist influence was so strong that the famous classical church historian Adolf von Harnack called it the "acute Hellenization of Christianity."[4] Indeed, the typical Platonic dualism of matter versus ideas, the view of the body as a prison of the soul, the idea of god as the source of all goodness, and the goal of human beings to progress in the knowledge of god have deeply shaped Gnosticism.

What Was the Gnostic Teaching?

Gnostic faith can be described along the following lines:

- God is the Supreme Being and is fully transcendent, immutable, unchanging, and good.
- God's original creation was a purely spiritual (i.e., nonmaterial) creation.
- All matter is evil. The material world is not a creation of God, but the creation of a so-called demiurge, one of the lowest spirit beings, a semi-god with limited power who created the world without the prior approval of the supreme unknown God.
- The present world in which we live is a mix of spiritual (also called pneumatic) elements and matter.
- Our human yearning for salvation is rooted in the fact that spiritual elements are imprisoned in our human bodies.
- The goal of Gnosticism is salvation. Salvation is the return of these spiritual elements from their exile in the world to their spiritual home through liberation from matter.
- Christian Gnosticism sees Christ as the divine messenger who leads the spiritual elements imprisoned in our bodies back to their divine origin.
- Salvation happens through the knowledge of our spiritual home, of which Jesus Christ reminds us. Salvation is not forgiveness of sin;

---

3. S. Lieu, *Manichaeism*.
4. Adolf von Harnack, here quoted from King, *What Is Gnosticism?*, 55.

rather, it is the liberation of the soul from exile, from slavery, and from imprisonment in the human body.

- Christ belongs fully to the divine world and is sent to lead the spiritual sparks of divine origin back to God, that is, to free them from matter. Gnosticism denies Jesus' humanity. Jesus was without a physical body. He *appeared* as a human being, but actually was not. What appeared to be Jesus' body was only a body that the heavenly messenger, the spiritual Jesus, took on as disguise and that he relinquished before the crucifixion. This teaching is also called *docetist christology* (from Greek *dokein*, "to seem, to appear").

Apocryphal Stories about Jesus' Childhood

In contrast to the canonical Gospels, which, with the exception of Luke 2:40–52, contain no stories about Jesus as a child, this story from the *Infancy Gospel of Thomas* (not to be conflated with the *Gospel of Thomas* that is equally of Gnostic origin) relates miraculous anecdotes from Jesus' childhood. The *Infancy Gospel* is regarded as part of the Gnostic literature; it may also be understood as part of popular religious interest in stories from Jesus' life.

> 3. And Jesus made of that clay twelve sparrows; and it was Sabbath. And one young child ran and told Joseph, saying, 'Behold your child is playing in the brook and has made sparrows of the clay, which is not lawful.' And having heard, he went and said to the child, 'Why do you do these things, profaning the Sabbath?' And Jesus did not answer, but looked at the sparrows and said, 'Go, fly away, and remember me while you live.' And at the word they took flight and went off into the air. And Joseph marveled when he saw it.
>
> 4. And after some days, as Jesus was going through the middle of the city, a certain child threw a stone at him and hit him on the shoulder. And Jesus said to him, 'You shall not go on your way.' And straightway he too fell down and died. And those who happened to be there were astonished, saying, 'Where does this young child come from that every word that he says has immediate effect?' They too went and complained to Joseph, saying, 'You will not be able to dwell with us in this city. But if you please, teach your child to bless and not to curse; for he slays our children and every word that he says has immediate effect.'

Source: *The Infancy Gospel of Thomas*, Greek Text B, III–IV, in Elliott, *The Apocryphal New Testament*, 81.

Gnosticism distinguishes further between different kinds of people. In the highest rank are "pneumatic" people, those who know about their spiritual divine origin. "Psychic" people are those who do not know about humans' divine origin but who at least have faith beyond matter. Finally, "hylics" (from Greek *hyle*, "matter") are those who know only about material life. This elitist view of the religious community sees followers of Gnosticism as the "elect" who know about the secret of personal salvation, while the majority of humankind remains ignorant of our origins.

Fig. 3.3: Graphic description of the Gnostic salvation story

What Was the Impact of Gnosticism and What Made It Attractive?

Gnosticism denied all positive value of matter, regarding it as illusory and all bodily needs as irrelevant. Such an attitude could lead to two contrasting moral attitudes: radical asceticism and libertinism. The former was a way of ignoring and killing all bodily needs, while the latter was a radical freedom to engage within the physical realm since it was irrelevant anyway.

Gnosticism competed directly with Christianity because it offered a view of matter that seemed relevant and plausible to many. Similar to Christianity, it appealed particularly to people of the lower classes—that is, those suffering in the body and in the physical world—by telling them that our physical being is simply an irrelevant illusion. Gnosticism attracted a significant number of followers by offering a meaningful and comprehensive alternative interpretation of the events that began with Jesus Christ. Its mysterious character appealed to those who enjoyed the combination of rich symbolism of ancient traditions and a narrow path to salvation. Its strict dualism of good and evil, of spiritual and material, of those belonging to God and those belonging to the world, gave a sense of superiority to all who regarded themselves as the elect, and it provided a clear compass of orientation in a world that appeared complex to many.

This is one of the reasons why Gnosticism has found a significant revival in recent times. Its basic and simple narration in richly symbolic and mythological language, its mysterious techniques, its openness to various religious sources, its individualistic approach, and its emphasis on one's own potential appeal to many religious seekers in the modern world.

What Was the Significance of Gnosticism and the Faith Crisis It Caused? In What Way Is It Relevant Today?

As a religious competitor, Gnosticism challenged basic elements of Christian faith. Although rejected by Christianity, the Gnostic interpretation indirectly influenced Christianity in several areas: the teaching about the value of the created world, the understanding of the meaning of suffering, and the question of how to understand God's revelation. These topics are of ongoing relevance.

(a) How should Christians view created matter?

The biblical tradition gives mixed answers. On one hand the creation story clearly tells how God (and not a low-level demiurge) created the world and found it good. However, some passages in the letters of Paul point toward a more negative view of matter.

The question is relevant because in rejecting the Gnostic challenge early Christianity may inadvertently have absorbed elements of it. Significant parts of the Christian tradition have a negative view of matter, caused not only by the Gnostic challenge but equally by Hellenistic influence in general.

(b) How should Christians view the suffering of Christ?

Gnosticism's docetist Christology stands in clear contrast to the Christian insistence that Jesus truly suffered on the cross. While Christianity in its earliest days emphasized that Jesus was truly divine, it later had to defend the humanity of Jesus against the Gnostic challenge. A Christology that denies Jesus' full suffering reflects a desire to avoid "failure" on the side of God. However, a crucial point of Christian faith is its paradoxical, upside-down pattern, discovering victory in the suffering and death of Christ where non-Christians see only failure. We may consider whether the attempt to eliminate the experience of suffering and failure in our image of God finds a parallel in triumphalist Christian teachings that deny the full reality of suffering.

(c) How should Christians read the Bible?

The Gnostic interpretation of the biblical scriptures claims that they are not really what they appear. Rather, the truth of the Bible lies in some deeper and allegorical or metaphorical truth. Such an allegorical interpretation of the Bible was equally advocated by many Christian theologians, first and most famously by Origen. While allegorical interpretation allows abundant new and meaningful interpretations of Scripture, it is dangerous because it is often applied whenever a biblical text is particularly disturbing. Allegorical Bible interpretation may thus eliminate the scandal at the center of the Christian message.

THE MARCIONITE CRISIS: WHAT IS THE RELEVANCE OF THE JEWISH TRADITION?

Marcionism (the teaching of Marcion) is a movement that seems in many ways similar to the Gnostic movement, but Marcionism and Gnosticism are not the same. The importance of Marcionism lay in raising crucial theological questions that the Christian tradition had to clarify. Its core question was about the relationship of Christians to Israel and the Hebrew Bible. The writings of Marcion have been lost. All that we know about his teaching has to be reconstructed from his so-called orthodox opponents, mainly Tertullian.

Marcion was a native of the region near the Black Sea, born at the end of the first century as the son of a bishop. Around 140 CE he was working and preaching in Rome, where his teaching caused conflict. In 144 CE he was excommunicated from the church and subsequently organized the Marcionite church, which became influential as it spread throughout the Roman Empire. During the second century, Christianity appeared to some observers as divided into two major groups, namely, the Catholics and the Marcionites. The Marcionite church disappeared in the fifth century but did influence Syrian monasticism and its asceticism.

What Was Marcion's Teaching?

Similarly to Gnosticism, Marcion had a negative view of creation; yet, unlike Gnosticism, Marcion found the God of the Hebrew Scriptures not evil but simply weak and incompetent. He emphasized the teaching of the New Testament as something radically new that needed no foundation in the creation story or in the story of the people of Israel. Marcion saw the gospel as entirely a gospel of love, and the God of love revealed by Jesus as different to the creator God or the God of Moses in the Old Testament.

As a result of such theology, Marcion redefined the canon to include only texts he felt actually expressed the truth of Christianity. He rejected the Hebrew Scriptures as a whole and eliminated all Jewish influences in the text of the Christian tradition. What remained was a reduced version of the Gospel of Luke and ten of Paul's epistles. All other parts were rejected.

The church founded by Marcion showed some interesting features, among them gender equality and the admission of women to the clergy, a democratically organized church without rigid distinctions between clergy and laity, and a non-permanent office of the bishop. Marcion himself had never been a bishop, and the churches of the Marcionite community built a loose federation of churches without one head church.

What Was the Difference between Marcionism and Gnosticism?

Although there are significant similarities between the two movements, particularly their dualist view of the world and their negative view of matter, it is generally agreed that the two movements were different. Different to Gnosticism, Marcion taught that the whole human being was corrupt, not just the body. He also lacked the mythical speculation so typical of Gnosticism, and he rejected the Gnostic idea of a special revelation or a secret tradition handed down to a small group, the elect. His teachings were based on the writings of the Bible, albeit a greatly reduced canon.

What Is the Relevance of Marcion's Teaching Today?

The historical importance of Marcion is that his was the first attempt to draw up a canon of the New Testament. He realized the important link between theology and canon. When the church began to define a New Testament canon in the second century, it was foremost due to the influence and stimulation of Marcion.

Marcion was also important in raising the question of how Christianity should relate to the Jewish tradition. Although the church rejected his solution of radically cutting off the Jewish tradition and the Hebrew Bible, he challenged the Christian movement to clarify its relationship to the Jewish heritage and to give a more convincing answer about its relationships to the Hebrew Bible, the Mosaic law, the old covenant, and Israel. In fact, one problem with the Hebrew Bible—then and now—is that it needs to be interpreted against the Jewish interpretation but also against Gentile criticism, which finds the anthropomorphism in the religious language of the Hebrew Bible and the cruelties described in it difficult to reconcile with the image of God as love. The anthropomorphic images of God in the Bible appear indeed as a scandal to many Christians.

Finally, the question that Marcion raised has ongoing relevance in discussions of contextualization, particularly in contexts far away from the ancient Near East. Intellectuals from contexts with their own rich tradition (e.g., Chinese intellectuals) may ask whether the classics of Chinese philosophy could not take up the same role as the Jewish tradition and the Hebrew Bible, namely, to give a partial revelation of Christ and to prepare the way to Christ.[5] What is the relevance of the Hebrew Bible for Christians in China who may instead prefer to draw from their own literary and intellectual traditions? To what extent are we ourselves anonymous Marcionites? How essential is the Hebrew Bible in our own teaching and preaching ministries?

THE MONTANIST CRISIS: WHAT ABOUT THE PROCLAIMED END OF TIME?

Although the Montanist movement was traditionally condemned as heretical, more recent interpretation regards it less as a heresy than as a fringe and a "rigorous, prophetic, women-tolerating" renewal movement within early Christianity.[6] The movement is interesting as part of an alternative church history, a history of dissent. Showing elements of charismatic revival, renewed eschatological expectation, radical communitarianism, and egalitarian social concepts, it may simply be understood as a revival of elements of the earliest Jesus reform movement and as a protest against the Hellenization of Christianity and the catholic streamlining of the church.

What we know about the Montanist movement is, like Marcionism, known only through its opponents, who eventually condemned it as

5. For instance Xie Fuya; for more on this and further references, see Lai Pin-chao, "Hong Kong Christians' Attitudes," 25–26.
6. See Trevett, *Montanism*, 41, with reference to what she calls "proto-Montanism."

heretical. It is thus a biased perspective that may not do full justice to Montanus and may have included certain elements simply to discredit him.

Montanus was a pagan priest in Asia Minor (present-day Turkey) who converted to Christianity around 155 CE. He was joined and supported by two female prophets, Priscilla and Maximilla. His teaching attracted many followers, most famously Tertullian, one of the most important patristic theologians of the West. Other supposed followers of Montanus were Perpetua and Felicitas, the famous martyrs. Such prominent supporters hint at the movement's orthodox character.

What Is the Teaching of Montanism?

The main tenets of Montanism are not different from those of mainstream Christianity. Where Montanus apparently moved beyond mainstream belief was in his eschatology. His opponents described him as expecting the imminent end of time and as declaring himself the expected *paraclete* as announced in John 14. He was accused of presenting his own person as final revelation and his own prophecies as surpassing and completing the previous prophecies and revelations. The movement initiated by Montanus and his followers was the beginning of a new age of the outpouring of the Spirit. He called on believers to gather in Phrygia, Asia Minor, and to lead a rigorous, ascetic, celibate, and vegetarian life. He also declared post-baptismal sins as unforgivable. Montanus tried to explain the twin problems of the continuing sin of Christians and the still-unrealized end of time by interpreting the church as an intermediate stage that was now superseded by the new age of the Spirit. His perfectionism opposed the increasing adaptation of Christian life to the world. The church saw in Montanus' teaching of a new age the danger of diminishing the significance of Christ, and subsequently rejected him.

What Is the Relevance of Montanism Historically and for Us Today?

Montanus' historical significance is that he raised two crucial questions Christianity had to clarify.

1. Are new revelations possible? Is it possible that God reveals himself in new ways beyond what has been revealed in Jesus' life and death?
2. Should we still expect an imminent end of time?

These questions are still relevant today. The question of new revelations has repeatedly been a contentious issue in the charismatic movement and in some independent and indigenous churches. The question of whether we should still expect an imminent end of the world has found new relevance in modern groups, again particularly in the Pentecostal-Charismatic and Fundamentalist traditions.

A further relevance of Montanism for today is that the movement may be interpreted as an early form of Pentecostal revival and as one chapter in a long history of charismatic revivals in the church. Such an interpretation of Montanism would stand in contrast to the traditional view, which has dismissed Montanism as forfeiting the uniqueness and ultimate authority of Jesus Christ. This reinterpretation would place Montanism within the bounds of Christian orthodoxy. Whether such a view is appropriate largely depends on how we judge the teachings of Montanus and his followers, which can, unfortunately, be recovered only from biased "orthodox" sources. Finally, Montanus stands in a long Christian tradition of thinkers who, with their moral discipline, protested against the growing laxity of the church.

An Ecstatic Vision by a Montanist Woman

Tertullian (c. 160–220) was the first major theologian who wrote in Latin, and his contributions to the dogmatic decisions of the early church were very important. The text below shows something of Tertullian's fascination with Montanism. His description of the Montanist woman's visions make them appear to resemble expressions common in modern charismatic Christian groups.

The text, an extract of chapter IX, is part of a larger argument, in which Tertullian argues for the corporeality of the soul, against Plato's teaching of the soul's incorporeality.

Chapter IX.—Particulars of the Alleged Communication to a Montanist Sister.

. . . We have now amongst us a sister whose lot it has been to be favoured with sundry gifts of revelation, which she experiences in the Spirit by ecstatic vision amidst the sacred rites of the Lord's day in the church: she converses with angels, and sometimes even with the Lord; she both sees and hears mysterious communications; some men's hearts she understands, and to them who are in need she distributes remedies. Whether it be in the reading of Scriptures, or in the chanting of psalms, or in the preaching of sermons, or in the offering up of prayers, in all these religious services matter and opportunity are afforded to her of seeing visions. It may possibly have happened to us, whilst this sister of ours was rapt in the Spirit, that we had discoursed in some ineffable way

about the soul. After the people are dismissed at the conclusion of the sacred services, she is in the regular habit of reporting to us whatever things she may have seen in vision (for all her communications are examined with the most scrupulous care, in order that their truth may be probed). "Amongst other things," says she, "there has been shown to me a soul in bodily shape, and a spirit has been in the habit of appearing to me; not, however, a void and empty illusion, but such as would offer itself to be even grasped by the hand, soft and transparent and of an etherial colour, and in form resembling that of a human being in every respect." This was her vision, and for her witness there was God; and the apostle most assuredly foretold that there were to be "spiritual gifts" in the church....

Source: Tertullian, *A Treatise on the Soul*, ch. IX (ANF 3:188).

CREED, CANON, AND APOSTOLIC SUCCESSION: TOWARD THE DEVELOPMENT OF A CATHOLIC THEOLOGY AND CHURCH

In response to these three major challenges to early Christianity, the church had to clarify its belief and authority structure. The developments of a creed, of a biblical canon, and of a system of apostolic succession were three steps by which the church responded to the questions raised by Gnosticism, Marcionism, and Montanism. They are crucial steps in the process of a unified faith, that is, a catholic and universally valid faith.

The Apostles' Creed

The Apostle's Creed, still used in the churches today, goes back to earlier creedal forms first formulated around the middle of the second century, most importantly the Old Roman Creed. They were based on questions that baptismal candidates had to answer. Christian faith's fixation on clarity and dogma was, first and foremost, a reaction to the mainly Gnostic interpretation of the Christian faith and its denial of Jesus Christ's humanity. The anti-Gnostic direction of the Apostles' Creed is clearly recognizable in its emphases on God the creator and on Jesus' human birth and real suffering on the cross.

The establishment of a creed summarizing the basic principles of our faith in a comprehensive way is a natural development of any faith community. It had, however, a deep impact on the Christian movement: Faith turned into belief. And belief distinguishes between right and wrong, between orthodox and heterodox. Being a Christian shifted from enjoying a trust-based relationship into affirming a specific propositional content.

The Christian Canon

The development of a Christian canon was an attempt to define which sources revealed the real teaching of Jesus. The criterion for inclusion in the canon was the apostolic character of the writing. The process of biblical canon-building lasted several centuries and, for the Roman Catholic Church, concluded officially only at the Council of Trent in the sixteenth century. Consensus about the New Testament canon, however, was reached already around the middle of the fourth century.

In the process of defining valid writings for the Christian tradition, the church made two crucial decisions. The first decision was to establish a canon *in addition to* (i.e., not in place of) the Hebrew Bible. A second decision was to maintain the plurality of the Gospels despite their internal contradictions, thus stressing the consensus and the openness of the apostolic tradition.

The development of a Christian canon was first directed against Gnosticism, which claimed that Jesus had entrusted his secret knowledge to one particular disciple, for instance, the apostle Thomas, as in the *Gospel of Thomas*. It was secondly aimed at the Marcionites, who rejected the whole of the Hebrew Scriptures and large parts of the New Testament. It was, however, also aimed implicitly at the Montanists, who claimed the possibility of new revelations. Defining a canon of documents that witnessed the revelation of God in Jesus Christ implied that revelation had come to an end in the apostolic time and that new revelations were not necessary and not possible. The church thus distinguished between the *apostolic age*, in which God spoke through prophecies and other special forms of revelation and empowered the apostles with special supernatural gifts, and a *post-apostolic age*, in which such special forms of revelation were not necessary anymore because the established canon was sufficient to reveal God. This theory was later called cessationism. It was rejected by the Pentecostal movement of the twentieth century, which claimed a continuing work of the Holy Spirit through supernatural gifts and revelations. The canon thus quashed the idea of new revelations and provided justification for cessationists to dismiss post-apostolic supernatural gifts as invalid.

Similar to the creation of a creed that summarizes our faith, the establishment of a canon of authoritative writings is a natural development of any faith community. In the same vein, it has deeply influenced what it means to be a Christian. While the earliest Christians were simply a community of people looking ahead in eager expectation to an imminent radical change in history, such an eschatological expectation had long since waned. Now, with a canon sufficiently defining the revelation of God, the Christian faith community turned into an established tradition that looked back to a past revelation. It was no longer a movement led by the Holy Spirit and relying on new inspirations by the Spirit, but a movement that found orientation in a creed and a clearly defined body of texts.

Apostolic Succession

A third crucial development in response to the faith crisis of the second century was the development of a system of apostolic succession. Gnosticism had claimed that a secret teaching had been passed down to the present without the knowledge of the mainstream church. The church responded to this claim by emphasizing that if ever there had been such a secret body of knowledge, Jesus surely would have entrusted it to the apostles to whom he also entrusted the church. The church's authority is, by the direct line of apostolic succession, linked to the apostolic time and to the apostles who were closest to Jesus. A bishop's authority thus derives—through a line of bishops—from one apostle, from whom the bishop and his predecessors have succeeded.

Until around the middle of the second century, the bishop was one among several presbyters leading the congregation. Now, by tracing the line of authority back to the first apostles, the monarchic episcopate (meaning a church led by one individual) developed. To further emphasize the direct connection to the apostolic time, bishop lists for the churches in the principal centers of Rome, Jerusalem, Alexandria, and Antioch were established. Church authority was unified under these bishops.

These organizational changes have had a far-reaching impact on the church. The monarchic form of church government became for many centuries the norm and is still dominant in many churches. By tracing the church's authority to the twelve apostles, women were increasingly eliminated from higher church ministry.[7] Traditional hierarchy and clearly defined church order were confirmed, against the prophetic spirit.

---

7. That this process was not such a simple process, and that a kind of ordained women's ministry continued for many years, is convincingly argued in Madigan and Osiek, *Ordained Women in the Early Church*, 203–6.

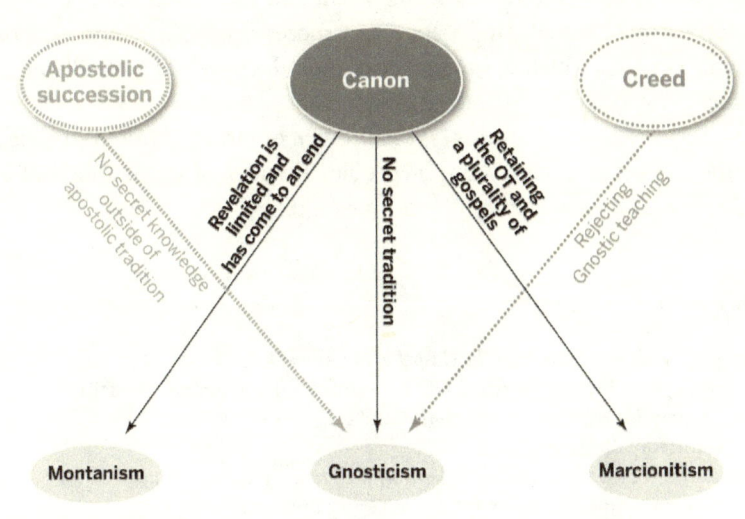

Fig. 3.4: Christian responses to doctrinal challenges in the second century

Creed, canon, and a system of apostolic succession deeply changed the appearance of the church and set it on a path of continuous institutionalization and order. To meet the test of apostolic orthodoxy, a movement or idea had to measure up to the norms set by the apostolic canon, the apostolic creed, and the apostolic episcopate. The Roman-Catholic concept of the joint authority of Bible and church tradition has its beginning in these decisions. The authority of the Holy Spirit was replaced by the established church authority. To be a Christian now meant accepting a particular creed, relying on revelation as contained in a specific body of writings, and submitting to the authority of the bishop. Christianity had effectively started to set up a home and a practical structure in the world. The danger of these changes was piquantly expressed by James Dunn, who described the danger of this tradition as "failure to realize that the biggest heresy of all is the insistence that there is only one ecclesiastical obedience, only one orthodoxy."[8]

What the movement toward a catholic (i.e., universally valid and relatively unified) theology meant for the development of the church as a whole can be summarized in a few words: The church turned into an increasingly well-organized body with regional and provincial synods and with an increasingly hierarchic organization—bishops in all major churches, a kind of

---

8. Dunn, *Unity and Diversity*, 400.

higher bishop (a metropolitan) in each provincial capital, and again higher bishops (patriarchs) in the most important and traditional centers. As the bishop was increasingly understood as a successor of Christ, and as apostolic succession formed the guarantee of right doctrine, the authority of the bishop grew throughout the third century.

The development of this "special" office of bishop introduced a clear distinction between clergy and laypeople. The idea of a priesthood of all believers was gradually lost.

For Further Reading

Harnack, Adolf von. *Marcion: The Gospel of the Alien God*. Translated by John E. Steely and Lyle D. Bierma. Durham, NC: Labyrinth, 1990. (German original 1924)

King, Karen L. *What Is Gnosticism?* Cambridge, MA: Belknap Press of Harvard University Press, 2003.

Lieu, Judith M. *Marcion and the Making of a Heretic: God and Scripture in the Second Century*. Cambridge: Cambridge University Press, 2015.

Lüdemann, Gerd, and Martina Janssen. *Suppressed Prayers: Gnostic Spirituality in Early Christianity*. London: SCM, 1998. (Sourcebook on heretical texts of the first centuries)

Rossing, Barbara R. "Prophets, Prophetic Movements, and the Voices of Women." In *Christian Origins*, edited by Richard A. Horsley, 261–86. Minneapolis: Fortress, 2005.

Roukema, Riemer. *Gnosis and Faith in Early Christianity: An Introduction to Gnosticism*. Translated by John Bowden. Harrisburg, PA: Trinity Press International, 1999.

Learning Activities

1) Review key elements of this chapter by answering the following questions:
   - What was Gnosticism?
   - What was the teaching of Marcion?
   - Was Marcion a follower of Gnosticism?
   - What was the teaching of Montanus? What attracted people to Montanism?

2) Probe your understanding by discussing the following questions:
   - Why did the Christian community regard as necessary the teaching of continuity with Israel (see also the discussion in ch. 1)?
   - Was the Montanist movement heretical? What was the answer of church tradition? How would you yourself answer?

- Discuss the Apostles' Creed and show how it was directed against the spiritual challenges of the time.
- What was the role of women in Gnosticism and in Montanism?

3) To deepen the significance of what we have learned about this period, discuss the following questions in small groups:
    - Where do you see elements of Gnosticism revived in modern esoteric traditions?
    - How relevant is Marcionite thinking today? In what ways is it still relevant?
    - Why do you think the Hebrew Bible is important? What is the relevance of the Hebrew Bible for you personally?
    - What do you think of some Christians' suggestion to replace the Hebrew Bible with the important philosophical texts of local cultures (e.g., with the classical writings of Chinese tradition)?
    - What is the theological significance of the establishment of the canon?
    - What do you think about the reaction of the church to the doctrinal threats in the second century? Do you think the church could have reacted better? If so, how?

Chapter 4

Christianity and Culture
The Encounter with Hellenist Philosophy

CHRISTIAN DOCTRINE DEVELOPED IN a context that was not only *religiously* mixed—popular religions and local cults, as we saw in chapter 3—but also *philosophically* mixed. The philosophical traditions that most strongly influenced the development of Christianity in the first centuries were Platonism, Neo-Platonism, the Jewish-Alexandrinian *Logos* philosophy, and, to a lesser extent, Stoicism.

The previous chapter introduced some of the challenges arising from the process of contextualization and explained some of the church's reactions—and contextualization is the topic of this chapter as well. More precisely, the topic is how Christianity entered the Greco-Roman *intellectual* world, what traditions it encountered, and how Christian thought reacted to this encounter. However, different to the last chapter, where we saw how Christianity mostly *rejected* alternative interpretations of faith, we see here how Christian theologians mostly *welcomed and absorbed* the intellectual traditions of the Hellenist world into their own theological interpretations. Inspired by this encounter, Christian thinkers began to develop elaborate systems of theological thought to present Christianity to the intellectual world and to defend Christianity as the better philosophy. The theological systems developed in this context are called apologetic theology and patristic theology. One result of this more systematic presentation of the Christian belief system was the emergence of Trinitarian interpretations of the divine relationship between Father, Son, and Holy Spirit.

This chapter focuses on the following questions:

- What were the major worldviews and philosophical traditions that challenged the Christian movement?
- How did Christianity respond to the challenges posed by these competing philosophies and worldviews? How did Christianity adapt, and how did it remain distinct?
- What are apologetic and patristic theologies? What are their characteristics and why did they develop in the second and third centuries?
- Compared to previous Christian writers, what changes did the apologetic and patristic theologians bring, and how did they influence later intellectual and cultural developments?
- How did the church in this era clarify its understanding of the relationship between God the Father and God the Son?

HELLENISTIC PHILOSOPHICAL TRADITIONS

The earliest Greek philosophers were driven by two central questions, one cosmological and the other anthropological, that set the stage for all later philosophizing. Philosophers in the sixth and fifth centuries BCE asked, What is it that remains the same, as all that is visible appears to be in constant change? Later, in the fifth and fourth centuries BCE, a period sometimes called the Greek Enlightenment, philosophers asked, Is there a universal standard for morals and truth beyond the changing opinions of individuals? Over the years, the framework for the discussion of these questions shifted gradually, and by the first centuries of the Christian era, these questions were debated mainly within a religious framework. The central philosophical questions had come to focus on the relationship between God and world: How can we think of God and world together? How can the gap between God and humankind be bridged? In other words, how can human beings receive an idea of God?

Plato

Although Plato lived around four centuries before Christ, Platonism was still a highly influential system in the time of the early church, and it continued to provide the basic philosophical outline for centuries to come. Platonism understood all being in a strict dualism: a realm of ideas separate from a realm of matter. Human beings live in a world of visible and intelligible things. This visible world is what surrounds us: what we see, hear, or experience. It is a world of change and uncertainty. However, *actual and true reality* is not this perishable material world but the world of immaterial ideas. All being, all that is, exists first as ideas, as concepts, or words. The invisible world contains the eternal "forms" (in Greek, *idea*) of things. An idea is the immaterial reality of all manifest and material things: for example, an individual horse is simply a material manifestation of the idea "horse"; an individual apple is a material manifestation of the idea "apple." True reality is not tangible things but instead these ideas, which are unchanging and imperishable. The things *derived* from these original ideas have lower status and less dignity.

Plato taught that these ideas are intelligible to humans because our soul sees the pure ideas before our material existence; the perception of similar forms in the material world then triggers remembrance (*anamnesis*). Human reason has the ability to remember these ideas and to understand their categorical and logical relationships.

According to Plato, the human soul has a middle position between the immutable world of being (*ousia*) and the changeable world of becoming (*genesis*). As part of human life, the soul is subject to change and decay; however, the soul has the ability to recognize immutable ideas and thus participates in that eternal world of being. Plato thus claims an immortality of the soul, a teaching that many Christians have mistakenly assumed is biblical. This soul is imprisoned in our human body—beautifully expressed in the pun of *soma* ("body") = *saema* ("grave, prison")[1]—but it eternally yearns to be led back to the vision (*theoria*) of the original ideas. Plato describes this human yearning for the vision of the eternal ideas in his famous *Allegory of the Cave*,[2] which became one of the most famous philosophical documents in Western civilization.

The allegory of the cave tells how human beings are like captives, chained in a cave and watching the shadows of various items reflected on the wall of the cave. The shadows are created by a fire that, like the items, is behind the humans and thus not visible. The process of knowledge is one of liberation from the captivity of the chains, of moving out of the cave—first to see the real things, later the light that caused the shadows, and eventually the light of the sun.

---

1. Plato, *Cratylus* 400c, in *Dialogues of Plato*, 1:343.
2. Plato, *Republic*, bk. VII.

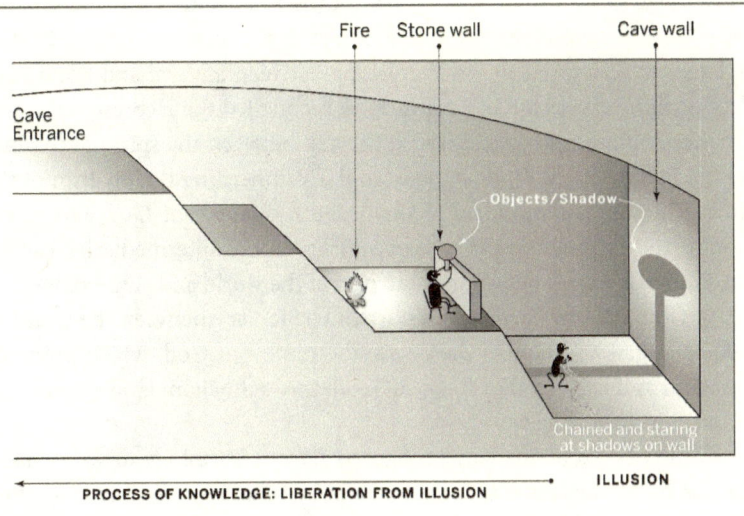

Fig. 4.1: Image of Plato's Allegory of the Cave

A further extension of the relationships between the different ideas brought Plato to the concept of a hierarchy of different ideas, with "the Good" as the highest idea. Influenced by earlier Pythagorean philosophies, Plato developed this concept which identified the idea of the good with the idea of the One, the Immutable, which is precisely the highest idea, the idea of God. He taught that from the One derives the Two, or the Other, and from there the Many. This gradation system, from the highest idea to the lower ideas, eventually led to the abolition of Platonism's originally strict dualism of ideas and matter in Neo-Platonism. It understood all being in a graded hierarchy from the highest being, the One, to the lowest reality of the physical world.

This provided one of the basic themes for centuries to come: How does the One, God, who is of pure spiritual nature, affect the material world? Conversely, how do humans get in touch with spiritual reality? Later philosophical and religious tradition responded to this question in various forms; Gnosticism was simply one of many answers to the question of the relationship between God and world.

Philo of Alexandria

Perhaps the most creative Hellenist answer—and the most influential on the Christian tradition—came from Philo of Alexandria. Philo was a Jewish philosopher who lived in the first half of the first century CE. He was the first philosopher to identify the god of Greek philosophy with the God of the Hebrew Scriptures. By distinguishing between a literal and a spiritual, allegorical interpretation of Scripture, he reconciled the Hebrew Scriptures with Greek philosophy and bridged the gap between the spiritual (divine) and the literal (worldly) meanings. Similarly, inheriting the dualism of the Greek-Platonist tradition, he reconciled the dualism of God and world through the introduction of *intermediaries*. These intermediaries can be called *ideas* or *angels of God*: they are part of the world and at the same time part of God. Among them, the highest intermediary between the world of ideas or angels and God is the *Logos*: the reason of God, which proceeds from God and is an icon or image of God, through whom God creates first the ideas and then the world.

Philo's *Logos* philosophy prefigured *Logos* christology to such an extent that he can be called a Christian before Christ. He is an important link between Plato and later Neo-Platonism, and also between Jewish and Hellenistic thought.

Neo-Platonism

Similarly, Neo-Platonism tried to reconcile the supposed dualism between God and the world, or between the realm of ideas and the realm of matter. Neo-Platonism was a philosophical movement originating in the third century CE. Important Neo-Platonist philosophers were Plotinus (204–70), Porphyry (234–305), and others. They further developed the thought—found in the late writings of Plato—that the realm of ideas is a hierarchy, with the highest idea, the idea of God, at the top. According to Neo-Platonist philosophy, the icon or the image of the One is reason; further down the hierarchy of the realm of ideas is the soul, not the individual soul, but a kind of universal soul. Through continuous differentiation, the realm of ideas descends to the lower ideas and eventually to the material world.

Three features of this philosophical concept are important:

i. Neo-Platonism describes the hierarchical relationships of the ideas as *emanation* from (*a*) the absolutely transcendent and immutable God, the highest idea, to (*b*) the Two, the otherness of the One, and from there to (*c*) the Many. The emanation into an increasing differentiation leads from the more general to the more specific, from the conceptual to the individual and material.

ii. The hierarchy of emanation and of increasing differentiation is paralleled by a hierarchy of being or a hierarchy of reality: The lower an idea in this hierarchy, the lower its "ontological reality," that is, its reality of being. God is absolutely real. The lowest level of the world is absolutely unreal.

iii. All lower ideas down to the material world participate in the highest being in descending intensity. This reconciles the radical Platonist dualism of God and world by describing the world as an emanation from God: the world is part of God, although in reduced quality.

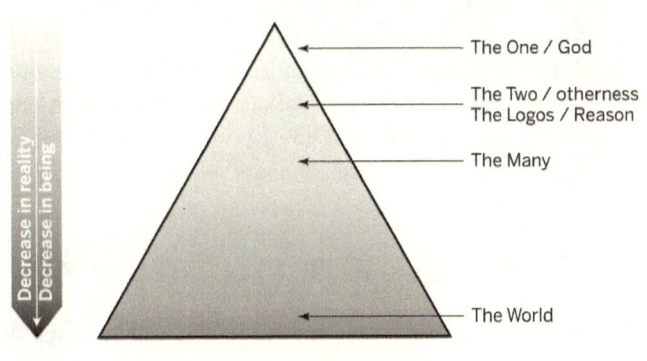

Fig. 4.2: Neo-Platonism's hierarchy of being

Stoicism

A fourth tradition that influenced early Christianity, although to a lesser extent, was Stoicism. The Stoa was a philosophical school that began in the fourth century BC. Its name derives from *stoa*, the Greek word for hall, because Zeno (c. 334–262 BCE), the founder of this school, used to gather his students in a hall to teach them. Other important representatives of Stoicism were Poseidonius (around 135–51 BCE), Seneca (4–65 CE), and Marcus Aurelius (the Roman emperor from 161–80; see ch. 2).

The relevance of Stoicism lies mainly in its moral teaching, but the Stoa also offered, as did other philosophical schools, a concept of reconciling God and world. The core idea was that of the *Logos* splintered into its smallest parts (*logos spermatikos*) and scattered throughout all being. God thus unfolds and differentiates himself in all that is, as a life-giving principle and as energy.

Hellenist philosophy, particularly the Neo-Platonist tradition, had a tremendous influence on Christian theology. Two points are particularly worth mentioning.

First, the concept of a hierarchy in the spiritual world led to a stronger emphasis on the absolute unintelligibility of God, his absolute beyondness and difference to all that is known. This thought eventually led to the Christian mystical tradition and to the concept of "negative theology," the idea that God is so far beyond everything that he can be expressed only in negative terms, and that every positive description of God limits His Being.

Second, knowledge is received by climbing up the hierarchy of emanations. The ultimate goal of knowledge is to see or envision (*theorein*) the origin of all knowledge, the One and Immutable. This tradition led to an emphasis on theory and on a visual approach to God, in contrast to the more auditory approach of the Hebrew tradition. Further influences will be evident after we look at patristic theology.

PERIODIZATION OF PATRISTIC THEOLOGY

The theology of the first centuries is usually called patristic theology. This term commonly describes the theological reflection from the end of the Apostolic era until the Council of Chalcedon in 451 (see ch. 7); the period can also be extended to the end of the eighth century, that is, the Seventh Ecumenical Council in 787. The term stems from the idea that these theologians are the "fathers" (Latin, *patres ecclesiae*) or teachers of the church because they laid the foundation for all later theology.

The patristic period can be further divided into

(*a*) a pre-catholic period, before the Gnostic and the Marcionite Crisis, roughly until 150 CE;

(*b*) a pre-Nicene period, until the Council of Nicaea in 325;

(*c*) a Nicene and post-Nicene period, until the Council of Chalcedon in 451.

Another model of periodization differentiates between different purposes of writing and thus distinguishes the following periods:

(*a*) The period of the Apostolic Fathers (late first century until around 150): Their writings dealt with specific problems of early Christian communities, just as Paul's letters responded to practical questions in early Christianity. Among the Fathers are Ignatius of Antioch, Clement of Rome, and Polycarp of Smyrna. Important writings of this period include the *Didache* and the *Shepherd of Hermas*.

(b) The period of the Apologists (around 120–220): Their main purpose was to defend the Christian faith against its intellectual critics and against persecution. The most famous apologetic theologian was Justin Martyr, whose most important writing was *Dialogue with Trypho*. Other apologists were Quadratus, of whom very little is known;[3] Aristides, who lived around 140 CE in Athens; Hegesippus; Melito of Sardis, whose petition to the emperor and list of the canonical books of the Old Testament have been preserved; Minucius Felix; and Tatian, a disciple of Justin, who after Justin's death was expelled from the church because of some heretical beliefs.[4]

(c) The period of the Catholic Fathers, the Teachers of the Church: Chronologically overlapping with the apologists, they appeared in the second half of the second century and introduced a new form of theological reflection, with a more systematic presentation of the whole of Christian thinking. This increasingly turned Christian *faith* into a Christian *philosophy*.

For the western part of the empire, this period extended until the middle of the fifth century; in the eastern part it merged with the later theology of the Eastern Orthodox Church without a clear demarcation. Among the important theologians during the earlier, pre-Nicene period were Irenaeus of Lyon, Tertullian, Hippolytus of Rome, Clement of Alexandria, and Origen; among the theologians of the later, post-Nicene period, the most important were the Great Cappadocians Basil the Great, Gregory of Nyssa, Gregory of Nazianzus, and Macrina, the sister of Basil and Gregory of Nyssa who, although not known for her own writing, played a crucial role in the development of monasticism. Also worth mentioning are the Latin Fathers Jerome, Ambrose of Milan, and eventually Augustine, who leads into medieval theology.

---

3. Only a fragment of his writing is preserved in Eusebius, *Church History*, IV:3.
4. Eusebius, *Church History*, IV:29.

	WEST	EAST	
Apostolic Fathers	Clement of Rome	Ignatius of Antioch	Polycarp of Smyrna
Apologists		Justin Martyr	Tatian
		Melito of Sardis	
Pre-Nicene Theologians	Irenaeus of Lyon / Hippolytus of Rome / Tertullian	Clement of Alexandria / Origen	
Post-Nicene Theologians	Ambrose of Milan / Jerome / Augustine	Macrina / Gregory of Nyssa	Basil the Great / Gregory of Nazianzus

Fig. 4.3: Important theologians of the first four centuries

A clear distinction between chronological periods or different purposes is not really possible because the different periods overlap and each theologian's writings naturally had several purposes. For the sake of better understanding, the rest of this chapter simply distinguishes between an earlier, more apologetic period and a later, more systematic period.

THE APOLOGISTS OF THE SECOND AND EARLY THIRD CENTURIES

The persecution of Christians in the first centuries was paralleled by most Greek and Roman intellectuals' rejection of the Christian faith as a superstition that was neither ancient nor intelligent. The most famous philosophical critic of Christianity was Celsus, who, in his book *The True Word*, written around 180, systematically attacked Christianity. He mocked Christians for not daring to preach among intellectuals, and he called Christianity a religion for the uneducated lower class, for people who were not satisfied with the status quo and who sought some sort of rebellion.

Apologetic theology was a response to such critics. Apologetic theology aimed first to reject these accusations from pagan philosophers, intellectuals, and public speakers and to defend Christianity against the allegations of atheism, immoral living, and superstition. It stressed both Christians' loyalty to the government and the moral character of Christianity. Secondly, it aimed to prove Christianity's fulfillment of ancient prophecies and its intelligibility to nonbelievers. Finally, it turned against the critics and showed the irrationalism and superstition of pagan polytheism and Greek philosophy.

The earliest form of apologetic theology can already be found in Paul's defense of Christian faith on the Areopagus in Acts 17. He preached that Christian faith fulfills rather than stands in contrast to Hellenistic thinking, a basic pattern that characterizes much of apologetic theology. Apologetic theology presented the Christian faith as the only true philosophy and emphasized its monotheistic character. Christian faith thus stood in continuity with and fulfillment of Greek philosophy. In order to connect God's revelation in the biblical tradition with the Greek tradition, the apologists distinguished between

(a) God's general revelation in creation and in human reason, accessible to all human beings, but clouded by the desires of the human flesh;

(b) God's special revelation to Moses and the prophets of Israel, but also to the ancient Greek philosophers (see excerpt from Clement below);

(c) God's full revelation in Jesus Christ.

At the center of the Christian faith was Jesus Christ, the *Logos*, the principle of reason who governs the world and who had ultimately been revealed by God. Pre-Christian Greek philosophy had spoken of this same *logos* even though it was not yet aware of the *Logos* as revealed in Christ. The *logos* of Greek philosophy and of human reason was ultimately the same *Logos* as fully revealed in Jesus Christ. Socrates and Plato were predecessors of Christianity, similar to Abraham and Moses.

Clement of Alexandria Writes about Philosophy as Handmaid of Theology

This extract from the fifth chapter of Clement's *Stromata*, book I, offers a historically important interpretation of Greek philosophy as preparation for the reception of the gospel. Interpreted in this way, Greek philosophy parallels the law of Moses and thus also leads to the reception of the gospel.

Chapter 5.—Philosophy the Handmaid of Theology

Accordingly, before the advent of the Lord, philosophy was necessary to the Greeks for righteousness. And now it becomes conducive to piety; being a kind

> *of preparatory training to those who attain to faith through demonstration. "For thy foot," it is said, "will not stumble, if thou refer what is good, whether belonging to the Greeks or to us, to Providence." [Prov 3:23] For God is the cause of all good things; but of some primarily, as of the Old and the New Testament; and of others by consequence, as philosophy. Perchance, too, philosophy was given to the Greeks directly and primarily, till the Lord should call the Greeks. For this was a schoolmaster to bring "the Hellenic mind," as the law, the Hebrews, "to Christ." [Gal 3:24] Philosophy, therefore, was a preparation, paving the way for him who is perfected in Christ.*

Source: Clement, *Stromata* I.5 (ANF 2:305).

While most Christian apologists, most famously Justin Martyr, stressed this harmony and continuity between Christianity and the Greek tradition, some theologians on the contrary emphasized Christianity's radical opposition to Greek and pagan philosophy. "What indeed has Athens to do with Jerusalem? What concord is there between the Academy and the Church?" asked Tertullian, who together with Tatian was critical of connecting Christianity and Greek philosophy.[5] Tertullian's critical view of human reason is best expressed in his famous phrase "And the son of God died; it is by all means to be believed, because it is absurd. And he was buried, and rose again; the fact is certain, because it is impossible" (*credibile est, quia ineptum est*).[6] This negative view of Hellenist philosophy stemmed partly from their realization that a too-close relationship between Hellenism and Christianity leads eventually to Gnosticism.

CHURCH FATHERS OF THE SECOND AND THIRD CENTURIES

Toward the end of the second century, a new kind of theological reflection emerged, offering a more systematic presentation of the whole of Christian thinking. This theology of the church fathers was part of the continuing contextualization of the gospel in the Greek world, and it likewise continued the process of turning Christian faith into something more like a philosophy. While this theology still defended the Christian faith against its critics

---

5. Tertullian, *Prescription Against Heretics*, ch. 7 (ANF, 3:246).

6. Tertullian, *On the Flesh of Christ*, ch. 5 (ANF, 3:525). The phrase is often wrongly quoted as "I believe because it is absurd" (*credo quia absurdum*) and is thus misused as evidence to present Tertullian as the father of fideism, faith against reason. The quote does not exist as such. However, the labeling of Tertullian as the father of fideism can still find support in his various criticisms of human reason.

and against heretical radicalizations like the Gnostic interpretation, its main purpose now was to present the Christian faith to educated non-Christians.

If Christianity wanted to be understood by people in the Greek context, it had to find expression within the framework of Greek thought, and patristic theology thus tried to do so. It can be understood as the merging of Christian spirituality with Greek education, or as a dialogue merging Christianity with Greek philosophy, the dominant philosophical and religious worldview of the time. It must be noted that philosophy and religion in that era were not clearly separated; philosophical schools also included elements of religious life, as for instance the ascetic practices of the Pythagoreans.

Patristic theology was still written mostly in Greek, the language of most church fathers until the end of the third century—Tertullian was the first theologian to write in Latin. Yet, already at the end of the second century, two distinct theologies, one more Western and the other more oriental, were emerging. Irenaeus and Tertullian stand for the former, Clement and Origen for the latter.

(a) Irenaeus of Lyon (c. 140–202), from Asia Minor, became the bishop of Lyon in the Rhone Valley of today's France. He resolved the Marcionite question regarding the relationship between the Hebrew Bible and the Christian faith through a salvation-historical interpretation: History is the process of a growing communion of humankind with God and a continuous development from creation to a higher status of redemption. The importance of Israel lies in its role in the unfolding of salvation history. The incarnation of Christ was not a result of human sin; rather, even before the fall, God had already intended to draw humanity into communion with Himself. Human sin merely gave God's incarnation in Jesus Christ an additional purpose—repairing the harm caused by the fall. Such an interpretation of the incarnation and of the history of salvation would later be called *supralapsarianism*, in contrast to *infralapsarianism*, which sees the incarnation solely as God's reaction to the fall.

(b) Tertullian (around 150–220) was a native of Carthage, North Africa, where he also spent most of his life. Tertullian's theological radicalism and his moral rigorism caused church tradition to see him critically, particularly because later in life he joined the Montanist movement. Nevertheless, he has had a deep influence on Western theological tradition. The relevance of his thought for Christian history is, first, that he introduced legal categories into the relationship between God and man. These legal categories subsequently became a hallmark of Western theology. Second, he interpreted grace not only as the remission of sins through baptism but also as the guidance and inspiration of the Holy Spirit after baptism. Third, and most important, Tertullian provided some of the crucial Trinitarian and christological formulations that became orthodox positions in the debates of the fourth and fifth century: the Trinitarian formula of God as one substance and three persons; and the description of Jesus Christ as two substances or natures, divine and human, in one person.

(c) Clement of Alexandria (around 150–215) was originally from Athens but spent most of his active time in Alexandria. He was a philosopher turned Christian who merged Christian spirituality with Greek philosophy and therefore developed a speculative Christian philosophy. This speculative character of oriental theology became very influential in the tradition of the Orthodox Church. Clement showed how Platonist philosophy and the Platonist understanding of truth and of God stood in harmony with the Christian understanding, because God had revealed himself in the *Logos*. Greek philosophy was shown to lead to Christ, just as the Jewish law did. Philosophy was necessary for the righteousness of the Greek. The logic behind Clement's argument was that, since there can only be one truth, both the *Logos* of Greek philosophy and the Mosaic law of the Hebrew tradition must lead to that truth.

Clement's theology presented Christ as a divine educator who transcends all that has appeared before in human history and who represents the true and full knowledge, the perfect *gnosis*. Salvation is thus a continuous process rather than a once-for-all redemption. Salvation is deification, a perfect union with God that may not be attained within this life. This idea later developed into the concept of *theosis*, which is important in the Orthodox tradition.

Similar to Philo of Alexandria, Clement reconciled the Mosaic law with the Greek philosophical tradition through an allegorical interpretation of Scripture. The allegory allowed him to transcend the literal sense to reach what he regarded as the higher spiritual sense. It also prepared the ground for the development of a negative theology, the first signs of which can be found in Clement's writings: speaking about God only in metaphors and avoiding any positive statement about God that would potentially define his infiniteness.

(d) Origen (c. 184–254) was from Alexandria, where he became a disciple of Clement. He continued his master's reconciliation of the Christian and Neo-Platonist traditions. He shared Clement's idea of Christianity as the new education (*paideia*) with the divine *Logos* as its resource.

A creative and independent-minded theologian and Christian philosopher, Origen appears in many ways more Platonist than Christian. His closeness to Platonist philosophy is particularly evident in his understanding of God's creation, where he distinguishes between a spiritual and a material creation. The sin that we committed during our previous spiritual existence led to God's second, material creation, Origen said, and the goal of human existence is to be led back to perfect contemplation (*theoria*) of God.

One of Origen's important contributions was in biblical scholarship. He combined exegetic exactness with allegorical creativity to show how the spiritual truths of the texts are hidden behind the literal meaning. In his systematic presentation of the Christian faith in *On First Principles*, he (similar to other patristic theologians) described the *Logos* as a bridge between the Greek and Hebrew traditions: Christ is the great teacher of divine origin and the perfect embodiment of the *Logos*. However, Origen understood this *Logos* as subordinate to God. Such subordinationist teaching prompted later church tradition to condemn Origen's teaching. Another reason for the church's rejection of Origen was his teaching that the whole creation would one day return to its original status and be saved, a doctrine known as *apocatastasis* (see Acts 3:21).

AN ASSESSMENT: THE IMPACTS OF PATRISTIC THEOLOGY ON CHRISTIAN THOUGHT AND OCCIDENTAL CULTURE

The opening of Christianity toward a non-Christian environment and the start of an intellectual dialogue with non-Christian philosophy were an expression of Christians' increased intellectual strength, maturity, and self-confidence. Apologetic theology was a new form of Christian literature, the first addressed to a non-Christian public: all previous Christian literature had been designed for the Christian community. Patristic theology was an inculturation of the gospel in a Hellenistic environment—a reinterpretation of the gospel and an attempt to make it understandable for people of non-Semitic contexts. However, this process of Hellenistic inculturation caused Christian faith to undergo some fundamental changes that affected all of later Christianity:

- One immediate impact of the patristic theologians' attempt to appeal to Hellenistic intellectuals was that Christian faith was narrowed down to what was understandable within Hellenistic thinking. As a result, Christian faith looked more and more like Greek philosophy.

- Closely related to this was an intellectualization of Christian faith: Patristic theologians saw Christian faith more as revealed doctrine and knowledge (*gnosis*) about God, not so much as new life or new hope or new being. Intellectual categories replaced relational ones—in other words, a shift from *pistis* to *gnosis*. Faith turned from a relational approach, abiding in a relationship of trust with God, to a cognitive approach, emphasizing knowledge and doctrine.

- The understanding of salvation saw a similarly significant change. The God of Israel's tradition was not only relational, but was also believed and proclaimed as saving in history. One of the foundational biblical narratives is God's salvation of the Israelites from their oppression in Egypt. This faith in God's saving intervention in history had remained the crucial framework for Israel and Jesus up to the time of early Christianity. The whole biblical perspective was historical, expecting salvation in time and distinguishing between "this age" and "the age to come." Under Platonist and Neo-Platonist influence, however, salvation came to be understood instead in spatial categories. It turned into salvation from the world, understood as eternal life. Patristic theology thus distinguished between time and eternity, shifting from historical to metaphysical thought. Platonism also influenced the understanding of salvation by leading many to believe that only the (immortal) soul would be saved.

- Greek philosophy regarded the highest goal of humankind as the vision of eternal ideas. This perspective also influenced patristic theology: The Christian spiritual journey, patristic theologians said, was aimed at leading believers to rejoice in the visual contemplation of the spiritual world. This stood in contrast to the more auditory perspective of the biblical tradition, where God reveals himself primarily through words rather than visions. We thus observe a shift from the auditory to the visual.

- The most significant change was perhaps in the understanding of God: The God of Israel was a passionate and relational God. How much different was patristic theology's description of God as the eternally immutable One! This understanding of God emphasized God's beyond-ness rather than God's involvement and interest in humanity. It spoke of God in philosophical categories that removed him from the Bible's relational descriptions of God.

The above assessment interprets the theological changes in the Hellenization of Christian faith as (*a*) the loss of an original faith relationship and (*b*) a shift to a more theoretical and doctrinal understanding of God. Still, patristic theology had a significant long-term impact on the intellectual development of the West. The most important may have been that later occidental theology and culture regarded God, in general, as standing in harmony with human rationality. God was believed to be above, not against, reason. This attitude caused European society to be generally open to human reasoning, to the scientific and technical fruits of intellectual development, and to progress overall. This positive view of human reason was based not only on the belief that human reason was part of God's good creation and, as such, a precious gift from God, but even more on the understanding of God as a *rational* supernatural being—in contrast to many religions' belief in God as an irrational supernatural power. The belief in the convergence of God and rationality, and the view of God as the epitome of reason,[7] became a characteristic element of later medieval theology, though the basic framework of this belief was formulated during the patristic period. The development of Western science, even though over long periods opposed by the church, was possible only because it was fundamentally supported by the theological insistence that God acts according to reason; that God has revealed himself not only in the word of the Bible but also in creation; and that human beings through their rationality are able to progressively understand God's revelation both in scripture and in nature.

PATRISTIC THEOLOGY SHAPING THEOLOGICAL DEBATES: EARLY TRINITARIAN POSITIONS

After the church had more or less successfully rejected the Gnostic, Marcionite, and Montanist challenges to the Christian faith, the most pressing theological issue was the question of the relationship between God the Father and God the Son. The problem emerged because the Bible does not spell out clearly how this relationship is to be understood. This so-called Trinitarian debate shows how Greek philosophical categories were used to clarify theological questions and, possibly, how new theological questions were triggered by Christianity's entry into a new context.

Around the year 200 CE we can find three positions in the Trinitarian debates: *Logos* christology, adoptionism, and modalism.

---

7. Stark, *Victory of Reason*, 11.

(a) *Logos christology* held that God created the *Logos*, who is of divine nature but clearly subordinate to God. The *Logos* can be understood in Neo-Platonist categories as a kind of emanation of God (though this is not a necessary link). The Spirit is again subordinate to the *Logos*. Both *Logos* and Spirit are of divine substance but only in derived form. This position was influenced by the Gospel of John, the middle Platonism of Philo of Alexandria, and the Neo-Platonist tradition. Problems with this interpretation are, first, the idea of Christ (and the Spirit) being subordinate to God and, second, the concept of emanation.

(b) *Adoptionism*, sometimes also called Dynamist Monarchianism, taught that Jesus Christ was fully human, but that God filled him with divine power (*dynamis*) and caused him to become divine. God adopted him as Son either through the virgin birth or through baptism. An important representative of this teaching was Paul of Samosata, bishop of Antioch.

Although later tradition clearly rejected this teaching because of its idea of Christ being subordinate to God, which eventually leads to Arianism (see ch. 6), it has solid grounding in the Bible, particularly in Mark, where Jesus' baptism can be seen as the moment where he acquired divinity. A further strength of this position is that it avoids the Neo-Platonist images of emanation.

(c) *Modalism*, also called Modalist Monarchianism, saw Christ as a form, an appearance, or simply a mode of God. This teaching emphasized the *identity* of God the Father and Christ, and, later, of Father, Son and Holy Spirit. God simply appeared, as in the theater, in three different roles (*prosopon*) or in three different forms. The most famous representative of modalism is Sabellius, because of whom modalism is sometimes also called Sabellianism.

Christian tradition rejected modalism as heretical because it dissolved the different persons of the Trinity into oneness. Yet many present-day Christians, mostly subconsciously, still follow a modalist interpretation of the Trinity, as evident in a popular image of the Trinity as a substance (like water) that appears in different states as ice, liquid, or as gas and yet always remains that same substance. Theologically, a more accurate image would be that of the sun as a physical body, the sun's light, and the heat that emerges from the sun.[8]

---

8. Based on Athanasius, *Against the Arians*, Discourse III, ch. XXIII, para. 3 (*NPNF* 2/4:395).

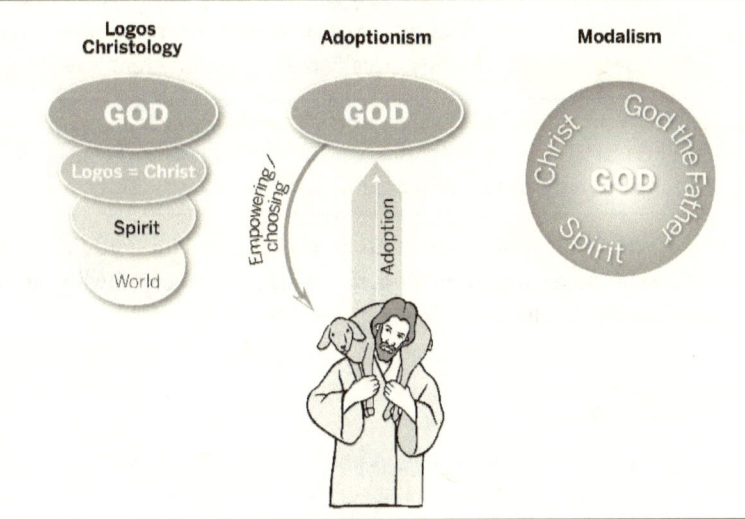

Fig. 4.4: Early Trinitarian models

Nowadays, Christians often regard dogmatic formulations as dry, unspiritual, overly intellectual, and irrelevant for practical faith life. This may be true; however, the purpose of trying to formulate correct dogmatic expressions is not to encourage believers in their daily lives but rather to guide theologians in their endeavor to communicate faith, and to find meaningful expressions in changing contexts while remaining faithful to previous faith language. Exact dogmatic formulations are attempts to put one's own spirituality into precise words—thus linking spirituality, knowledge, and communication.

What Is the Relevance of a Trinitarian Understanding of God?

Several points may be considered:
- The Trinity is a way of speaking of the one God that maintains God's diversity. The different Trinitarian concepts of God respond to the criticism of tri-theism by refining Christian monotheism in Trinitarian form.
- When Christians speak of God in Trinitarian language they ultimately give testimony to the mystery of a God who at the center of his being is *paradoxical*, One in Three. Christians thus express that at the heart of their faith there is a mystery.

- Trinitarian speculations are a way of expressing the Christian belief that God not only ontologically exists in different persons or relationships but that God is also historically revealed in different ways.

> For the specialist: This difference between God in his being and in his revelation-history is called the difference between the immanent Trinity and the economic Trinity.

The Trinitarian understanding of God thus links faith in a God who is at the beginning of all that is with faith in a God who can be encountered in the unfolding of history.

For Further Reading

Bosch, David Jacobus. *Transforming Mission: Paradigm Shifts in Theology of Mission*, 190–214. Maryknoll, NY: Orbis, 1991.
McGrath, Alister E. *Christian Theology: An Introduction*, 3–25 (ch. 1). Oxford: Blackwell, 1994.
Osborn, Eric Francis. *The Emergence of Christian Theology*. Cambridge: Cambridge University Press, 1993.
Smith, Andrew. *Philosophy in Late Antiquity*. London: Routledge, 2004.
Wilken, Robert Louis. *The Spirit of Early Christian Thought: Seeking the Face of God*. New Haven: Yale University Press, 2003.
Young, Frances, Lewis Ayres, and Andrew Louth, editors. *The Cambridge History of Early Christian Literature*. Cambridge: Cambridge University Press, 2004.

Learning Activities

1) Review key elements of this chapter by answering the following questions:
    - What are the key elements of Platonism?
    - What is the difference between Platonism and Neo-Platonism?
    - What were the three periods of theology until the middle of the fifth century? What was the purpose of theological writing in each period?
    - Name five Christian theologians of the second and third centuries.

2) To probe your understanding of what we have learned about this period, to deepen the understanding of its significance, and to apply it to your present experience, discuss the following questions:

- Think about the impacts of Platonism on Western thinking and theology:
    - What were the long-term impacts of Christianity's contextualization in Hellenist culture?
    - How did Hellenism influence Christianity?
    - How did Christians' image of God change?
- Do you think Christianity adapted too much to Hellenist thought?
- What is the difference between infralapsarist and supralapsarist theology? What is the significance of this difference?
- Think about the early Trinitarian speculation: What can you learn from it? How would you try to explain the Trinity within your own context? What is its importance and relevance nowadays?
- Patristic theology regarded Greek philosophy as preparation for the gospel. What if Asian theologians regarded classical Asian philosophy, be it Chinese or Indian, Daoist or Hindu or Buddhist or other, as preparation for the gospel? How would such contextualization look? What would be its potential insights? What would be its potential dangers?

Chapter 5

Christianity Becomes the Religion of the Empire

At the end of the third century, the Roman Empire was split into eastern and western halves, each ruled by a senior emperor and a deputy emperor. Constantine became senior emperor in 306 and pursued a military strategy that would gradually make him the sole ruler of the empire. Then, in the year 312, something happened that would change Christianity forever: The night before a decisive battle against his opponent Maxentius, Constantine had a dream in which he received a promise that he would win the battle if he entered it under the symbol of Christ's cross. After emerging victorious, Constantine began to implement religious policies that radically changed the history of Christianity. Once a persecuted faith, Christianity became a religion officially supported by the imperial government. Once an intellectually questioned faith, it became the popularly accepted faith. Once small communities of people at the fringes of society, the church became a major pillar of European society.

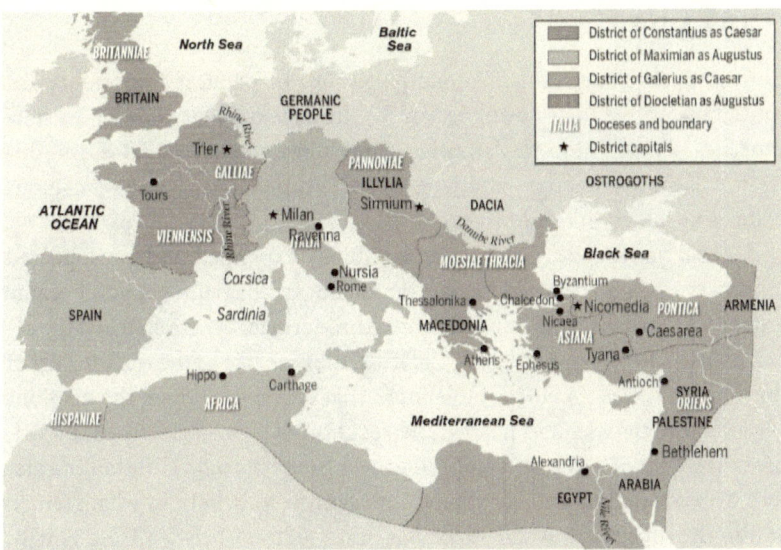

Fig. 5.1: Map of the Roman Empire before Constantine at the end of the third century

Yet, parallel to Christianity's move to the center of occidental society, a countermovement gained strength—a significant number of Christians withdrew from the church to pursue an alternative form of spirituality. This is the history of Christian monasticism, and although its roots predated Constantine, it turned into a significant movement as the church gained power.

This chapter describes that shift, the religious policy behind the shift, and Christianity's changes under the new political conditions. In particular, the chapter asks the following questions:

- How did the changes in the emperor's religious policy unfold?
- Why did Constantine convert to the Christian faith?
- How should the emperor's conversion be understood? As a strategic calculation? As a spiritual renewal? As a superstitious reaction to a dream?
- How did the emperor's conversion affect the church's life and theology?
- How did Christians react to the emergence of an imperial church?
- What is Christian monasticism?

The crucial question—the desirability of an emperor converting to Christianity—will not find an answer in this chapter but will accompany us through the subsequent centuries.

WHAT CHANGED?

Constantine's changes in religious policy are of greatest importance for church history, as they paved the way for the development of so-called state churches. Constantine was emperor from 306 to 337 CE, and during his reign as senior emperor—and later as sole emperor—these new religious policies unfolded in three stages.

From 306 to 324: Constantine gradually expanded and consolidated his power until he defeated his last opponent, Licinius, in 324 and became the sole emperor of the Roman Empire. Three crucial events changed the official status of Christianity: First, Galerius, the emperor of the eastern part of the empire, issued an edict of toleration that effectively ended the previous emperor Diocletian's and his own persecution of Christians. Then, in 312, the crucial Battle of the Milvian Bridge near Rome brought Constantine victory over Maxentius and convinced Constantine to believe in what seemed to him the supernatural and victorious power of the Christian God. Finally, in 313, Constantine and Licinius put a formal end to Christian persecution by jointly issuing the Edict of Milan. The edict not only officially granted full tolerance to Christianity but also restored property that Diocletian had taken from the churches. Any one of these three events could be regarded as the beginning of a new era.

During this first period, Christianity's legal status did not surpass the legal status of other religions, but Christianity was privileged in several respects: The government supported church construction, made efforts to reconcile different church factions, and issued laws that reflected the interests of Christians (e.g., prohibiting gladiator fights).

From 324 to 330: As sole emperor, Constantine leaned more heavily on Christianity and discriminated against non-Christian faith groups. His government introduced laws prohibiting the erection of images, the practice of divination, and the offering of private sacrifices. Resources were allocated for building or restoring churches at public expense. At the same time, Constantine intensified his efforts to reconcile competing doctrinal factions and called for an ecumenical council in Nicaea in 325 (see ch. 6).

From 330 to 337: The Roman government began to actively combat Christian heresies and eliminate paganism, in particular by destroying centers of pagan religion. In 330, a new capital for the eastern part of the Roman Empire was established in the Greek city of Byzantium and was named Constantinople ("the city of Constantine," present-day Istanbul, Turkey). The new capital signified the beginning of a new era and a break with pagan Rome. Several famous shrines and temples in the Aegean region were looted for treasure to decorate the new city. The old religion became a sort of quarry for the new and victorious religion.

An Imperial Epistle of Constantine, in which Money Is Granted to the Churches

The following text documents how Constantine offered help to the churches. It is from the last book of Eusebius' *Church History*, where he praises the Emperor Constantine and records various legal imperial documents that outline the new religious policies benefiting the Christian church. The subsequent extract is an imperial law promulgated in a letter of Constantine to Bishop Caecilian of Carthage. It shows how Constantine made generous financial contributions to the church.

> *Constantine Augustus to Caecilian, Bishop of Carthage. Since it has been our pleasure that in all provinces—namely, Africa, Numidia, and Mauretania—certain specified ministers of the legal and most holy catholic religion should receive some contribution for expenses, I have sent a letter to Ursus, the most eminent finance officer of Africa directing that he pay three thousand folles to Your Constancy. When you have received this sum, you will arrange that it is distributed among all the above-named persons according to the schedule sent you by Hosius [Bishop of Cordova in Spain and important adviser to Constantine]. If later on you find that you lack anything to fulfill my intentions regarding them, do not hesitate to ask Heraclides our procurator for whatever you need. When he was here I gave him orders that if Your Constancy should ask any money from him, he was to hand it over without question.*
>
> *And since I have learned that certain people of unstable mentality are eager to lead the laity of the most holy catholic church astray by foul inducements, know that when they were here, I instructed Anulinus, the proconsul [of Africa] and also Patricius, the vicar of the prefects, that especially in this matter they are not to overlook such incidents. Therefore, if you observe any such men persisting in this madness, you must not hesitate to bring this matter before the aforementioned judges so that, as I instructed them when they were here, they may turn these people from their error. May the divinity of the great God keep you safe for many years.*

Source: Eusebius, *Church History*, bk. X, ch. 6, 326–27.

After the death of Constantine, religious policy moved further in the same direction. This development was interrupted only for a short period by Julian the Apostate (361–63), who tried to abolish all the privileges of Christianity and restore what had been destroyed by Constantine. With the exception of Julian's reign, however, the church gradually increased its power and became a state church.

We may distinguish various forms of governmental support for the official church. The most basic form, as generally happened during the first period under Constantine, was the church simply enjoying a certain advantage: public funding for church construction, the government raising church taxes on behalf of the church, or a Christian practice receiving general recognition, as in 321, when Constantine's government declared Sunday a public holiday.

A stronger form of support for the officially recognized church emerged during the second period of Constantine's reign: the government began to destroy non-Christian religious sites and suppress or prohibit alternative faith practices like sacrifices. Such policies affected not only other religions but also Christian groups outside the Catholic Church. This kind of policy was also common in the time after Constantine's death.

The highest level of support is, of course, when one religious faith (and usually one church) is made mandatory for all subjects of the state. This happened in 380 under Theodosius the Great, who declared the faith of the Catholic Church compulsory for the entire Roman Empire.

WHAT MOTIVATED CONSTANTINE TO MAKE CHRISTIANITY THE OFFICIAL RELIGION?

Constantine's motives are still being debated, with all suggested answers mere speculative guesswork. Still, we can distinguish personal, religious, and political aspects that seem to have contributed to Constantine's religious policies.

Personal Motives

We may assume that Constantine was overwhelmed by his victory in the Battle of the Milvian Bridge, which verified his dream of a Christian cross that he was called to carry into battle. In a way that may appear superstitious to modern eyes, Constantine seemed to see the Christian God as more powerful than any other god. As a consequence, he felt compelled to show loyalty to this powerful God. However, did Constantine indeed become a Christian or was he simply impressed and subsequently compelled to be loyal to this Christian God? That remains unclear. At any rate, he received baptism only on his deathbed. Was Constantine simply an opportunist, a spiritual pretender who exploited Christianity for its benefits? Although Christians did not have significant political or economic power, Constantine had good reasons to think that the adoption of Christianity as the official state religion could bring political advantages. What were they?

Political Motives

The heyday of the Roman Empire was a period of great stability and prosperity, lasting for two hundred years until the middle of the second century. Since then, the empire had faced an increasing risk of disintegrating into different regions. People groups at the fringes of the empire were eager to reclaim their independence and move away, and migrating tribes brought disruption into the heartlands of the empire. This is a situation typical of any large political entity. Governments counter such centrifugal tendencies through the hard power of the military and through the soft power of ideology or common thought. Religion can be a powerful way of providing cohesion on a spiritual level. This could have been one motivation for Constantine to rely on Christianity as a spiritual bond for his vast empire.

But why did Constantine, rather than turning to traditional Roman religions, adopt a new faith? Perhaps Christianity seemed more likely to provide spiritual unity within a socially and ethnically diverse empire. What, then, made Christian faith seem better suited to this task than traditional religions and cults?

Religious Motives

One strength of Christianity was that it had a strong universalistic capacity while at the same time an ability to find expression in various contexts. Belief in Israel's god, Yahweh, creator of the universe and God of all nations, and in Jesus Christ, the *Logos* and Pantocrator, implied a universalism that did not deny local relevance. Christian monotheism thus reached beyond pagan myths and cults that were often only locally relevant. Linking universalist and contextual potentials has remained a feature of Christianity up to the present, and it is one of the core factors for its continuous growth. A further factor is a lack of alternatives: Christianity was nearly the only faith that was known throughout the whole empire. There were only two other alternatives with similar empire-wide popularity—the cult of Mithras, which had many followers in the army, and Manichaeism—but neither had the same ability to merge with Hellenistic thinking and relate to old philosophical traditions. Third, Christianity was successful not only in integrating Hellenistic philosophy, but equally in absorbing pre-Christian popular religious elements. It linked the particular history of Israel and the ancient wisdom of the Middle East and of ancient Greece with the present age and with its universalistic outlook. Fourth, Christianity employed a powerful and relatively unified organization, the church. This organizational religious structure conveniently promised to parallel the empire-wide political structure. Fifth, Christianity was popular among the poor, as it offered them social help. This social ministry supported and strengthened the cohesion of the empire. Sixth, Christian faith offered a convincing bridge between this world and life after death. The teaching of a God incarnate in Jesus linked this life with the next; and the sacraments made this bridge accessible to all believers. Such a solid connection between this world and the other world fostered confidence in a better and generally accessible life after death. Finally, Christian faith showed spiritual strength, visible not only in the way martyrs were able to face torture and death but also in countless stories of healing and of victory over demonic possession. Seemingly powerful demons appeared powerless against Christ, and in a culture that feared demons, this was genuinely relevant. This brings us back to the beginning of our discussion: Constantine being touched by the victorious strength of the Christian God.

What really motivated Constantine to support Christianity and to gradually establish it as the official religion of the state remains shrouded in mystery. We may, however, assume that all the factors mentioned above offer partial answers.

HOW DID CONSTANTINE AFFECT THE RELIGIOUS LIFE AND THEOLOGY OF CHRISTIANITY?

The immediate impact of the changed political situation was that, for the first time in three centuries, persecution ended and, with it, the feeling of living under threat. The new political and social context also affected how the church expressed its message through worship and art, as well as how the church appeared in society at large. The new context of Christianity also influenced theological thought.

Liturgy and Art Reflecting the New Social Status of the Church

When the emperor and high government officials started to join Christian worship services, social distinctions and hierarchies increasingly entered the liturgy of the church. Worship became influenced by imperial protocol: processionals, elaborate choirs, and colorful liturgical clothes were introduced.

Artistic representations emphasized the victorious image of Christ and depicted him as creator and ruler of the universe in the position of Pantocrator, sitting on a throne like a Roman emperor and ruling the world from there. Egyptian sun disks became the gloriole of Catholic saints. Churches were built after the model of impressive public buildings, for example, the basilica, whose basic architectural shape is based on the Roman public building for justice and administration.

However, an even more important change might have been Christian worship accommodating popular religious practices.

Absorbing Elements of Popular Religion

As more followers of popular religion turned to Christianity, the churches had to satisfy traditional folk religious needs. They began to incorporate elements of popular faith and traditional ideas into the Christian framework. People continued to venerate local pagan deities who were in charge of specific areas of life, though now within the Christian framework. Beliefs in local deities were absorbed into beliefs about "angels" or "saints." They acted as intermediaries between the two spheres of God and world and mitigated the strict separation between the two. Indeed, popular believers found a strictly monotheist god too remote to be bothered with their daily needs. The introduction of nonhuman intermediaries helped bridge this gap.

Mother Mary similarly satisfied people's spiritual yearning by providing a motherly divine figure and absorbing many features of female goddesses. She became an important intermediary, interceding before God on humans' behalf. Priests also assumed the role of mediator between God and the world. When conducting the eucharistic celebration, they actually re-presented (literally, "to make present again") the sacrifice of Christ on Golgotha and offered a sacrifice on humans' behalf. The Eucharist was thus increasingly understood as a sacrifice.

In addition, pagan festivals were absorbed into the Christian calendar and turned into Christian celebrations. The most famous festival with roots in popular religious faith is Christmas. Religious scholars assume that two earlier religious festivals lie behind our celebration of the birth of Christ, namely, the celebration of the Unconquered Sun (*Sol Invictus*) that happened around the winter solstice and Saturnalia, an originally Roman carnival-like festival that included gift-giving, partying, and lawlessness.

Some elements of the Christian liturgy are likewise rooted in popular faith; one example is incense, which originally served to chase away demons. Even the social hierarchy reflected something of popular religious backgrounds: As the primacy of the pope was not yet established, the emperor assumed highest authority in religious matters as a kind of high priest, similar to the position of an ancient Roman king.

Theology from a New Perspective

An important motive to establish Christianity as official religion was the hope that the Christian faith would provide spiritual cohesion to a vast and diverse empire. The problem was that Christianity itself was deeply divided—different views about how to understand Jesus Christ existed side by side. The government had a vital interest in overcoming such divisions and encouraged the unity of the church by whatever means possible. It was against this background that Constantine invoked the first ecumenical council, in Nicaea (325), to overcome the Arian controversy. This conflict about the relationship of Jesus Christ to God the Father had divided Christianity throughout the Roman Empire (see ch. 6). Now, for the first time in Christian history, decisions about right and wrong in matters of faith could be enforced by political (and, eventually, military) power. It is from this very moment that we can speak of orthodoxy and heresy; only after the council in Nicaea could the decision of the "majority" (at least of those present) be sanctioned and dissent punished. The history of orthodoxy and heterodoxy thus starts with Christianity becoming a religion of political power. Unity of the church became a primary concern. This was the first important theological change.

Second, theology always reflects the social context from which it emerges. As Christianity became the official religion, the interpretation of religious experiences and matters—what we call "theology"—became equally a concern of the state. The government began to employ intellectuals as theologians whose duty it was (besides providing spiritual services to the court) to clarify theological issues. A famous theologian of this early time was Eusebius of Caesarea. We may call him the first historian of Christianity. His theology may also be called a form of "court theology" because it lent spiritual legitimacy to political power. Eusebius described the history of the church as a triumphal salvation-historical development, from early persecution to the present time of triumph, with Christian faith reaching the peak of political power and the emperor bringing peace to the church.

History thus appeared as gradually evolving, finding its culmination and ultimate goal in the present rule of Constantine.

Eusebius' history of the church drew on previous theological thought like that of Justin, Clement, and Irenaeus, who saw a progressive development of human history and a progressive revelation of God from creation to its goal in Christianity. Both Justin and Clement interpreted ancient Greek philosophy and the Hebrew Scriptures as preparation for the gospel. Irenaeus saw human history as a progressive development from creation and fall to redemption in Christ and the church. Such theology obviously lent tremendous legitimacy and spiritual value to the emperor and portrayed his rule as part of a divine plan that stretched from creation through the low points of history to the present "golden era." Salvation-historical thinking, seeing history as gradually revealing a divine plan, has remained a crucial feature of Western theology throughout the centuries, and we will rediscover it in later periods.

Closely related to such interpretation of history is a third point, a new understanding of the end time (eschatology). As Christianity historically triumphed and became a common faith, it became much less appealing to talk of a sudden end of history and the beginning of a new time that would stand in radical contrast to the present time. Why should the time end now when everything seemed so good? As a result, eschatological expectation—the hope for a radical change in history and for the coming of God's kingdom—faded even further from view. Now, the *present* was indeed regarded as the fulfillment of God's promise. The millennium was not expected to come at some point in the future but was already here, made visible in the church. Such a view of history is called *amillennialism*.

ALTERNATIVE CHRISTIAN MOVEMENTS EMERGE: ASCETICS AND MONKS

Most Christians enjoyed the new status and privileges of the church, but a small number of Christians felt uncomfortable in such an association with political power. They separated from the church, either as individuals or as small ascetic and monastic communities. Christian asceticism and monasticism did not suddenly fall from heaven—it had grown out of a rich religious tradition, was influenced by political experiences, and preceded the changes in religious policy under Constantine. However, it was because of the changed political landscape that Christian asceticism and monasticism became an important alternative movement of Christianity that remained in critical yet fruitful tension with the Christian mainstream.

What Spiritual Movements Influenced Christian Asceticism and the Monastic Movement?

The Jewish tradition regarded the desert as a privileged place for encountering God. Various figures in the Jewish tradition, among them Elijah and Moses, had experienced special divine encounters in the desert. In more recent times John the Baptist had preached in the desert; radical Jewish groups like the Essenes lived in the desert; and, most importantly, Jesus retreated to the desert at the beginning of his public ministry.

Earlier Christians followed these models and chose an ascetic lifestyle. The most famous example was Origen, who lived as an ascetic teacher, sleeping on the ground, going about barefoot, drinking no wine, and contenting himself with only one garment. At the peak of his ascetic career, he famously chose to castrate himself, thus taking the words of the gospel (Matt 19:12) quite literally (although he otherwise was very skillful in interpreting the Bible allegorically). Origen thought that good Christians and true teachers should be able to fully control their desires. Origen's teaching strongly influenced Christians in Egypt.

The movement of ascetics and monks was further influenced by Hellenist philosophical traditions. The Platonic tradition had always taught a negative view of the body and the material world, and it saw transcending the transient world of matter as a goal of human life. The Stoa taught interior detachment and tranquility (*atharaxia*) and held that human beings could reach happiness by suppressing the desires of the body. Manichaeism also contributed to a negative view of the material world and thus stimulated asceticism.

What Motivated Ascetics and Monks in Their Spiritual Quest?

During the time of persecution, Christians had the chance to show the power of their faith through martyrdom. Now, as Christianity became a common belief, the opportunity for such extraordinary witness was lost. Christianity forfeited its distinctiveness and became a matter of course: Christians became part of the social mainstream, and it was not difficult or dangerous to believe. The churches lived in the midst of society and became increasingly wealthy.

Opposing this loss of spiritual fervor that came with the church's enhanced social status, a small number of Christians yearned for a renewed religious experience, for a more radical faith practice, and for a higher quality of Christian life that would reflect the original radicalism of the Jesus movement. They hoped to find Christian perfection by living a strictly ascetic life, by killing all desires, and by completely withdrawing from family and the world. Some went even further and tortured or imprisoned themselves. Others withdrew into the desert where they exposed themselves to the demons supposedly living there. The desert was where, in earlier times, those persecuted by the authorities had hidden. Now, a new generation of Christians voluntarily withdrew from society. In solitude, they hoped to grow closer to God. Their radical faith was a protest against the accommodation of the church to the world, and a testimony to the original, countercultural Jesus movement.

How Did the Monastic Movement Develop?

The earliest forms of monasticism may be found in Asian Christianity, in Syria, with people like Tatian (c. 110–80) who withdrew from society with a small number of followers. Historically more influential was its emergence in Egypt, from where it spread toward the West. We may distinguish different forms of the movement.

Individual monasticism or Anachoretism (from Greek *anachorein*, "to withdraw") became popularly known first through Anthony, whose life spanned over a century, from around 250 until 355. His spiritual journey is described in the book *Life of Anthony*, which his friend Athanasius wrote shortly after his death. The story goes that, when Anthony was around twenty years old, he heard the call of Christ and sold his estate, saving only enough for his sister. He then heard the words "be not anxious for tomorrow," gave away what was left, and sent his sister to a nunnery. He withdrew into the desert where he lived a life of solitude, continuous fasting, manual work, and repetitive praying. He memorized the Bible and fought demonic temptations. His radical discipleship attracted many followers, from whom he repeatedly withdrew by moving further into the desert.

Individual monasticism took on some extreme forms, particularly in Syria where some hermits began to live on columns or in open spaces where they were exposed to the sun with a minimum of clothing and physical protection. One of them, Symeon the Stylite ("pillar-dweller"), is said to have lived on a column for thirty-seven years. The stylites and other radical hermits expressed their countercultural testimony as fools for Christ.

Communal monasticism was an alternative form of ascetic life. The joint discipline of life in a community was supposed to help hermits in their spiritual quest. Communal monasticism was also called Pachomianism after its founder, Pachomius (c. 290–346), who initiated the ordered communal life by transforming loosely grouped hermits into an organized community subject to strict hierarchical discipline and obedience. Each monastery was designed as a large self-supporting settlement that carried on various trades and occupations. Communal monasticism spread through Asia Minor into the West, where it further developed. The monastery became a center of spirituality, prayer, and community service, and some monasteries established schools for children and hospitals. This social function of monasticism was an important factor in the later spread of Christianity.

At the end of the fourth century Athanasius introduced the idea of monasticism to the West, where it was supported by many important Christian leaders and thinkers, among them Jerome, Ambrose of Milan, and Augustine. Western monasticism found its most famous expression in the teaching of Benedict of Nursia (c. 480–c. 550), who belongs rather to the early medieval period. Benedict became a hermit in 500 and established twelve monasteries that all followed his rule. Most subsequent monasteries in the West were based in some way on the Benedictine rule. Benedict devised monasteries as self-sufficient communities where monks followed a balanced, well-organized, and humble lifestyle. Benedict's rule was pragmatic and did not require exceptional holiness. A significant element was that the monks were advised to spend equal time for worship, spiritual reading or intellectual work, and manual work. This emphasis on manual work stood in contrast to traditional views that saw labor as distracting from higher and immaterial pursuits and a quest for holiness. Instead, gardening, cleaning, cooking, and washing were all seen as standing in harmony with a life dedicated to the pursuit of holiness.

Another element of Benedictine monasticism was its strict obedience. The Benedictine rule holds that "the first step of humility is unhesitating obedience, which comes naturally to those who cherish Christ above all.... For the obedience shown to superiors is given to God, as he himself said: *Whoever listens to you, listens to me* (Luke 10:16)."[1] To be clear, Benedictine monks owed obedience to their abbot; obedience to the pope as claimed head of the universal church was a later development (more about the Benedictines in ch. 11).

From the Benedictine Rule

Written in the middle of the sixth century, the Benedictine rule is based on an earlier anonymous text called *The Rule of the Master*. Features of the Benedictine rule are its simplicity and its emphasis on obedience

---

1. Benedictine Rule, ch. 5, in Holzherr, *Rule of Benedict*, 113.

to the abbot, clear discipline, and a balance between individual asceticism and communal life. Benedictine monasticism became particularly famous for the principle of work and prayer ("ora et labora"). It should be noted, however, that work was soon understood as including scholarship. The Benedictine rule was critical of the wandering hermits that were popular in the Eastern churches and also in Irish monasticism.

Benedict of Nursia (c. 480–c. 547) was from Italy and founded several monastic communities, among them the monastery of Monte Cassino, where he eventually died. The Benedictine rule consists of seventy-three chapters. The text below shows three of the rules.

> *Ch. 8. Divine worship at night [vigils].* — *During the winter; that is, from the first of November to Easter, the monks should rise at the eighth hour of the night; a reasonable arrangement, since by that time the monks will have rested a little more than half the night and will have digested their food. Those brothers who failed in the psalms or the readings shall spend the rest of the time after vigils (before the beginning of matins) in pious meditation. From Easter to the first of November matins shall begin immediately after daybreak, allowing the brothers a little time for attending to the necessities of nature.*
>
> *Ch. 22. How the monks should sleep.* — *The monks shall sleep separately in individual beds, and the abbot shall assign them their beds according to their conduct. If possible all the monks shall sleep in the same dormitory, but if their number is too large to admit of this, they are to be divided into tens or twenties and placed under the control of some of the older monks. A candle shall be kept burning in the dormitory all night until daybreak. The monks shall go to bed clothed and girt with girdles and cords, but shall not have their knives at their sides, lest in their dreams they injure one of the sleepers. They should be always in readiness, rising immediately upon the signal and hastening to the service, but appearing there gravely and modestly. The beds of the younger brothers should not be placed together, but should be scattered among those of the older monks. When the brothers arise they should gently exhort one another to hasten to the service, so that the sleepy ones may have no excuse for coming late.*
>
> *Ch. 33. Monks should not have personal property.* — *The sin of owning private property should be entirely eradicated from the monastery. No one shall presume to give or receive anything except by the order of the abbot; no one shall possess anything of his own, books, paper, pens, or anything else; for monks are not to own even their own bodies and wills to be used at their own desire, but are to look to the father [abbot] of the monastery for everything. So they shall have nothing that has not been given or allowed to them by the abbot; all things are to be had in common according to the command of the Scriptures, and no one shall consider anything as his own property. If anyone has been found guilty of this most grievous sin, he shall be admonished for*

the first and second offence, and then if he does not mend his ways he shall be punished.

Source: Petry, *History of Christianity*, 157–58.

COUNTERCULTURAL AND MAINSTREAM CHRISTIANITY: AN ASSESSMENT OF CHRISTIAN ASCETICISM

Monasticism can be regarded as the creation of an alternative community when the previous alternative community has joined the mainstream. From this basic principle, further aspects of the significance of monasticism can be highlighted.

Relation to the Church as a Whole

Monastic groups were financially, politically, and ideologically self-sufficient communities that were, to a large extent, independent from mainstream Christianity. This allowed monasteries to occasionally build a power base of groups opposed to the Catholic Church. Monasteries thus diminished the power of the official church.

Indirectly, though, monasteries strengthened the power of the church, particularly during the medieval church's investiture controversy (see ch. 9). Withdrawing into monasteries, the hard-pressed church was able to regain strength, to reconsider its fundamentals, and to create visions for reform. A famous church reform movement that emerged from monastic life was the Cluny reform movement in the tenth and eleventh centuries (see ch. 9).

Relation to the State

The independence of monasteries allowed them to stay in critical opposition to the political government. Throughout the history of Christianity, monasteries and ascetic groups have served as support and hiding places in times of conflict with political authorities. An example was Athanasius, who repeatedly found refuge among monastic groups when he escaped the government's persecution.

Relation to Society and Culture

Monasteries, particularly in the West, were important centers of learning and of shaping culture. Studies pursued at monasteries were crucial for passing down ancient knowledge to later generations as the Roman Empire disintegrated during the period of migratory waves from Central Asia.

Monasteries also contributed economically to the welfare of society through their social and care ministries, through agricultural production on marginal lands, and, perhaps most importantly, by reshaping the understanding of physical work as something in accordance with spiritual achievement.

Basis of Theology and Mission

Monasticism was theologically important because mystical theology (a theologically countercultural tradition) developed in monasteries. Yet, more than just mysticism, most theology was monastic theology, as monasteries were the foremost economic and social place for the production of theology, the role played today by universities and Bible schools.

Monasteries played also an important role in the spread of Christianity. During the first millennium, missionary outreach to new areas often began with a monastery built in an area that was not yet evangelized. From this economic and spiritual basis the hermits reached out to the surrounding areas.

Challenges

Yet, Christian asceticism also faced serious challenges: First, monasteries attracted many people—and not always the best. Some people found refuge from persecution even where persecution might have been justified. Many persons who sought admission to a monastery did so for less than spiritual reasons. Monasteries frequently faced the problem of how to maintain their spiritual and educational standards.

Furthermore, monasteries received generous donations from believers and became wealthy. Their wealth jeopardized the ideal of poverty and potentially corrupted the monks. Whether a monastery developed well often depended on the spiritual power and leadership ability of the abbot.

Finally, for many monasteries and ascetic groups it was difficult to find the right balance between withdrawal from the world and participation in political affairs: If monastic groups separated too much from the world, they lost their impact. When participating too much in political or ecclesial affairs, even in critical opposition to political or ecclesial mainstream, they risked losing their purity and countercultural uniqueness.

For Further Reading

Digeser, Elizabeth DePalma. *The Making of a Christian Empire: Lactantius and Rome.* Ithaca: Cornell University Press, 2000.

Drake, Harold Allen. *Constantine and the Bishops: The Politics of Intolerance.* Baltimore: John Hopkins University Press, 2000.

Louth, Andrew. *The Origins of the Christian Mystical Tradition: From Plato to Denys.* Oxford: Clarendon, 1981.

MacMullen, Ramsay. *Christianizing the Roman Empire (A.D. 100–400).* New Haven: Yale University Press, 1984.

Roldanus, Johannes. *The Church in the Age of Constantine: The Theological Challenges.* London: Routledge, 2006.

Learning Activities

1) Review key elements of this chapter by answering the following questions:

    o Name three Roman emperors of the fourth century who were important for the history of Christianity.

    o What were the crucial events in the change of religious policies affecting Christianity?

    o When and with what event did the changes of religious policy regarding Christianity begin?

    o Why did Constantine introduce policies that privileged Christianity? What were his possible motives?

    o How did Constantine's conversion affect the church? Systematically present different aspects of this change.

    o What elements of popular faith did the church absorb? Name some examples.

    o What philosophical and religious traditions influenced the emergence of monasticism?

    o Why and how did monasticism emerge? In what forms?

    o What have been the effects of monasticism on church history?

2) To deepen your understanding and the significance of what we have learned about this period, discuss the following questions:

- Was Constantine's conversion good for the church? Try to distinguish the positive and negative effects of Christianity becoming an established religion. What can we learn from this for our own ministry?
- Try to imagine: What would happen theologically and in church life if Christianity became China's official or quasi-official religion?
- Try to understand religious policies in the modern world: What different forms of state religion can you distinguish? Where do you find low levels of state church systems? Where do you find high levels? Try to find the answers by making yourself familiar with the religious policies of Asian countries like China, India, Malaysia, Iran, Turkey, and Israel.
- Religion can be a powerful way of bringing cohesion to a socially or ethnically diverse state or community. What other "spiritual" or ideological tools can similarly create such social cohesion? Again, try to find the answer by thinking of China, Singapore, Malaysia, and Indonesia: What techniques to create identity and cohesion can you discover in these communities?
- Discuss the absorption of elements of popular faith, as happened in the fourth century in the West. Can you find similar processes in your local context?
- Protestantism traditionally strongly rejects any intermediary between God and the world besides Jesus Christ. Think critically: Do Protestants still have such intermediaries?
- How do you see history? Is history gradually evolving? Does it contain a divine plan? What are the dangers of such a view?
- Try to describe: What is a salvation-historical interpretation of history? What are its strengths and weaknesses? Could you imagine later periods of time that reveal a salvation-historical interpretation of history?
- What is official theology or court theology? What are its elements? What are its shortcomings? Where do we in our theological thinking have elements of official theology? How do official theologies look nowadays?
- What are the strengths and weaknesses of monasticism?

Chapter 6

Theological and Ecclesial Controversies in the Fourth Century

THE LAST CHAPTER SHOWED how the new political situation influenced Christian church life, spirituality, and theology. As the threat of persecution ceased, intra-Christian differences turned into major divisions and fellow Christians turned into bitter enemies. The possibility for conflicting theological parties to call on the government or enter into a political alliance further exacerbated internal differences.

This chapter presents two major theological and ecclesiological debates that deeply divided the church of the fourth century and that also had significant social and political dimensions: the Donatist controversy and the Arian controversy. Constantine and later emperors played active roles in both conflicts, trying to end them and using political power to enforce their decisions. The chapter asks the following questions:

- What was the Donatist controversy about? What were the interests of the opposed parties, and what was at stake theologically?

- What was the Arian controversy about? What were the interests of the different parties, and what was at stake theologically?

THE DONATIST CONTROVERSY

The origin of Donatism precedes the period of Constantine, but the conflict was strongly influenced by the political dynamics created by Constantine's religious policies.

How Did the Issue Emerge and Unfold?

The Donatist controversy was similar to the earlier Novatian schism (see ch. 3) in that it concerned the question of what to do with those who had weakened in their faith under persecution.

When in 311 Caecilian was elected as the new bishop of Carthage, some rejected him because the bishop consecrating him was accused of having betrayed his faith during the Diocletian persecution. They instead elected Majorinus as bishop, who soon after was succeeded by Donatus, hence the name of the movement. This meant a schism, a division in the church not so much over doctrine as over right authority. A council invoked by Constantine in 314 confirmed the election of Caecilian, but this did not end the schism.

Behind the religious conflict stood different political and social interests, and a deeper conflict between social and geographical groups. Donatists were popular in the agricultural areas of north and northwest Africa. The eventually victorious (and thus called "orthodox") party, supported by the emperor, had its power base more in the urban center of Carthage. In this regional business center, a more affluent class of landowners enjoyed good relationships with Rome and exported the agricultural goods of North Africa to Italy.

The conflict lived on and the Donatists were both partly tolerated and partly persecuted as a schismatic church that threatened the unity of the empire. The persecution led the Donatists to link their *theological* opposition to the Caecilian party with their *political* opposition to the urban elite and the Roman government. When a new synod was called in 411 at Carthage to resolve the conflict, the two parties stood against each other, with the catholic (or "orthodox") delegation slightly larger in number. The imperial commissioner who supervised the dispute declared—not surprisingly—the catholic party as winner. This new decision against the Donatists still did not end the conflict, and the group continued to exist at the social margins in more radical opposition to the catholic party. It lived on under constant persecution, dying out only with the Islamic conquest of North Africa in the seventh century. The division of the church in this vast territory is often seen as one of the reasons why the Muslims attained victory so easily.

How Did the New Political Context, with Christianity as the Official Religion of the State, Influence the Resolution of the Conflict?

Social tensions between urban and rural classes, as well as between affluent landowners and poor agricultural laborers, existed long before Constantine, and these social differences were carried into the church because there were Christians among both groups. However, the conflict within the church was initially ameliorated by the fact that many upper-class Christians had to break with their previous social contacts. When Christianity became the official religion of the empire, however, upper-class Christians naturally assumed the dominant position in both church and society. Social tensions became more visible. From the perspective of the lower class, those who had previously controlled politics and the economy now also controlled the church. The moral rigorism of the Donatists was a form of protest against a church that had become part of mainstream society.

What Was the Theological Importance of the Conflict?

The core theological question was whether an ordination or a consecration performed by an unworthy bishop (if in fact he had been) was still valid. In other words, was an ordination dependent on the personal qualities of the one who performed it? At stake was not only the conducting of ordinations or consecrations but whether *any* sacrament depended on the virtue of the person officiating.

The answer that became recognized—and that later tradition followed—was that the validity of the sacrament is independent of the worthiness of the one performing it. The validity of the sacrament instead depends only on whether the sacrament was properly conducted, that is, with the right words and acts. This was theologically and practically a wise decision. Any retrospective discussion about the dignity and validity of a priest or bishop who had dispensed a sacrament would have caused unending turmoil.

The Donatist conflict was also important because, in the synod of 411 in Carthage, Augustine for the first time formulated the principle that it is right to force a schismatic church into the fold of the catholic church, although he made clear that heresy should not be punished by death.[1] Augustine supported the catholic party with reference to Luke 14:23: "*Urge them to enter!*"[2] This historically significant decision became a model for much of the medieval church's expansion and its suppression of dissent.

THE ARIAN CONTROVERSY

The more important conflict of this period was the Arian controversy. The traditional depictions of Arianism as a movement and of Arius as a person are, similar to those in other conflicts, biased by catholic tradition and by what became known as orthodoxy. This tradition regards Arius as the most important heretic of the fourth century, who was fortunately defeated by Athanasius, the defender of orthodox faith. What we know about Arius thus comes mostly through the negative orthodox depiction of him. Few of his own writings have been preserved.

Although the conflict seems rather abstract and difficult to understand, the controversy between Arius and Athanasius was one of the most important theological debates in the history of Christianity. It was not at all a mere disagreement among aloof intellectuals and theologians but one that triggered heated popular debate. At the center of the conflict stood the question about how God the Father and Christ the Son relate to each other.

What Was the Arian Controversy About?

At its core, the problem was (and is) simple: How can Christians believe in both God the Father and in Jesus Christ, while still upholding the basic biblical belief that there is only one God? *How can Christians avoid bi-theism* (or even tri-theism, if the Holy Spirit is included)? How does Christ, the Son of God, relate to God the Father: Is the Son of God equal to God or inferior? Does Christ have a beginning in time or is he eternal? Was there a time in the beginning when Christ was not?

The conflict is exacerbated by ambiguous biblical texts. Passages like Colossians 1:15–20 speak of Christ as the image of the invisible God and firstborn of all creation. The question thus arises: Is Christ now part of creation and a creature, or not? The Philippian hymn emphasizes how Christ did not count equality with God a thing to be grasped. Doesn't such a passage suggest that Christ is *not* equal to God? The Gospels offer a similar

---

1. Augustine, Letter 100: Augustine to Donatus (408 CE), *NPNF* 1/1:412.
2. Augustine, Letter 93: Augustine to Vincentius (408 CE), *NPNF* 1/1:383.

ambiguity. On one hand, John emphasizes the divine character of Jesus, who is in everything equal to the Father. The Synoptic Gospels, on the other hand, focus more on Jesus as a human being. Mark, in particular, is often said to have an adoptionist Christology, seeming to suggest that Jesus became the Son of God only through his baptism.

The purpose of Arius' theology was first to maintain a strict monotheism. He therefore emphasized strongly that Christ is subordinate to God. He insisted that the separation between a transcendent, eternal, and unchanging God and humanity was a fundamental part of the created order. God, being eternal and unchanging, could not suffer—suffering belongs to the created order. Thus if Jesus suffered, he could do so only if he belonged to the created order.

But more than this, the Arian controversy was really about soteriology. At the center of the Arian soteriology was a redeemer who was obedient to his Creator's will, whose life of virtue is a model of the perfect creature and hence the path of salvation for all Christians. The humanity of Jesus Christ is important for salvation because it is Jesus' humanity that shows us how a creature should be obedient to the Father and could be elevated to the status of God. We are thus called into a process of deification. We are called to *imitate Christ* and consequently become sons like him. We have, in principle, the same chance as Christ of being declared sons of God. In short, salvation is imitation of Jesus Christ—imitation of his humanity, of his humility, and of his free subordination under the will of God the Father.

Arius expressed his belief this way:

> And God, being the cause of all things, is Unbegun and altogether Sole, but the Son being begotten apart from time by the Father, and being created and found before ages, was not before His generation, but being begotten apart from time before all things, alone was made to subsist by the Father. For He is not eternal or co-eternal or co-originate with the Father, nor has He His being together with the Father, as some speak of relations, introducing two ingenerate beginnings, but God is before all things as being Monad and Beginning of all.[3]

In contrast to this stood the soteriology of Athanasius, which subsequently became the recognized (orthodox) position: *Only God can save.* If we believe in salvation through Jesus Christ, his full divinity is therefore required or presupposed. Athanasius rejected Arius' view because it claimed a human ability to achieve the same status as Jesus Christ. Christ is the natural

---

3. Letter to Alexander, Bishop of Alexandria (c. 320), in Athanasius, *On the Councils of Ariminum and Seleucia* (359), ch. 16 (*NPNF* 2/4:458).

and one son of God. His sonship is eternal and he was born in eternity. A century earlier, the famous Christian theologian Origen had already affirmed this belief; there was no time when the Son was not: "God is the Father of His only-begotten Son, who was born indeed of Him, and derives from Him what He is, but without any beginning."[4] Christians are equally children of God, yet not natural children like Jesus Christ, but adopted in and through God's grace.

How Did the Conflict Begin?

The conflict erupted in the year 318, in Alexandria, when a synod led by Bishop Alexander of Alexandria excommunicated the presbyter Arius (c. 250–336) for his teachings. The following events (up to and including the First Ecumenical Council in the history of the church, the Council in Nicaea in 325) were strongly shaped by political factors and political maneuvering. Constantine played a crucial role in the resolution of the conflict because he was interested in a united church that could serve as a cohesive bond for the empire. In other words, he was driven more by political considerations than by theological ones.

The conflict did not end with the excommunication of Arius. He had been supported by several notable theologians, most importantly Eusebius of Nicomedia (not to be confused with the church historian Eusebius, who was from Caesarea), a highly influential Eastern bishop who had a good relationship with the emperor. The conflict soon threatened to split the church, making it a matter of public concern and causing the emperor to intervene. To overcome the divisions in the church, which threatened the unity of the empire, the emperor called a council in Nicaea, not far from the soon-to-be capital, Constantinople.

What Happened in Nicaea?

Constantine invited all of the approximately eighteen hundred bishops of the church and offered them free travel and lodging. Eventually 318 bishops attended, only five of them from the Western part of the empire. This weak representation of the Western churches reflected two things: the church in the West was not as strong as in the East, and the conflict was more an issue in the eastern part of the empire (see ch. 7).

Three parties were present at the council:

---

4. Origen, *De Principiis*, bk. I, ch. 2.2, "On Christ" (*ANF* 4:246).

i. The Arians, also called the Eusebian party (because of their chief representative, Eusebius of Nicomedia).

ii. A middle party with an Origenist theology, led by Eusebius of Caesarea.

iii. The Alexandrine party, later called the orthodox party, led by Alexander of Alexandria and others. Emerging as important within this party was Bishop Alexander's secretary, Athanasius.

Athanasius' Image of the Relationship between the Father and the Son

Athanasius had become the most important opponent of Arian Christians. In the following section of his book *Against the Arians*, he refers to the image of the sun and the radiation of the sun to argue for the co-eternity of the Father and the Son: although the two are distinguishable, they are of the same being.

> *For the Son is in the Father, as it is allowed us to know, because the whole Being of the Son is proper to the Father's essence, as radiance from light, and stream from fountain; so that whoso sees the Son, sees what is proper to the Father, and knows that the Son's Being, because from the Father, is therefore in the Father. For the Father is in the Son, since the Son is what is from the Father and proper to Him, as in the radiance the sun, and in the word the thought, and in the stream the fountain: for whoso thus contemplates the Son, contemplates what is proper to the Father's Essence, and knows that the Father is in the Son.*

Source: Athanasius, *Against the Arians*, Discourse III, ch. XXIII, para. 3 (*NPNF* 2/4:395).

The middle party maintained that the Son is subordinate to the Father, but agreed with the Alexandrine party that Christ's sonship is eternal. The Council of Nicaea decided in favor of the Alexandrine party and adopted an older baptismal creed with the inclusion of anti-Arian keywords: Christ is begotten, not made, and he is *homoousios*, of one substance with the Father (from Greek *homo* = "same, equal"; *ousia* = "being, essence"). The creed thus stressed the ontological unity—a unity of being—between the Father and the Son. This was the first time that a nonbiblical word was used in a creed. The teaching of Arius was condemned and he was sent into exile; however, the Arian faith continued to spread for several centuries, as we will see in a later section.

In addition to this decision about Arius' teachings, the Council of Nicaea made three other significant decisions. First, the church had traditionally followed the Jewish Passover in setting the date for the celebration of Easter. Throughout the years, a number of Christians began to feel dissatisfied with the way the Jewish community defined the month in which the Passover was to be held. The council decided that the church should not follow the Jewish definition but should independently establish it uniformly throughout the church. However, the exact date of Easter remained a contentious issue for centuries to come.

The council also decreed that the patriarchs of Alexandria, Antioch, and Rome should have highest authority in their respective regions. The honorary right of the patriarch of Jerusalem was also recognized.

The council further sought an end to the Meletian schism. Meletius was a bishop in Egypt known for his moral rigorism and his rejection of those who had yielded to persecution during the reign of Diocletian. This caused a schism in the church similar to the Novatian and the Donatist schisms. The Council of Nicaea tried to find reconciliation with Meletius and his followers by allowing him to keep his bishop's seat; however, those whom he had ordained needed to undergo renewed ordination. The conflict did not end with the council, nor did the death of Meletius soon after the council bring a resolution. Instead, the followers of Meletius joined the excommunicated Arians.

How Did the Controversy Continue after Nicaea?

It might be debated whether a compromise—or an effective persuasion of one side by the other—in such a difficult yet crucial question was ever possible. It might equally be discussed whether the church could have accommodated and embraced two widely different theologies. In any case, Nicaea did not establish a real compromise; instead, the victorious party, supported by the emperor, imposed a doctrinal decision on the minority. This could not bring an end to the controversy, and thus the Arian and other theological positions lived on. They continued to offer an alternative theology and soteriology to resolve the dilemma between the insistence on a strict monotheism and the assertion that only God can save.

In addition, the central problem of the Nicene Creed was the word *homoousios*, "of the same being." This word, used in the attempt to clarify doctrine, only triggered new questions. If God the Father and Christ the Son are of identical "being," what remains then as distinction between Father and Son?

> *The debate*: Some people therefore preferred the term *homoiousios*, "of a similar being" (from *homoios* = "similar") as a better description of the relationship between Father and Son. According to these so-called *homoiousians*, the essence or the being of the Son is "like" the Father's, a perfect image, resembling its archetype but not identical. An important representative of this position was Basil, bishop of Ancyra. Meanwhile the Arians—who did not simply disappear—were called *heterousians* or *anomoions* (from Greek *heteros* = "different" and *a-* or *an-* = "non-"). The orthodox party was called the *homoousians*.

From Nicaea to the Death of Constantine (325–37)

After the Council of Nicaea, Eusebius of Nicomedia, who still held a prestigious position at the imperial court, continued to support the Arian teaching. He enjoyed so much influence at the court that he was chosen to baptize Constantine at Pentecost in 337, shortly before the emperor's death. He regularly spoke out on behalf of the excommunicated Arians and found a strong ally in Constantia, the sister of Constantine.

Eusebius knew that the Nicene Creed could not simply be changed, but he began attacking the leading representatives of orthodoxy, first among them Athanasius, who had become the patriarch of Alexandria in 328. As a result of these maneuverings, Athanasius was excommunicated in 335, though on the basis of non-theological accusations. This was the first of five excommunications and reinstatements in Athanasius' long and colorful career.

Controversy during the Reign of the Sons of Constantine (337–61)

After Constantine's death, the empire was split among his three sons. Soon enough, civil war broke out and Constantius became the sole emperor. During this time, the Arian party increased its influence at the imperial court and used it to attack the Athanasians. In 340, Bishop Julius of Rome restored Athanasius to the Catholic church after he had once again been deposed. The bishop claimed that he had the canonical right and duty to act as a court of appeal, or even a final court, in case of controversies. This event was an early sign of Rome's claim of primacy.

Later synods—Arles in 353 and Milan in 355—continued to condemn Athanasius and put pressure on the Athanasians (the *homoousians* or orthodox party). The supporters of Athanasius, among them the bishop of Rome, were exiled. Suddenly, it looked as if the Arian theology and soteriology would prevail.

From the Death of Constantius to the Council of Constantinople (361–81)

After Constantius' death, the influence of the Arians went up and down, as did that of their opponents. In general, though, the influence of the Arian party was stronger. Athanasius remained a focal point of the Arians' criticism until his death in 373; he had been the last survivor of those directly involved in Nicaea. From then on, Nicene theology was represented by the great Cappadocian theologians Basil the Great, his brother Gregory of Nyssa, Gregory of Nazianzus, and the oft-forgotten fourth, Macrina the Younger, the sister of Basil and Gregory. They introduced important Trinitarian terms like being, nature, individual reality, and personality (*ousia, physis, hypostasis,* and *prosopon*).[5] These terms helped establish a balance between the three-ness and the one-ness of Father, Son, and Holy Spirit: one could believe Christ to be of the same being with the Father, though maintaining a different identity.

Macrina Converts Basil to the Ascetic Life

Macrina (c. 320–79) was the older sister of Basil the Great and Gregory of Nyssa. Although we have no knowledge of her writings, she had a deep influence on her brothers, particularly on Basil, whom she led to the monastic life. The story of Macrina's life is preserved in a biography written by her brother Gregory, which combines biography with instruction in the monastic life. Macrina was engaged at a young age; her fiancé suddenly died, however, and subsequently, Macrina committed herself to a life of contemplation and celibacy.

The text below tells how Macrina led Basil to the monastic life. It sheds light on the dynamics of the siblings. One wonders whether Basil would have agreed with his brother's description of his pride.

> *When the mother had arranged excellent marriages for the other sisters, such as was best in each case, Macrina's brother, the great Basil, returned after his*

---

5. Jenkins, *Jesus Wars*, 56.

> long period of education, already a practiced rhetorician. He was puffed up beyond measure with the pride of oratory and looked down on the local dignitaries, excelling in his own estimation all the men of leading and position. Nevertheless Macrina took him in hand, and with such speed did she draw him also toward the mark of philosophy that he forsook the glories of this world and despised fame gained by speaking, and deserted it for this busy life where one toils with one's hands. His renunciation of property was complete, lest anything should impede the life of virtue.

Source: Stevenson, *Creeds, Councils and Controversies*, 96.

When Theodosius I came to power in 379, the tide turned again, this time in a more lasting way, as Theodosius began to pursue religious policies against the Arians. In order to unify the church and reconfirm the church's rejection of Arian theology, he convened the Second Ecumenical Council, the Council of Constantinople, in 381.

What Was the Theological Contribution of the Council of Constantinople?

What became recognized as the Second Ecumenical Council of the church was attended by only 150 bishops, all of them from the eastern part of the empire. The most important decision of the council was to confirm the Nicene Creed, including the contentious word *homoousios*. The creed agreed upon was called the Niceno-Constantinopolitan Creed, with two significant changes to the earlier Nicene Creed. The first was that the section on Jesus Christ was extended to include more elements regarding Jesus' earthly life and his suffering. The human figure of Jesus thus gained a higher profile. This emphasis on the humanity of Christ can be seen as an early attempt to balance the humanity and divinity of Christ, a topic that would occupy the church in the fifth century. Too much emphasis on Christ's divinity would inevitably lead to modalism, the Trinitarian view that God-Father, God-Son, and Holy Spirit are simply different appearances, or modes, of the same. This teaching, also known as Sabellianism, was condemned by the Council of Constantinople. The other important change was a cautiously worded article concerning the Holy Spirit, who in the earlier creed had been only mentioned, not really described. This step was directed against the so-called Pneumatomachians ("those who fight against the Spirit"), a theological tradition that agreed on the equality of Father and Son, but denied the equal status of the Spirit.

Besides these amendments to the Creed, the council condemned the teaching of Apollinaris, the bishop of Laodicea, in present-day Turkey, who anticipated something of the debates of the fifth century when he emphasized Christ's divinity to an extent that the reality of his human life appeared lost. Among the other decisions of the council, the most fateful was an agreement that "the Bishop of Constantinople, however, shall have the prerogative of honour after the Bishop of Rome; because Constantinople is New Rome."[6] Although this decision was actually aimed at diminishing the status of the patriarchies of Antioch and Alexandria (and, ironically, on this ground was criticized by the bishop of Rome), it contributed to the Roman claim of primacy.

	Arianism	Orthodoxy
OTHER NAMES	Subordinatianism; Eusebianism	Homoousians
REPRESENTATIVES	Arius; Eusebius of Nicomedia	Athanasius
THEOLOGICAL POSITION	Christ is subordinate to God	Christ is essentially equal to and of the same substance with God (homoousios)
DECISION	Excommunication of Arianism in the ecumenical council of Nicaea (325) and Constantinople (381)	
LATER DEVELOPMENT	Surviving many centuries and spreading to the Goths, ultimately disappearing	Further development into the Catholic Church

Fig. 6.1: Summary comparison between Arianism and Orthodoxy

Concluding Thoughts on the Two Councils' Doctrinal Decisions

One of the problems in the Arian controversy was that it was mainly about soteriology, that is, about how we as human beings can be saved. But the soteriological debate was carried out in an external field, that of Christology and Trinitarian theology.

---

6. "The Second Ecumenical Council," in *The Seven Ecumenical Councils* (NPNF 2/14:178).

The unfolding of the controversy and the decisions of the two councils raise several fundamental issues:

(*a*) Regarding the necessity of spiritual developments: What we said in chapter 3 when discussing the development of the creed can also be said here. One may regard it as unavoidable and natural that a faith-based community should develop a common doctrinal basis in order to give a clearer and more systematic account of central elements of their faith where the biblical basis is ambiguous. However, such a development implies a shift in the perception of what is essential for salvation: less emphasis on personal trust in God, more on belief in and adherence to a fixed creed.

The question remains: Despite appearing to be a natural process, is it historically necessary for a faith community to define a joint creedal basis? If this is necessary, how, then, could belief be defined in a way that still allows diversity? More critically, one may ask, is the *iota* in a word like *homoiousios* so crucial as to impede a person's salvation? And contrarily, could the Christian faith be thought of as without such "essentialism"?

(*b*) Regarding the randomness of history: The Nicene Council was far from a free exchange of views. Arius himself was not able to present his theology, and some bishops had been condemned or excommunicated even before the council began. The council achieved unity at least partly through political coercion, disregarding plurality within the church. Critics may argue that the council was a failure because it was unable to end the conflict. Supporters, however, may maintain that later tradition largely validated the victorious position and did not attempt to revive earlier positions.

The question remains: Was the victory of what became known as orthodoxy the will of God or a historical coincidence?

(*c*) Regarding the role of politics or non-theological factors in the development of belief: The emperor played a crucial role and influenced the council at various points. His family, and bishops close to the throne, likewise influenced the emperor.

The question remains: What is the value of a doctrinal expression that has been so strongly influenced by politics?

(*d*) Regarding the Holy Spirit: Although the theological debates of the fourth century provided the basic Trinitarian doctrines and beliefs, the discussion about the role and meaning of the Holy Spirit seems rather subordinate. In other words, the Holy Spirit was included as the third person of the Trinity but did not receive equal doctrinal space.

The question remains: How much of the present-day disagreement over the role of the Spirit (e.g., charismatic gifts) can be traced to the relative undervaluing of the Spirit in those first few centuries of the church? Could it be that both the view of the church as an embodiment of the Spirit, adopted by later generations, as well as ecclesial appropriation of the Spirit were possible because of the lack of doctrinal definition regarding the Spirit?

For Further Reading

Barnes, Timothy D. *Athanasius and Constantius: Theology and Politics in the Constantinian Empire.* Cambridge, MA: Harvard University Press, 1993.

Gregg, Robert C., and Dennis E. Groh. *Early Arianism: A View of Salvation.* London: SCM, 1981.

Jenkins, Philip. *Jesus Wars: How Four Patriarchs, Three Queens, and Two Emperors Decided What Christians Would Believe for the Next 1,500 Years.* New York: HarperOne, 2010.

Young, Frances M. "Monotheism and Christology." In *The Cambridge History of Christianity*, vol. 1, *Origins to Constantine*, edited by Margaret M. Mitchell and Frances M. Young, 452–69. Cambridge: Cambridge University Press, 2006.

Learning Activities

1) Familiarize yourself with the geography of early Christianity by studying the following map:

114　Part I: The History of the Early Church

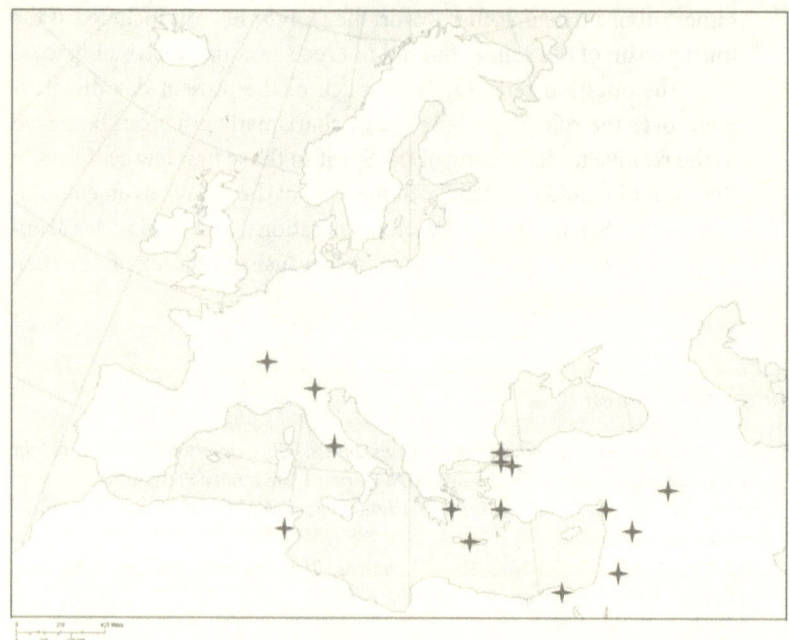

Link the locations (+) on the map to the geographical names below: Athens; Carthage; Edessa; Constantinople; Rome; Ephesus; Lyon; Milan; Alexandria, Jerusalem; Damascus; Antioch; Nicaea; Crete; Chalcedon.

2) Review key elements of this chapter by answering the following questions:

- Discuss the background and the unfolding of the church's conflict with Donatism:
  - What were the reasons for this conflict?
  - What were/are parallels to this conflict?
  - What role did the emperor play?
- What was the theologically crucial question of the controversy between Donatism and the wider church?
- What were (a) the theological and (b) the soteriological concerns of Arius?
- What three positions were debated at the Nicene Council?
- What steps can be distinguished in the historical process from Nicaea 325 to Constantinople 381?
- Discuss and clarify the different positions in the Arian controversy:
  - What is Arian christology? What is Arian soteriology?

- What is Orthodox christology? What is Orthodox soteriology?
- What was the middle position of the Origenists?

3) Probe your understanding by discussing the following question:
    o Compare the Nicene Creed with the Niceno-Constantinopolitan Creed. What were the important changes? What was the reason for their inclusion?

4) To deepen the significance of what we have learned about this period, discuss the following questions:
    o How do you assess the significance of the orthodox tenet that Christ is of the same substance as the Father? How important is it for you? Would an Arian position have been good enough for you?
    o What do you think about the relationship between the sacrament and the one administering it? What relevance does the theological issue raised by the Donatists have in today's church?
    o Think about your local church culture: Can you find any parallel/relevance to the Donatist concern about the worthiness of the one administering the sacrament? What does this mean for Christian doctrine? What does it mean for local Christians?
    o Think about the problem of orthodoxy and the relation of our faith to orthodox (right) doctrine:
        - How important is it?
        - How should faith and belief relate?

CHAPTER 7

Theology and Christological Debates in the Fifth Century

THE FIFTH CENTURY WAS in many ways the peak of the early church, and it gave rise to the most important theological systems for centuries to come. The different interests and the different theological patterns of the Greek-speaking Eastern churches and the Latin-speaking Western churches had become increasingly visible. The Eastern churches were more influenced by Hellenism and by metaphysical and philosophical interests, developing a more speculative theology that was more concerned with the understanding of the Trinity and the question of Christ's origin and his different natures. In contrast, the Western Latin tradition showed more interest in anthropological and soteriological questions: What is a human being? How can a person be saved? How can fallen humanity be repaired? The Western church thus expressed a stronger concern for ethical and psychological issues.

This chapter takes these disparate interests into account, dedicating one part to the continuation of the Trinitarian and christological debates, more relevant for the East, and another part to the theology of Augustine, who could be called the father of occidental theology.

The Council of Constantinople did not end the process of theological clarification. However, the focus in the following decades shifted from the relationship between God the Father and God the Son to the question of how Christ's humanity can be described, if he is fully of the same being as God. The fifth century brought intense theological debates regarding the relationship between the divine and human natures of Christ and offered various theological answers to the question. The emerging orthodox belief came at the expense of alternative understandings of the two natures of Christ, his humanity and his divinity. Many features of the theological debates of the fifth century were similar to those of earlier ones: The church's decisions were again strongly influenced by political and ecclesial maneuvering; and as before, the debates, apparently so abstract for modern people, aroused strong popular interest and the participation of all social groups. The first part of the chapter will summarize the different aspects of the debate.

The second part of the chapter offers an introduction to the theology of Augustine. Augustine is without question the single most important theologian of the Latin (Western or Roman) church tradition. We should note, however, that the veneration of Augustine came largely from the Western church. In the Eastern churches, he was recognized but never played the same preeminent role; in the West, all later theology was influenced and shaped in one way or another by Augustine's thought.

The chapter, then, asks the following questions:

- What were the motives and interests that led to the christological debates of the fifth century? What were the outcomes?
- What was Augustine's contribution to the development of Christian theology? Why was he so important?
- What was Augustine's understanding of sin and salvation?

THE CHRISTOLOGICAL DEBATES OF THE FIFTH CENTURY: EPHESUS, CHALCEDON AND BEYOND

The christological debates lasted several centuries and were carried out under varying titles. The crucial question debated throughout the whole period was how much Jesus Christ was human and how much he was divine. The most radical positions had been previously condemned as heresies—most importantly Ebionitism, which saw Jesus as following in the tradition of the prophets of Israel, simply as specially empowered and anointed by the spirit of God; and Gnosticism, which regarded Jesus Christ as fully divine and as a messenger of the spiritual world who had not really become human or entered the material world.

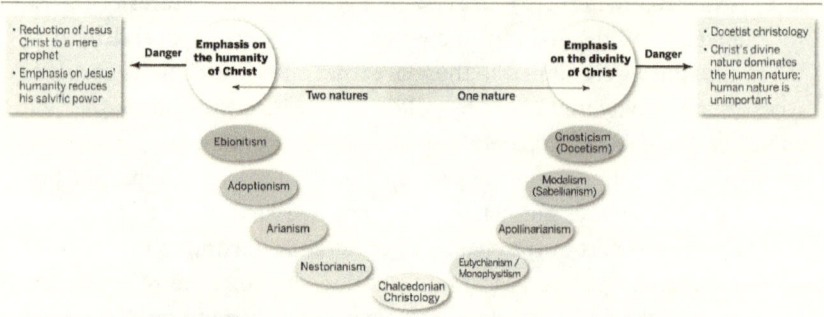

Fig. 7.1: Five centuries of Trinitarian and christological debates under different names

What Were the Different Positions in the Fifth Century?

For the sake of simplifying the complex debate, we can distinguish three positions, each with its support base in one major church.

(a) The School of Antioch taught that in the person of Jesus Christ two natures came together with two persons maintaining some independence.

This would, in the chart above, correspond to the Nestorian position. The connection between the divine and immutable *logos* and the perfect man Jesus was not a *substantial* connection but merely an *ethical* one based on the attitude and, one may say, the free decision of the two persons. This connection can be understood as the indwelling of God in a temple or in a saint, only that the intensity of God's indwelling was of course stronger in Jesus. Christ seemed like a being with two heads, God and man, and the unity between the two appeared somehow accidental—a moral unity, not ontological or essential—with two separately effective wills.

The danger of this position was that the loose connection between the human and divine nature of Jesus Christ reduced the uniqueness of Christ and made him look like an inspired prophet on whom the Spirit of God had descended. Its background lay in the adoptionist understanding of Christ, that is, that Christ was a man and, at one point in time, was adopted by God the Father and thus elevated to divine rank. Important representatives of this school were Diodore of Tarsus and Theodore of Mopsuestia.

(b) In radical contrast to this, the Alexandrian School taught that Christ was one person and one divine nature.

This is, in the chart above, the position of Eutychianism or of Cyril of Alexandria. The divine being dwelt in the individual person of Jesus Christ in a way that connected the divine and human nature completely and in a substantial unity. The human nature appears to have been swallowed by the divine nature—it loses its distinctiveness and does not play a role anymore. This position can be compared to a being in which one side, the human nature of Christ, has disappeared. The one remaining person is God himself; therefore, when Jesus acts it is not the unity of something divine and something human that is acting, but the *Logos* of God. All the struggles and uncertainties, all the despair and loneliness that the Gospels present, only *appear* to have been experienced by Jesus—they were not truly real.

The obvious danger of this position was that the life of Jesus lost its physicality, with Jesus seeming to merely play-act in his temptations and suffering. Such a position veered dangerously close to the docetist Christology of the Gnostics.

(c) Between these two positions stood the Occidental School of the Roman Church, suggesting that in the one person of Jesus Christ two natures are closely connected without being mixed. This important doctrine was first formulated by Tertullian and became the official teaching of large parts of later church tradition, known as Chalcedonian Christology.

How Did the Conflict Unfold?

The conflict unfolded in two stages and with different alliances. The first stage ended with the Third Ecumenical Council of Ephesus in 431 and with the excommunication of Nestorius and his followers. The second stage ended with the Fourth Ecumenical Council of Chalcedon in 451 and with the excommunication of the so-called monophysite (or, more neutrally, the Non-Chalcedonian) churches.

The First Stage: The Nestorian Debate and the Council of Ephesus (431)

The conflict emerged around 428 when Nestorius, the newly elected Patriarch of Constantinople and a representative of the School of Antioch, began to criticize the title *theotokos* (God-bearer or mother of God), commonly used for Mary. Nestorius disapproved of this title because it implied that she had given birth to God. Instead, he advocated the more appropriate title *christotokos* (Christ-bearer or mother of Christ). He argued, quite understandably, that it simply does not make sense to call Mary the mother of God because God is before all creation and cannot have a mother. Nestorius' teaching targeted Apollinaris of Laodicea (c. 310–c. 390), who emphasized the divinity of Christ to an extent that Christ appeared unable to truly experience temptation. Nestorius' opponents, led by Cyril, the Patriarch of Alexandria, accused him of taking the divine character of Christ lightly and thus implicitly subordinating Christ to God.

Of course, the conflict was as much about politics as about different theological perspectives. What energized it was an old rivalry between two of the three most important centers of church authority—Alexandria and Constantinople. Alexandria was more important in terms of theological and spiritual tradition; Constantinople's prestige was due to its status as new capital of the empire.

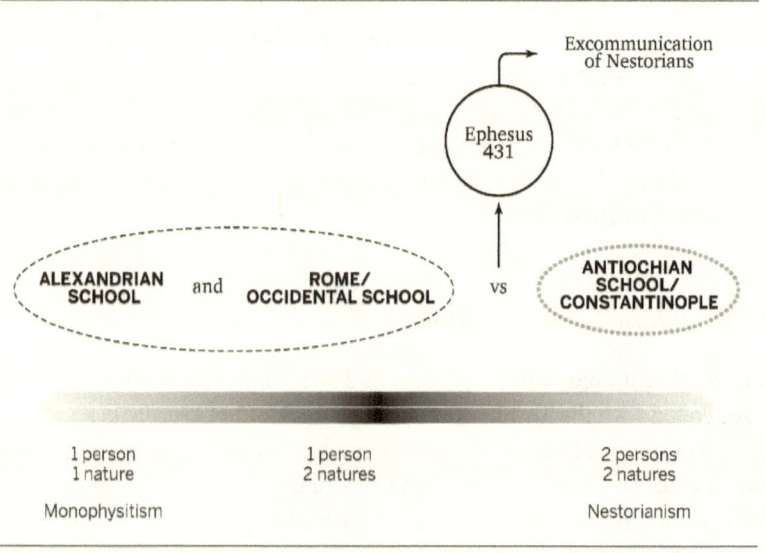

Fig. 7.2: *Conflicting positions in the christological debates of the fifth century: Part I*

The solution to the controversy again had deep political implications: Celestine, the bishop of Rome, supported Cyril against Nestorius, at least partly because he was irritated that Nestorius had received Pelagian refugee bishops (see the discussion of Pelagianism, below) who had been expelled from the West. Another reason for his support of the Alexandrians was that he was trying to limit the influence of the patriarchate of Constantinople.

Emperor Theodosius II wanted to resolve the conflict, which once again threatened to divide the unity of the empire, and called an ecumenical council at Ephesus in 431. What became (in official counting) the Third Ecumenical Council resulted in the condemnation of Nestorius' teaching and in his removal as patriarch of Constantinople. Nestorius himself withdrew into a monastery near Antioch and was later sent into exile. His tradition lived on, based in Persia (present-day Iraq). It developed into a major church tradition that, at times, extended as far as China and India, far beyond any other form of Christianity of that time. China's first encounter with Christianity, in fact, was with the Nestorian tradition. The tradition later became known as the Church of the East and, in modern times, as the Assyrian Church of the East.

The council of Ephesus was in no way a free exchange of ideas and can hardly be described as fair. The council opened before the important Antioch delegation, which should have given support to Nestorius, had arrived. Not surprisingly, the conflict continued after the council. Two years later, Theodosius II, more interested in unity than in the subtleties of theological debates, urged the conflicting parties into a union in which the Antioch party successfully introduced a declaration that came close to its own theology. Both Patriarch John of Antioch and Cyril of Alexandria accepted this Formula of Union of 433, which maintained the excommunication of Nestorius, accepted the title *theotokos* for Mary and at the same time assented to a more Antiochian christology. For some years the conflict seemed resolved.

	Nestorianism	Orthodoxy
SUPPORTING CHURCH	Antioch	Alexandria, Rome
REPRESENTATIVES	Nestorius, Patriarch of Constantinople	Cyril, Patriarch of Alexandria
THEOLOGICAL POSITION	Mary gave birth not to God, but only to Christ	Mary gave birth to God
DECISION	Excommunication of Nestorians in the ecumenical council of Ephesus (431)	
LATER DEVELOPMENT	Eventually spreading into India and China – now a small minority in the Middle East and in the diaspora	Further development into the Catholic and the Eastern Orthodox Church

Fig. 7.3: Comparison between Nestorianism and Orthodoxy

The Second Stage: The Eutychian Debate and the Council of Chalcedon (451)

After the death of Cyril of Alexandria, a widely respected monk named Eutyches began to teach a form of Christology that advocated the doctrine of the one nature of Christ (*mia physis*), a position clearly condemned in the union of 433. According to his teaching, the body of Christ looked like a human body, but actually had a divine nature. Patriarch Flavian of Constantinople, who tended toward an Antiochian position, condemned Eutyches' teaching. As a consequence, both Flavian and Patriarch Dioscorus of Alexandria asked the Roman Pope Leo I to make a judgment. Based on the occidental dogmatic tradition, in particular on the writings of Tertullian, Leo I upheld Flavian's position: In Christ there are always two natures (or substances), but they are in full union, theologically called a "hypostatical union." The church leaders of Rome and Constantinople thus became allies against Alexandria. The doctrinal appeal to the bishop of Rome and the subsequent success of the Roman position later became an important precedent for the claim of papal primacy.

In 449 the emperor, Theodosius II, called a general synod at Ephesus to restore Christian unity. Patriarch Dioscorus of Alexandria presided and, with the support of Theodosius, used his authority to rehabilitate Eutyches. The monophysite position of the Alexandrians was declared orthodox, and the representatives of Rome were ignored; Flavian was deposed and later mortally wounded when mobs tried to remove him from his church. This synod thus came to be known as the "robber synod."

Only one year later Theodosius II was thrown from his horse and died. A horse thus changed church history: the Alexandrian position, which had depended on the support of the emperor, began to wane. Theodosius' sister Pulcheria and her husband Marcian inherited the throne. Both were merely moderate in their support of the Alexandrians, and they convened a new council to be held in 451 at Chalcedon. This assembly (the largest in the history of the early church) became known as the Fourth Ecumenical Council. It condemned Eutyches and Dioscorus and adopted as orthodox the position that Pope Leo I had spelled out in his letter to the earlier council.

The council produced a definition of faith that defined the belief of the church:

> This one and the same Jesus Christ, the only-begotten Son [of God] must be confessed to be in two natures, unconfusedly, immutably, indivisibly, inseparably [united], and that without the distinction of natures being taken away by such union, but

rather the peculiar property of each nature being preserved and being united in one Person and subsistence, not separated or divided into two persons, but one and the same Son and only-begotten, God the Word, our Lord Jesus Christ, as the Prophets of old time have spoken concerning him, and as the Lord Jesus Christ hath taught us, and as the Creed of the Fathers hath delivered to us.[1]

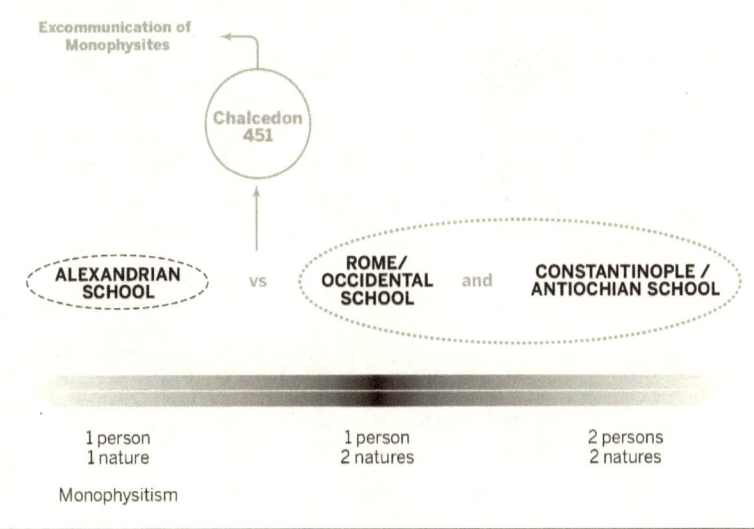

Fig. 7.4: *Conflicting positions in the christological debates of the fifth century: Part II*

The key point of the decision was that the union of the two natures of Christ, human and divine, is *without confusion, without change into one another, without separation, and without division.* The monophysite belief was condemned; however, it lived on and spread through the Middle East and North Africa, often carried on by national groups and independence movements in opposition to the Byzantine emperor.

At present, various churches belong to what they themselves call the miaphysite tradition, distinct from the Monophysites because Miaphysites refer to the teaching of Cyril of Alexandria, which does stress only one nature of Christ but which was found orthodox in Ephesus and in the later union of 433. Among them are the Armenian Orthodox Church; the Coptic Orthodox Church, which is the most important Christian church in Egypt; the Ethiopian Orthodox Church, which counts large parts of the Ethiopian

---

1. *The Seven Ecumenical Councils* (NPNF 2/14:264–65).

population as its members; the Malankara Jacobite Syrian Orthodox Church in India, often referred to as the Thomas Christian Church; and the Syriac Orthodox Church. These churches are also called Non-Chalcedonian churches or Oriental Orthodox churches.

	Eutychianism	Orthodoxy
OTHER NAMES	Monophysites; Miaphysites; Henophysites	Dyophysites
REPRESENTATIVES	Eutyches; Dioscur, Patriarch of Alexandria	Leo I (Leo the Great), Pope of Rome
THEOLOGICAL POSITION	Christ is of only one nature, i.e., docetic view of Christ's human nature, denying his full humanity	Christ is truly God and truly man; the two natures are united in one person, yet without confusion, conversion, division, and separation
DECISION	Excommunication of Eutychians in the ecumenical council of Chalcedon (451)	
LATER DEVELOPMENT	Spread of miaphysite churches in Middle East and Africa, known as Non-Chalcedonian or Oriental Orthodox Churches	Further development into the Catholic and the Eastern Orthodox Church

Fig. 7.5: Comparison between Eutychianism and Orthodoxy

Besides these important christological decisions, several other important decisions were taken at Chalcedon, among them two that remained historically significant. First, the earlier synods of Nicaea (325), Constantinople (381), and Ephesus (431) were formally recognized as ecumenical and orthodox councils and declared valid. Second, the bishops of Rome and Constantinople were given equal rank (the famous 28th Canon of Chalcedon). The political background to this decision was that the emperor had defeated the powerful Alexandrian patriarch only with the support of the pope of Rome, and now the emperor was trying to limit the growing power of the Roman bishop.

Concluding Thoughts on the Christological Debates of the Fifth Century

Most of the thoughts at the end of the last chapter (regarding the necessity of historical processes, the randomness of history, faith turning into belief, the role of non-theological factors and the problem of discussing soteriology in the context of Christology) also apply here. Some further thoughts:

(*a*) It may be natural for a growing church to develop some definition of its belief, in order to hold together its diversity of faith expressions.

However, we need to ask, could it be that Christianity had already become too diversified to be united by one single formula? Could it be that the (necessarily) contextual character of Christian faith actually makes it impossible to define unity through one joint statement of faith?

(*b*) Some of the conflicts had to do with different understandings of contentious words (e.g., the word *physis*). Other conflicts could be seen simply as different levels of sensitivity regarding such words. It would have been good to remember the biblical advice, "Warn them [God's people] before God against quarreling about words; it is of no value, and only ruins those who listen" (2 Tim 2:14 NIV).

The question remains: Was it really necessary for some parties to insist so strongly on the word *theotokos*? Could *christotokos* not have served as a compromise?

(*c*) The Nestorius who was condemned was not necessarily identical to the "real" Nestorius. At the end of the nineteenth century, an old Syriac translation of a text written by Nestorius, *The Bazaar of Heracleides*, was discovered. The text takes a position close to that of Leo I, which became orthodox, showing that Nestorius neither advocated adoptionism nor denied the divinity of Christ or the unity of the person of Christ. The only point where he might fairly have been criticized is that he did not sufficiently understand the *communicatio idiomatum*, the idea later promoted by Lutheran theologians that the attributes of God the Father and God the Son are interchangeable. What can be said of the Father can also be said of the Son, and vice versa; and what applies to the human Christ also applies to the divine Christ (e.g., it is theologically correct to say that God was suffering on the cross).[2]

(*d*) The divisions of the past live on—they have not really been healed. Yet, it is encouraging to see that recently, partly in reaction to a new understanding of unity and diversity, relations between Chalcedonian and Non-Chalcedonian churches, as well as between the Assyrian Church of the East and the rest of the global church, have become closer. Many

---

2. See regarding the whole Nestorian controversy Moffett, *History of Christianity in Asia*, 1:170–80 (175–76 about the *Bazaar of Heracleides*).

Non-Chalcedonian churches have even become active members in the World Council of Churches.

On the Path of Reconciliation: Common Christological Declaration between the Roman Catholic Church and the Assyrian Church of the East (11 November 1994)

Although not belonging to the period of the early church, the text below is an important document that shows something of the recent reconciliation between long-separated parts of the church.

This joint declaration was signed by Pope John Paul II for the Roman Catholic Church and by Patriarch Mar Dinkha IV for the Assyrian Church of the East. It shows sensitivity to the different traditions by not insisting on the controversial title of "Mother of God." At the same time it emphasizes the true union of the two natures of Christ, upholding the Chalcedonian definition of the relationship between the two natures of Christ as without confusion or change and without division or separation.

> *Therefore our Lord Jesus Christ is true God and true man, perfect in his divinity and perfect in his humanity, consubstantial with the Father and consubstantial with us in all things but sin. His divinity and his humanity are united in one person, without confusion or change, without division or separation. In him has been preserved the difference of the natures of divinity and humanity, with all their properties, faculties and operations. But far from constituting "one and another," the divinity and humanity are united in the person of the same and unique Son of God and Lord Jesus Christ, who is the object of a single adoration.*
>
> *Christ therefore is not an "ordinary man" whom God adopted in order to reside in him and inspire him, as in the righteous ones and the prophets. But the same God the Word, begotten of his Father before all worlds without beginning according to his divinity, was born of a mother without a father in the last times according to his humanity. The humanity to which the Blessed Virgin Mary gave birth always was that of the Son of God himself. That is the reason why the Assyrian Church of the East is praying [to] the Virgin Mary as "the Mother of Christ our God and Saviour." In the light of this same faith the Catholic tradition addresses the Virgin Mary as "the Mother of God" and also as "the Mother of Christ." We both recognize the legitimacy and rightness of these expressions of the same faith and we both respect the preference of each Church in her liturgical life and piety.*

Source: Neuner and Dupuis, *Christian Faith in the Doctrinal Documents of the Catholic Church*, 254 (ch. 683).

THE THOUGHT AND IMPACT OF AUGUSTINE (354-430)

Augustine is like a bridge connecting the early church with the medieval church. He is still the single most important teacher of the Western church. In his work, he connects different traditions of the earlier period and lays the foundation for all medieval theology. His theology tried to find an answer to crucial spiritual challenges that came to him from his context.

A first challenge was the sacking of Rome in 410 by the Gothic troops of Alaric, which led Augustine to ask, in the light of God's history of salvation, what is the significance of this destruction of a centuries-old capital, the pride of the Roman Empire?

A second challenge came from the Donatist movement and led Augustine to ask, what is the church? On what does the authority of the church's clergy rest?

A third challenge came from Pelagius, a monk from Britain, whose view of humankind and of the process of salvation challenged Augustine to ask, how is God's grace to be understood?

Other challenges came to him from his personal life. Augustine dealt with them in his *Confessions* and in his wide correspondence with various people.

Augustine's Life

Augustine of Hippo was of North African origin, born in 354 in present-day Algeria. His mother, Monica, who had a strong influence on him, raised him as a Christian and helped him receive a solid education in classical philosophy and rhetoric. Yet Augustine moved away from the faith of his mother and found inspiration in different spiritual and philosophical movements, first in Manichaeism and later in skepticism. At the age of thirty he assumed a prestigious position as professor of rhetoric at the imperial court in Milan. While there, he came into contact with Bishop Ambrose, who had a deep impact on Augustine and brought him back to the Christian faith.

At the age of thirty-four, while living and working in Milan, Augustine experienced a conversion—he heard a voice calling him to "take up and read" the Bible, and upon doing so, he read Romans 13:13-14:

> Let us behave decently, as in the daytime, not in carousing and drunkenness, not in sexual immorality and debauchery, not in dissension and jealousy. Rather, clothe yourselves with the Lord

Jesus Christ and do not think about how to gratify the desires of the flesh.

This passage stood quite in contrast to his earlier hedonistic lifestyle, when he had famously prayed, "Grant me chastity and continency, but not yet."[3] One year later, he and his son (born of a concubine) received baptism from Bishop Ambrose. After the death of his mother and his son, he converted his family house into a Christian community and gave up all other property. He was ordained as a priest and a few years later, in 395, was consecrated as bishop of Hippo.

Augustine is nowadays known largely through his two most important writings, the *Confessions* and *The City of God*.

Augustine on His Struggles with Worldly Desires

Book VIII of the *Confessions* recounts Augustine's conversion to Christ. This section, from the seventh chapter (7:16–17), offers a strong example of Augustine's sense of sin and his resistance to spiritual change. Ponticianus was a court official who visited Augustine and told him about the conversion of Anthony and others. These stories moved Augustine deeply and triggered renewed self-scrutiny. Augustine compellingly describes his inner turmoil and struggle and his wish to maintain a life dedicated to the satisfaction of worldly desires.

> 16. Such was the story Ponticianus told. But while he was speaking, thou, O Lord, turned me toward myself, taking me from behind my back, where I had put myself while unwilling to exercise self-scrutiny. And now thou didst set me face to face with myself, that I might see how ugly I was, and how crooked and sordid, bespotted and ulcerous. And I looked and I loathed myself; but whither to fly from myself I could not discover. And if I sought to turn my gaze away from myself, he would continue his narrative, and thou wouldst oppose me to myself and thrust me before my own eyes that I might discover my iniquity and hate it. I had known it, but acted as though I knew it not—I winked at it and forgot it.

> 17. But now, the more ardently I loved those whose wholesome affections I heard reported—that they had given themselves up wholly to thee to be cured—the more did I abhor myself when compared with them. For many of my years—perhaps twelve—had passed away since my nineteenth, when, upon the reading of Cicero's *Hortensius*, I was roused to a desire for wisdom. And here I was, still postponing the abandonment of this world's happiness to devote myself to the search . . . But, wretched youth that I was—supremely

---

3. Augustine, *Confessions*, bk. VIII, 7:17.

wretched even in the very outset of my youth—I had entreated chastity of thee and had prayed, "Grant me chastity and continence, but not yet." For I was afraid lest thou shouldst hear me too soon, and too soon cure me of my disease of lust which I desired to have satisfied rather than extinguished. And I had wandered through perverse ways of godless superstition—not really sure of it, either, but preferring it to the other, which I did not seek in piety, but opposed in malice.

Source: Augustine, *Confessions and Enchiridion*, 168–69.

What Religious and Philosophical Traditions Influenced Augustine?

Augustine's theology reflects influences from the stages of his spiritual search.

Neo-Platonist influences are particularly evident in his understanding of God, whom he describes as the highest being, the highest good (*summum esse, summum bonum*), and the one beyond all words. The real world is to be found in the spiritual world, ultimately in God, and this spiritual world is of higher reality than everything of the visible world. Evil is not a substance in itself or a reality, but a deprivation, a lack of good. The goal of human existence is the ecstasy that comes with the perfect contemplation of God, famously expressed in his words, "You have formed us for Yourself, and our hearts are restless till they find rest in You."[4] In Augustine's later life, the Neo-Platonist influence was less prominent.

For about nine years Augustine regularly followed Manichaean teaching. This Manichaean influence is particularly visible in his negative view of matter and of bodily desires, something that became important in his doctrine of original sin. Yet, these views can also be interpreted as a reaction to his struggle with sexual desire. Another influence, monasticism, led him in the same direction. He encountered monastic teaching through Athanasius' book on the life of the desert father Saint Anthony, which prompted Augustine to set up a monastic community himself. Finally, Augustine was influenced by orthodox teaching through Bishop Ambrose of Milan, who taught Augustine to understand the Bible—particularly passages in the Old Testament—through allegorical interpretation.

4. Augustine, *Confessions*, bk. I, 1:1.

Why Was the Teaching of Augustine So Important for Later Theology?

Augustine's teaching deeply inspired medieval Roman Catholic theology and the theology of the most important Protestant reformers.

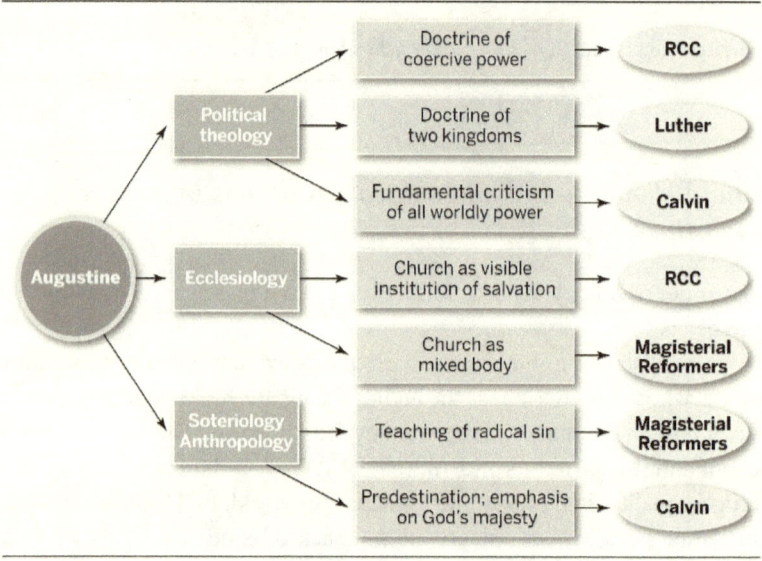

Fig. 7.6: Topics in Augustine's theology and its influence on later Western theology (RCC = Roman Catholic Church)

Augustine's Soteriological Teaching

The center of Augustine's theology is his position on sin and salvation. Augustine was the first theologian to take seriously Paul's teaching on justification by faith (or, rather, Protestant theology has tended to read Paul through the eyes of Augustine). Augustine emphasized the reality of total human depravity and sinfulness. Due to this total power of sin, a radical conversion is needed, and only through the irresistible power of God's grace can such a conversion come about. In strong contrast to Eastern theology, which regarded humanity as impaired by sin and weakness but still able to be restored by an upward process of theosis, Augustine argued the following:

i. In Adam, man was created good, with the freedom and the free will not to sin.

ii. Through Adam's sin we all have lost community with God and have fallen into the power of death: We *formally* still have the freedom of will and are still created in the image of God, but effectively, or *materially*, we have lost the image of God. We have equally lost the ability not to sin unless God's grace frees our will.

iii. God has chosen a number of people for eternal salvation (predestination). He calls them to faith, justifies them and leads them to sanctification.

iv. Our faith, that is, our acceptance of God's grace, is already part of God's grace. The initiative in human conversion is not human but divine. God's grace is irresistible: God gives it to those who are chosen.

Augustine outlined his soteriology in response to the challenge that arose from the teaching of Pelagius, a monk from Britain. A comparison with Pelagian teaching can further clarify the special emphases of Augustine.

Augustine and Pelagius

Augustine taught that the original sin committed by Adam completely incapacitates man. We are born into sin and lack the power to do what is good. This view did not come to Augustine as an abstract thought but was based on his own experiences, his own spiritual struggles, which reminded him of what Paul had said in Romans 7 about the radical nature of sin—knowing what is right, yet doing what is wrong. As sinners we may still be free to choose between different alternatives, but we are unable to choose *not* to sin. How can we find salvation from this entanglement in sin? Our sinful condition is so radical that only God can change it. Yet, at the same time, since we are human, somebody human needs to save us, and since all humans are sinners, the redeemer must be someone without sin. Thus, God redeemed us through Jesus, who was without sin.

Pelagius agreed with Augustine that the human will is the source of evil. However, he insisted that human beings have the ability to overcome their sin, the moral freedom to choose between good and evil. This freedom is part of every human's capacity, since God would never have commanded people to do what they cannot do. Sin is thus always an individual act and not a status, as the concept of original sin implies. Man without sin is possible; faith is the free choice of humans to accept God's grace. If humans were unable not to sin, then they could not be held morally responsible, something that would undermine the whole concept of moral responsibility. In other words, humanity's tragic imitation of Adam can be overcome by the imitation of Christ.

How Did the Conflict between Augustine and Pelagius Unfold?

Pelagius came from Britain, moving around 400 to Rome and later to North Africa, where his teaching spread and came into conflict with Augustine's. A synod in Carthage in 418 condemned Pelagianism. However, the conflict lasted beyond the death of both proponents. Later followers of Pelagius' teaching, monks from southern France led by Abbot Cassian, supported the church in the condemnation of Pelagius' teaching and agreed that human freedom was indeed badly damaged through the fall of Adam; however, they said that Augustine underemphasized man's role in the salvation process. They held that humans can still make the first step in a faith process, but that God's free gift of grace is necessary for the increase of faith and for salvation (a position that much later, at the end of the sixteenth century, became known as semi-Pelagianism). A later synod in Orange (southern France) in 529 condemned this theology, but it remained alive and was taught implicitly in much of medieval Catholic soteriology.

What Is the Relevance of the Conflict?

Three points deserve to be mentioned. First, the two positions of Augustine and Pelagius (and his later semi-Pelagian followers) point to a fundamental dilemma between a spiritual (and possibly experience-based) need to emphasize the radical nature of human sin and a practical need to emphasize some human responsibility and participation. Such a dilemma cannot be resolved through ecclesial authority and doctrinal decisions. The continuing existence of the two contradictory positions throughout later theological development may thus be regarded as necessary and natural. To simply ban one position is a typical theological error, claiming to abolish ambiguity and establish clarity of right and wrong instead of acknowledging that two positions can paradoxically both be true even when standing in contradiction to each other.

Second, the Pelagian conflict was largely played out in the Western, Latin-speaking church, and the issue was addressed more in legal and moral categories than in ontological ones. It is interesting to note, however, that the conflict overlaps somewhat with the christological discussions carried out among the Eastern churches. We have already seen some closeness between the Nestorian and the Pelagian party, that is, when Constantinople received Pelagian refugee bishops.

Third, contextualization in the East Asian context, where Confucianism has deeply influenced religion and culture, will challenge the church's doctrinal decisions: Generally speaking, Confucianism is more in line with Pelagius. Confucianism, especially the theory of human nature proposed by Mencius, asserts that all human beings have the ability to do what is good and thus achieve moral perfection. When Christianity was introduced into China, Confucianism criticized Christianity on the grounds that it neglects the inherent ability of human nature to do what is good. Christians in the East Asian context might thus ask whether the old yet long-lasting tension between these two positions needs to be critically revisited. In such a process an originally *intra*-religious issue would turn out to be relevant to *inter*-religious dialogue as well. This would apply even to Confucianism itself, as the teaching on the essential goodness of human nature is questioned by other Confucian philosophers such as Xunzi.[5]

Augustine's Political Theology

The fall of Rome at the hands of the Gothic invaders in 410 led to widespread doubts about the success and effectiveness of Christian faith. In order to address these doubts, Augustine wrote the book *The City of God*. Written over a long period (413–26), it gives a narrative account of God's providence in history and an apologetic response to the question of whether the destruction of Rome in 410 was due to Rome's conversion (i.e., under Constantine) to Christianity.

Augustine describes the history of the world as a history of two antagonistic societies or orders, the City of God (*civitas Dei*) and the City of the World (*civitas terrena*), both of supernatural origin—the City of God of divine origin, the City of the World of infernal origin. Augustine rejected a nostalgic view of the past and its paganism. Instead, he showed how the "most glorious City" of praise and thanks to God, the heavenly Jerusalem, stands in contrast to the ruins of historical decline of *all* worldly empires. The fall of Rome is thus also seen as part of God's provision.

Augustine described the church as a historical and worldly image of the heavenly City, but not identical with it, for the City of God will never be fully realized on earth. Yet the church that is related and pointing to the

---

5. See as an example of such a discussion Lai, "Cong da cheng fo xue kan jiakedun jidulun" (賴品超。〈從大乘佛學看迦克墩基督論〉。《輔仁宗教研究》).

heavenly City stands in contrast to the state and is superior to it; the worldly City is subservient to the City of God and, by extension, should also be subservient to the church. This strong self-confidence against any political pressure laid the ground for the later conflict between church and state.

What Is the Significance of Augustine's Political Theology?

First, Augustine provided a concept for the coexistence of church and political power in a crucial historical moment when growing turmoil was undermining society and when political power was decaying. He thus tried to make sense of a new political situation by interpreting it in the light of the Bible.

Furthermore, Augustine's political theology contained a fundamentally critical view of political government, seeing it as closely related to the City of the World, which is of infernal origin. He maintained that no worldly social order or political entity can equal the City of God, which always stands in critical tension to worldly order. Augustine thus introduced an element of critical opposition to all political power as based on human power, not on divine power. Any chance to divinize political rule was eliminated. This was perhaps the most important long-term impact of Augustine's political teaching. This opposition to political power extended even to the church. It meant that the idea of a Christian empire, such as Eusebius of Caesarea saw in the rule of Constantine, was wrong. Even if the church directly assumed political power, it would not mean that the City of God had been realized because no worldly reality can be identified with the City of God. Its citizens always remain pilgrims.

Augustine's opposition to the idea of a progressive salvation history overcame the millennialism of the earliest church (and its later revival in Montanist teaching) and introduced the occidental amillennialist tradition. He interpreted the prophecy of the millennium (Rev 20) as an ongoing conflict between the kingdom of Christ and the demonic forces within this world.

Augustine's Teaching on the Church

Augustine's ecclesiology shows elements that built the basis for contradictory understandings of the church. In the conflict with the Donatists (see ch. 6), Augustine stressed that the church is the visible and hierarchically organized institution of salvation, which people may even be compelled to enter. He criticized the Donatists' moral rigorism as self-righteousness and worse than sin. This view deeply influenced the popular Roman Catholic understanding of the church.

On the other side, he described the church as a mixed body (*corpus mixtum*) of sinners and elect. The invisible community of the saints is hidden in the visible church, comparable to the ark of Noah, where both clean and unclean animals were mixed. The separation of the good from the wicked is reserved for God at the end of time, as illustrated by the parable of the field of wheat mixed with weeds (Matt 13:24–30). This view inspired the Magisterial Reformers' understanding of the church and supported them in their opposition to the Radical Reformers' understanding of the church.

Augustine's Impact on Occidental Culture

Besides deeply influencing theological reflection, ecclesial self-understanding, and political relations between church and state for centuries to come, Augustine had further, though more subtle, impacts on later occidental culture.

The psychological introspection evident in his *Confessions* laid a basis for the later development of psychology and for the whole occidental tradition of psychological reflection. We could call it the principle of inwardness, looking for the truth in the interior of human beings, in the interior of our soul. Augustine expressed this thought quite clearly in one passage: "Do not go abroad. Return within yourself. In the inward man dwells truth. If you find that you are by nature mutable, transcend yourself."[6]

This psychological self-probing and this searching for assurance have profoundly shaped the atmosphere of occidental thought. In his search for assurance Augustine positively engaged with his doubts, acknowledging that even if he were deceived and completely wrong, at least one thing was for sure: to be wrong, I have to live and to be. Or in other words, "For if I am deceived I am!"[7] (*Si enim fallor, sum*). Descartes' later "I think, therefore I am" (*Cogito ergo sum*) clearly stands in this tradition of eventually finding existential self-assurance in the midst of uncertainty.

A second point has to do with the ecclesial mediation of truth, which laid the ground for the Western church's hegemonic role in public affairs. Humans can have an understanding of God, Augustine said, because they are created in God's image; yet, due to humans' radical corruption, only through God's grace can they receive understanding of the laws of reason. At this point the grace offered through the church becomes a needle's eye for

---

6. Augustine, *Of True Religion*, xxix:72, 69.
7. Augustine, *De Civitate Dei*, bk. XI, ch. 26, 76.

all aspects of secular life as well—politics, law, morality, aesthetics, reason. All have their ultimate ground in God as the highest good and the highest reason, and access to them passes through the church's dispensation of grace.

Another impact of Augustine on occidental culture is his negative view of sexuality. Augustine saw sin essentially as concupiscence, that is, a sexual desire that cannot be controlled by human will. His own biographical experience of failing to control his sexual desire has deeply influenced occidental attitudes toward sexuality. By identifying the grace of God with liberation from sexual concupiscence, Augustine initiated the tradition of narrowing sin to its sexual element.

Finally, Augustine reinforced the tendency of Christian faith to be strongly theocentric and to put an overwhelming emphasis on the soul's salvation. Such theocentrism—whether necessarily so or due only to the form that Augustine gave it—comes with the inherent danger of neglecting social justice. In other words, Augustine's theology is a far cry from the Jewish communal renewal movement of Jesus. In this sense, Augustine stands in line with the occidental tradition of neglecting the physical world, which has contributed to the negligence of social and ecological dimensions of theology.

For Further Reading

Brown, Peter. *Augustine of Hippo: A Biography*. Berkeley: University of California Press, 1967.

Gregorios, Paulos, William H. Lazareth, and Nikos A. Nissiotis. *Does Chalcedon Divide or Unite? Towards Convergence in Orthodox Christology*. Geneva: World Council of Churches, 1981.

Harrison, Carol. *Augustine*. Oxford: Oxford University Press, 2000.

Jenkins, Philip. *Jesus Wars: How Four Patriarchs, Three Queens, and Two Emperors Decided What Christians Would Believe for the Next 1,500 Years*. New York: HarperOne, 2010.

Learning Activities

1) Review key elements of this chapter by answering the following questions:

    o What is the meaning of "monophysite"? Who stood for a monophysite christology? What are other names for the monophysite churches?

- What basic dogmatic position did the Nestorians stand for?
  - What was the spiritual basis of the Nestorians?
  - What is their historical significance?
- Name three present-day churches that are known as miaphysite churches.
- What was the core question at the ecumenical council of Chalcedon?
- What correct christological formulations were agreed upon in these ecumenical councils?
- What different schools of thought stood against each other in the christological debates of the fifth century?
- Summarize important elements in Augustine's biography: Which thought movements influenced him most strongly?
- In what areas did Augustine most strongly influence later theology?
- Augustinism, Pelagianism, semi-Pelagianism—what are their respective understandings of human beings and of how salvation happens?
- What are the basic principles of Augustine's political theology?
- In what areas and through what elements of his thought did Augustine influence occidental culture?

2) To probe your understanding of what we have learned about this period, to deepen the understanding of its significance, and to apply it to your present experience, discuss the following questions:

- Though the christological debates are undoubtedly difficult to understand, for students of theology as for ordinary church people, can you see their significance? How do they relate to doctrinal debates you have experienced, or to controversies in the church today?
- Discuss Augustine's understanding of sin and of evil. How do you understand the problem of evil? Where does it come from? Discuss by taking Augustine's own view into account.
- Remember the basic dilemma of Augustine's and Pelagius' teaching on salvation. Where do you stand? Discuss the dilemma with reference to the reality of non-Christians: How can we theologically understand their disbelief?
- How can you make positive sense of the doctrine of original sin?

- How would traditional Confucian thinking understand categories like human freedom, original sin, the goodness of human nature, or the human ability to do good? Discuss with reference to intra-Confucian differences.
- For readers in East Asian contexts shaped by Confucianism: How would you explain Augustinian and later Protestant understanding(s) of sin and salvation?
- Is there such a thing as a Christian nation? Why or why not? What is problematic about this concept? What do you think of some Christians' hope that China will one day become a Christian nation?

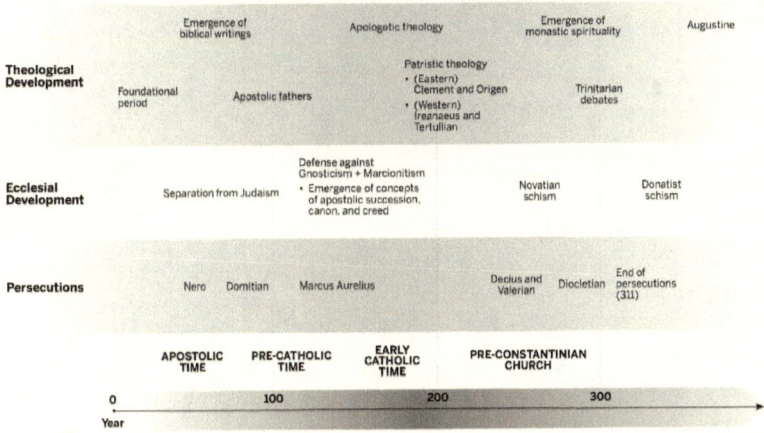

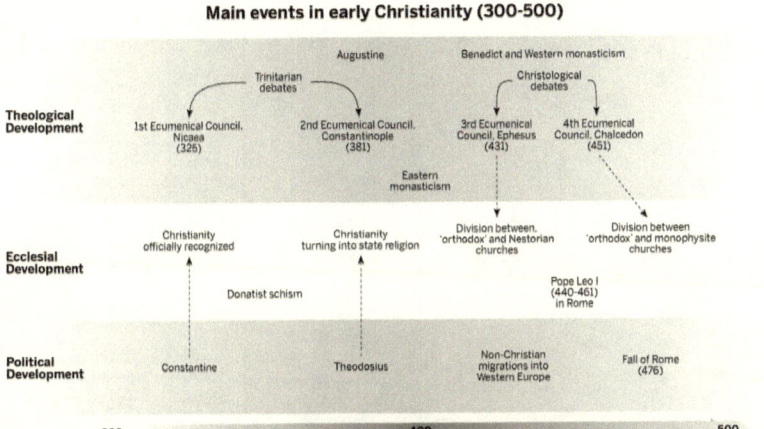

Summary of main events and developments in the first five centuries

PART II

The History of the Medieval Church

THE LONG PERIOD FROM the fifth to the fifteenth century is usually called the medieval era. Its beginnings are seen in the collapse of the western part of the Roman Empire; its ends are found in the Renaissance of the fifteenth century, the Age of Discovery (commonly linked to Columbus' first voyage to the Americas in 1492), or in the Reformation Period, starting in 1517. Most historians subdivide the period further into the Early Middle Ages (from the fifth to the end of the tenth century), the High Middle Ages (from 1000 to around 1300), and the Late Middle Ages (fourteenth and fifteenth centuries).

The term "medieval" has traditionally evoked negative connotations, in secular history as in religious history; it has become a synonym for backward and antiquated. The medieval time has been seen as a "dark age" of little progress—or even of cultural regress—with people living under the hegemonic tutelage of a church that regulated all aspects of society, and with classical learning decaying and cultural achievements of Greek and Roman antiquity being lost. We should, however, be careful about such judgments. In particular, the use of a single term ("Middle Ages") to describe so many centuries should not mislead us to think of the time as a static and homogenous period. It was not. The Middle Ages had its own achievements and regional variations. It was a time that laid the foundations for modern Western civilization, with modern languages, universities, and the idea of Europe emerging, as Jacques Le Goff, one of the foremost historians on medieval times, has emphasized.

In the following chapters, with the exception of chapter 10, we focus on the western part of Europe. The church in the eastern part of the

Mediterranean maintained more continuity with the early church until the fall of Constantinople in the fifteenth century.

It is impossible to reasonably cover one thousand years of history in a few chapters without radically simplifying both the abundance of material and the shifts that took place. To deal with such a diversity of developments and events, and such a long period of time, we will proceed thematically more than chronologically. This will help us both find systematic order in the plenitude of historic details and draw deeper insights in a few specific areas. Thus each of the following chapters will consider the whole period from one of several different perspectives:

- Mission
- Papacy
- The division between the Roman Catholic and the Orthodox churches
- Alternative Christian communities
- Growing internal and external tensions
- Philosophy and Christian thought

Chapter 8

Mission History
The Extension of the Catholic Church and Its Inculturation in New Contexts

From the fourth century on, and with growing intensity throughout the fifth century, ethnic groups from Central Asia entered Europe and hastened the end of the Western Roman Empire. The invasions brought a deep sense of crisis. As a consequence, people who were already hard-pressed by the local aristocracy began to suffer not only from the invaders' attacks but also from imperial efforts to maintain Constantinople's power. The period was marked by tremendous social and political turmoil throughout Europe and a clear break with the previous historical period. Christianity was strongly affected by these social and political shifts but eventually succeeded in expanding to the tribal groups that had settled in western Europe.

The following centuries saw not only an expansion of Christianity and a diffusion among ethnic groups outside the Mediterranean area, but also a shift in Christianity: While the center of Christianity until around the year 500 was clearly in the eastern part of the Roman Empire, by around 800 the situation had changed. The Western church became more significant, and over time even dominant, in worldwide Christianity.

This chapter asks the following questions:

- What were some of the important political and social developments in Western Europe after the end of the Roman Empire?
- Through what means did Christianity spread to the nations outside the Roman Empire?

- How did Christianity adapt to cultures outside of the Hellenist and Roman worlds?

THE CHRISTIANIZATION OF THE INVADING GERMANIC STATES—FIFTH TO SEVENTH CENTURIES

The migration of Germanic tribes from eastern and northern Europe into southern Europe was triggered by the invasion of the Huns from Central Asia and their military victories over the Germanic tribes. At their peak in the fifth century, the Huns, under their leader Attila, reached as far as northern France, where they were eventually defeated in the Battle of the Cattalaunian Fields (near today's Châlons-en-Champagne). While the Huns withdrew from the heartland of Europe, the Germanic tribes—among them the Ostrogoths, the Visigoths, the Vandals, the Burgundians, the Lombards, and the Franks—continued to move west and south and entered the Italian and the Iberian peninsulas. These places, still nowadays the goal of annual migratory waves of Nordic people yearning for warm places, were attractive both for their milder climate and the quality of their infrastructure, such as roads and aqueducts. Although these Germanic attackers were much smaller than the resident population, both in overall population and in military strength, they were fierce fighters and easily gained ground.

The most important events and developments of this period were the following:

378	The Battle of Adrianople, with victory for the Visigoths, who were of Arian faith: This year marked the beginning of the Germanic invasions.
410	The first fall of Rome, as groups of Visigoths attacked the city. This experience became an important background to Augustine's ideas about God's presence in history.
From 400 on	Vandals from the northwestern Balkans were pushed westward by the Huns and moved into Gaul (present-day France) and the Iberian Peninsula, where some of their groups settled more permanently. In 429 they entered North Africa, where they conquered the Roman province of Africa and established Vandal kingdoms, with their capital in Carthage and their territory including islands of the western Mediterranean Sea formerly controlled by Rome. The rule of the Vandals in North Africa lasted until 533, when the Byzantine Emperor Justinian I reconquered the province and annexed it to the Eastern Roman Empire. Yet groups of Vandals continued to live in the Iberian Peninsula and in northern Africa. The Vandals were, like the Visigoths, of Arian faith.

| Fifth century | Angles and Saxons from what is today northern Germany moved into the British Isles and overthrew the Romans. The original Celt population was pushed into the western corners of Britain: Cornwall, Wales, Ireland, and Scotland. |

Fig. 8.1: Map of invasions of the Roman Empire

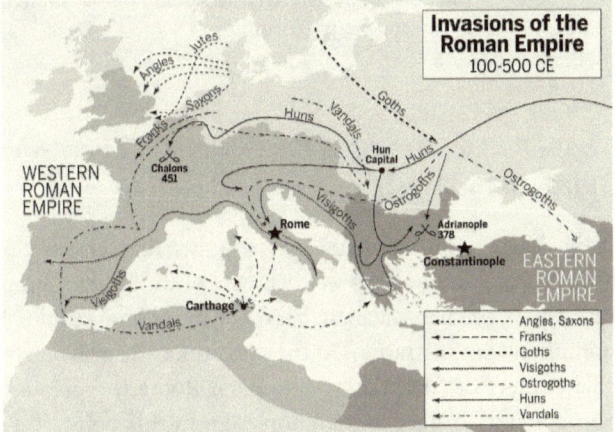

| 451 | The defeat of the Mongolian Huns under Attila in the Battle of the Cattalaunian Fields in northern France brought an end to the expansion of the Huns. |
| 455 | From their North African kingdom, the Vandals sacked the city of Rome (hence the term *vandalism*). |
| 476 | Odoacer, an invading Germanic soldier, overthrew Romulus Augustulus, who as a young boy had been recognized as the emperor of the western part of the Roman Empire. By declaring himself king of Italy, Odoacer brought the office of the emperor in the West—and with it the entire Western Roman Empire—to an end.

However, the idea of continuity with Rome lasted long after, with later Frankish or German leaders, like Charlemagne in the eighth and ninth centuries and Otto the Great in the tenth century, being crowned as Roman emperor and thus inheriting the tradition of the Roman Empire. The Holy Roman Empire of the German Nation, which began with the coronation of Otto the Great in 962, remained a feature of European politics until the early nineteenth century. It was not a centralized empire but a loose federation of central European territories under an elected monarch. |
| From 488 on | Ostrogoths of Arian faith settled in Italy and founded the Ostrogoth Kingdom under Theoderic. |

From 530 on   Justinian I (527–65) temporarily reconquered the originally Roman territories that had been taken by the Vandals in North Africa and by the Ostrogoths in Italy, thus restoring Byzantine rule over large parts of western Europe. Justinian aimed to restore the unity of the church through the whole empire by eliminating Arianism and paganism.

What Did the Attacks of the Germanic Tribes Mean for the Church of the West?

As the Roman Empire disintegrated under the various Germanic attacks, the catholic church of the western part of the Roman Empire, with Rome as its center, became the main bearer of traditional culture, knowledge, and communal administration. At the same time, the growing tensions with the other centers of Christianity prompted Rome to operate more and more independently from Constantinople. From this point, it makes increasing sense to speak of a Roman Catholic Church, meaning a Rome-centered church that claimed catholicity, that is, universal validity. The Roman Catholic Church built a link between the past and the present; it connected the old empire and its culture with the invading conquerors. One of the reasons for the religious and social dominance of Roman Catholicism in subsequent centuries was exactly this very role—guaranteeing a sense of stability, continuity, and the preservation of values.

How Did the Church Respond to the Invading Germanic Tribes?

We can distinguish four responses as Christianity dealt with the migratory waves entering Europe: re-evangelization, assimilation, catholicization, and centralization.

Re-evangelization

In those areas of the old Roman Empire where Christianity had not been deeply rooted, the invading tribes obliterated the thin Christian presence. Christianity thus needed to be reintroduced through re-evangelization. Re-evangelization was also continuously necessary to counter pagan revivals, which were a response to the feeling that the fall of Rome and the invasion of foreign tribes had revealed the weakness of the Christian God compared to pagan gods. Monks—Irish, Benedictine, and others—played a major role in the process of re-evangelization (see more below).

Assimilation

In the areas where Christianity had deeper roots, Catholic Christianity gradually won over the pagan immigrants from the Germanic states. Several factors played a role in the invading groups' assimilation to the faith of the indigenous people: First, immigrant groups admired the old Roman civilization and culture and took over many of its features, including Christianity. This is similar to what happened in other parts of the world—when, for example, the Manchus established their rule among the Han in China in the seventeenth century. Second, the religious faith of the invaders suited their nomadic life in the grasslands of eastern Europe or Central Asia but seemed less developed compared to the faith of the indigenous population in western Europe. Finally, Christianity contained within itself a powerful missionary vitality that could not be extinguished by the invasions.

Catholicization: Spreading Orthodox Faith among Germanic Tribes of Arian Faith

One of the major challenges of the Germanic invasions was that most of the invading groups—particularly the Visigoths, the Vandals, the Ostrogoths, and the Burgundians—were of Arian faith. In fact, after the Arians had been condemned in Nicaea, they did not simply disappear but continued to spread beyond the boundaries of the Roman Empire. Most famous among the Arian missionaries was Wulfila, also called the apostle to the Goths. The Arian areas were those where imperial power was unable to implement orthodoxy, and it is from these very areas that many of the invading tribal groups emerged. When the Germanic tribes moved toward western and southern Europe, they naturally brought with them their Arian faith and reintroduced it in areas where Christianity was predominantly Trinitarian, Nicene and "orthodox." Traces of this Arian Christianity can today still be seen in the northern Italian city of Ravenna, where the Ostrogoth king Theoderic the Great ruled from 493 to 526. The Arianism brought to Spain and established there by the Vandals was one reason why medieval Spanish Christianity was so militantly opposed to doctrinal dissent, as we will see later.

As a result, the main religious conflict between the invaders and the indigenous population was in fact a conflict between Arian Christianity and Catholic Christianity. Roman Christianity won an important victory in 496 when the pagan Clovis, the Merovingian king of the Franks, turned to the Catholic faith. His conversion seemed to have been instigated by his (Catholic) Christian wife Clotilde, a Burgundian. However, Clovis may also have had political reasons: The change of religious affiliation allowed Clovis to ally himself with the Catholic Church both inside and outside Gaul. It strengthened his rule in Gaul because he gained the support of the Catholic indigenous population, and it led to a harmonization between the Germanic invaders and the resident population, which ultimately strengthened the Frankish state.

With Clovis' decision, the Roman Catholic Church had gained the upper hand in its conflict with the invaders' Arian Christianity. Gradually, the Catholic Church, backed by Clovis, overcame the Arian faith of the other Germanic states. In 517, the Burgundians converted from Arianism to Catholicism. The successful catholicization of the Germanic tribes enabled the Catholic Church to focus on the evangelization of northern Europe.

A similar event was the 587 conversion (again, from Arian to Catholic) of Recared I, the Visigoth king of Spain. This was a turning point for the church in Spain—at least until the Arab conquest of the Iberian Peninsula.

The Conversion of Clovis

Clovis (or Chlodowech; c. 466–511) was the king who united the different Frankish tribes under one ruler and the founder of the Merovingian dynasty, which lasted until the eighth century, when Pepin of the Carolingian dynasty overthrew the last Merovingian king. His conversion to Catholicism was significant for the development of the church in Europe. It brought a major ruler into alliance with the Catholic Church and stopped the spread of Arianism.

Gregory (538–93) was bishop of Tours, the most important see in France. The text below about the conversion of Clovis is from Book II of the *History of the Franks* (Latin: *Historia Francorum*) and must be taken with caution—it may be legendary. The baptism of Clovis was probably a process of deliberation that had begun long before his marriage with Clotilde.

> *Ch. 30. The queen (Chrotechildis [i.e., Clotilde]) ceased not to warn Chlodowech that he should acknowledge the true God and forsake idols. But in no way could he be brought to believe these things. Finally war broke out with the*

Alemanni. Then by necessity was he compelled to acknowledge what before he had denied with his will. The two armies met and there was a fearful slaughter, and the army of Chlodowech was on the point of being annihilated. When the king perceived that, he raised his eyes to heaven, his heart was smitten and he was moved to tears, and he said: "Jesus Christ, whom Chrotechildis declares to be the Son of the living God, who says that Thou wilt help those in need and give victory to those who hope in Thee, humbly I flee to Thee for Thy mighty aid, that Thou wilt give me victory over these my enemies, and I will in this way experience Thy power . . . Then will I believe on Thee and be baptized in Thy name. For I have called upon my gods but, as I have seen, they are far from my help. Therefore, I believe that they have no power who do not hasten to aid those obedient to them . . ." As he thus spoke, the Alemanni turned their backs and began to take flight. But when they saw that their king was dead, they submitted to Chlodowech and said: "Let not, we pray thee, a nation perish; now we are thine." Thereupon he put an end to the war, exhorted the people, and returned home in peace. He told the queen how by calling upon the name of Christ he had obtained victory. This happened in the fifteenth year of his reign (496).

Ch. 31. Thereupon the queen commanded that the holy Remigius, bishop of Rheims, be brought secretly to teach the king the word of salvation. The priest was brought to him secretly and began to lay before him that he should believe in the true God, the creator of heaven and earth, and forsake idols, who could neither help him nor others. But he replied: "Gladly do I listen to thee, most holy Father, but one thing remains, for the people who follow me suffer me not to forsake their gods. But I will go and speak to them according to thy words." When he met his men, and before he began to speak, all the people cried out together, for the divine power had anticipated him: "We reject the mortal gods, pious king, and we are ready to follow the immortal God whom Remigius preaches." These things were reported to the bishop, who rejoiced greatly and commanded the font to be prepared. . . . The king first asked to be baptized by the pontiff. He went, a new Constantine, into the font to be washed clean from the old leprosy, and to purify himself in fresh water from the stains which he had long had.

Source: Ayer, *Source Book for Ancient Church History*, 572–73.

Centralization of the Power of the Catholic Church against National Churches

Another challenge of the invading tribes had less to do with theology than with church administration and church authority. Many rulers of the new kingdoms, both Arian and Catholic, established churches that were based on royal authority. Such church-state relations built the roots of the European Christendom concept. These churches were independent from the Catholic Church, had no formal relation to it, and did not recognize any jurisdiction of the Roman bishop. After integration into the Roman Catholic Church, the national rulers maintained a strong influence on the organization of the church. The bishop of Rome was respected but was not recognized as having legal authority or primacy over local bishops. His edicts became effective only when the king confirmed them, and the political rulers maintained the authority to introduce church laws and to appoint bishops, a practice called secular investiture. This led to problems of church administration: Senior church positions were treated like feudal fiefdoms that were bought and sold, a practice called simony (see below, ch. 9), and the appointment of laypersons to the position of bishop (so-called lay investiture) was a common practice. Church synods lost their purely ecclesial character because they were subject to the authority of the king.

The Catholic Church tried to counter these developments by centralizing and consolidating papal power against the secular rulers' claims of ownership of religious affairs. This was a slow process that took several centuries. The long conflict later became known as the medieval investiture controversy (see ch. 9).

Independent Christian Groups and Monastic Alternatives: The Case of Britain

At the fringes of the former Roman Empire, another Christian reaction to the Germanic migration emerged. This was particularly the case in Britain. Since the fourth century, Britain had been overwhelmingly Christian, but when the Roman army withdrew and Germanic tribes entered, Christianity decayed. The invasion of Germanic groups pushed the remnants of the earlier church to the western mountain areas. Their connection to the Catholic Church was interrupted and the church developed independently.

Later, it was from these fringe areas of the European continent, that is, the west and north of the British Isles (Ireland and Scotland), that Christian groups emerged which were administratively independent from Rome and autonomous from secular or episcopal oversight but which followed orthodox faith. This Irish and Scottish church was mainly a monastic church. The founding father of this special branch of Christianity was St. Patrick, who, according to legend, came from Britain to Ireland in 432. At the center of these churches were monasteries that emphasized an ascetic faith. The Scottish and Irish monks understood themselves as pilgrims; they practiced homelessness and remained on a constant journey as part of their discipline of penance. As a result, the Irish and Scottish monks became a strongly missionary church that had a significant impact on the spread of Christianity (see below).

SHIFTS IN WORLD CHRISTIANITY

From the seventh century on, two more important developments radically changed world Christianity and caused its center of gravity to move westward: First, in the eastern part of the Mediterranean world, the Islamic faith expanded and conquered previously Christian areas. Second, in the western part of Europe, the Frankish kings emerged as a dominant power supporting the Western church. As a result, the Roman Catholic Church, backed by Frankish rulers, spread into western, northern, central, and eastern Europe. The two developments can be linked to two persons: Muhammad in Asia and northern Africa and Charlemagne in the West.

Islamic Advances in the East and in Africa

Already during Muhammad's lifetime the faith he had founded began spreading quickly through vast parts of the Arabian Peninsula. Within another thirty years, during the reign of the first four caliphs (the supreme military, political, and religious leaders of the Islamic Empire), Islam spread through parts of North Africa, through the whole of the Middle East and into Central Asia. Within another century, during the time of the Umayyad caliphs, the Islamic Empire expanded further into Central Asia and conquered the whole of North Africa and most of the Iberian Peninsula. It also advanced far into the Frankish Kingdom, where in 732 it was eventually defeated by the Frankish king Charles Martel, who has since been regarded as a savior of Western Christianity and occidental culture.

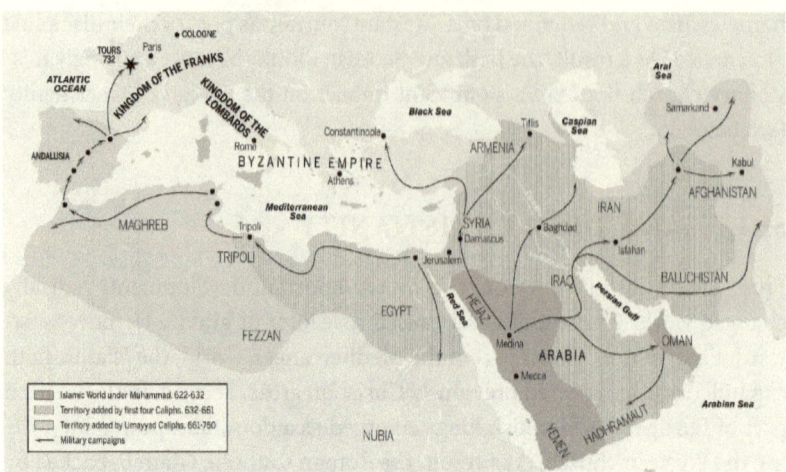

Fig. 8.2: The expansion of the Islamic Empire during the first 130 years

The expansion of the Islamic Empire mainly through military means was rapid: by 635 Damascus and Syria were conquered, by 638 Jerusalem, by 642 Alexandria, by 651 all of the Persian Empire, and by the end of the seventh century all of North Africa.

What Nonmilitary Factors Contributed to the Success of Islam?

The success of Islam was due not only to military power but also to other factors relating to the Christian population. We may therefore ask, What failures of Christianity contributed to its near disappearance in vast parts of North Africa and Asia?

Muhammad himself was at first very open to the witness of the Old and New Testaments.[1] He saw no conflict between Judaism, Christianity, and his own teaching. However, at the time of Muhammad there was still no Arabic translation of the New Testament. Although Christians had already translated the Scriptures into many different languages—even partly into Chinese—nobody, whether Chalcedonian, Nestorian, or Monophysite, had made the effort to translate the New Testament into Arabic. Was it a form of prejudice against Arabs? It seems that, at least partly, Christianity lost Arabia because of its own failure to inculturate the Christian message in the local context.

---

1. See on this and the following Moffett, *History of Christianity in Asia*, 1:332.

However, the most important factor may have been the splintered nature of Christianity and the political affiliations of its different factions. The divisions between Chalcedonians, Nestorians, and Monophysites, and the continuing existence of schismatic churches like the Donatists, weakened Christianity, particularly in places like North Africa. The different Christian factions were politically connected to Arabia's imperialist neighbors—most importantly, the dominant Chalcedonian faction to the Roman Empire and, to a lesser extent, the Monophysites to Ethiopia. Muhammad's plan to develop Arab unity needed a convincing monotheist faith in opposition to the neighboring political powers and their affiliated Christian groups.[2]

Some Christian groups, in fact, welcomed the Arab victories over the Christian Roman Empire because, for those who didn't follow Chalcedonian orthodoxy, Arab conquest and Islamic rule were seen as liberation from Roman (i.e., Chalcedonian) oppression. For instance, only after Arab rule was established in Egypt could the Coptic (Miaphysite) church establish itself without oppression from imperially enforced orthodoxy. The same could be said for the Nestorians, who had lived under Persian rule, under religious pressure from Persia's dominant Zoroastrians. Christian life under Islamic rule did change, but it worsened only slowly.

How Did the Advance of Islam Affect Christianity?

In short, the impact of the advance of Islam was that the center of gravity of Christianity moved to the west and to the north. Christianity in North Africa, with the exception of Egypt, disappeared slowly but gradually, surviving only in small and sometimes hard-pressed communities. For the first time in six hundred years of gradual expansion, the growth of Christianity was halted and countered by a gradual process of regional eradication. Although most Islamic rulers of the following centuries showed some religious tolerance and were absolutely different to today's radical Islamist movements, Christianity could never recover its dominant presence in the Middle East, even less so in Central Asia, where it had never had any strong position.

As a result, three of the five traditional patriarchates—Jerusalem, Antioch, and Alexandria—lost their political and religious relevance, overseeing only some small remaining communities. Constantinople, the capital of the East, lost most of its traditional heartland and was reduced to what is now Turkey. The only patriarchate that was left basically unchanged by the advance of Islam was Rome, the traditional capital of the church in the

2. Ibid.; see also Watt, "Muhammad," 33–35.

west, and Rome from then on tremendously increased its influence in world Christianity.

Nestorian Christianity, which had spread beyond the Roman Empire into the Middle East, and Miaphysite Christianity, which had similarly spread in the Middle East and in North Africa, were severely weakened and, in the case of the former, nearly wiped out.

Christian Advances in the West

While Christianity was hard-pressed in the eastern and southern parts of the Mediterranean world, things were different in the west and north. Political rulers and a vibrant monastic movement (see below) spread Christianity across all parts of Europe and into Russia. The decisive moments in these processes of religious change were usually the conversions of territorial rulers, decisions often influenced by political considerations such as making alliances. Once the political leader converted to Christianity, Christian belief quickly became the dominant belief of that leader's territory.

In the western and central parts of Europe, the Christian expansion after the decay of the Roman Empire began with the conversion of the Frankish king Clovis in 496 and the subsequent conversion of the Burgundians. The following centuries brought two other important events: First, in 754 the pope anointed the Frankish leader Pippin as king, thus conferring divine legitimacy on a political ruler; half a century later, in 800, after the Frankish leader Charlemagne had extended the power of the Franks over most of western Europe, including the Italian peninsula and Rome, Pope Leo III crowned Charlemagne emperor. This meant that Rome had moved away from Byzantine rule and regarded another emperor as supreme ruler over the western part of the former Roman Empire. This coronation was merely the end of a long process—the weakening of the nominal Byzantine rule over Rome. The popes of Rome, facing the turmoil of the Germanic invasions, had found themselves increasingly without real political support from the Byzantine emperor.

Fig. 8.3: Europe at the end of Charlemagne's reign (814)

The Christianization of the Eastern Frankish Kingdom, covering much of present-day Germany, happened partly through Irish missionaries and partly through Benedictine ones. The two most famous were Benedictine: Willibrord (658–739), who was active in the north, in Frisia, and Boniface (c. 675–754), who established his base in the central town of Fulda, in today's Hesse.

The extension of Christianity to eastern Europe and the Slavic world coincided with the growing conflict between Rome and Constantinople. The two centers of Christianity competed for influence in eastern Europe, and missionaries from both sides brought Christianity to these territories.

From the middle of the ninth century on, central parts of eastern Europe received the Christian message through two brothers from Thessaloniki, Methodius and Cyril. Their mission became famous because of their use of the Slavic language and their invention of an alphabet (based on the Greek alphabet) for the language.

- In the ninth century, the church in Moravia (today part of the Czech Republic and Slovakia) came under the authority of Rome, while other churches in eastern Europe remained under the authority of Constantinople.

- Neighboring Moravia, Bohemia (roughly today's Czech Republic) was influenced by the developments in Moravia, with its political leader converting to Christianity in 884. The Bohemian church soon came under Roman authority.

- The Christianization of Bulgaria during the ninth century was shaped by a tension between Rome and Constantinople. The process began with Photios, Patriarch of Constantinople, baptizing Boris, the king of the Bulgarians. The Bulgarians subsequently shifted their alliances back and forth between the two centers until finally remaining with Constantinople.

- Bohemian and Moravian influence brought the Christian faith also to Poland, which until then had been pagan. It began with the baptism in 966 of Miecislav, the ruler of Poland, under the influence of his Bohemian wife. The subsequent Christianization of Poland took several centuries.

- Russia turned to the Christian faith under the authority of Constantinople through Czar Vladimir the Great (980–1015), who received baptism in 988 and subsequently imposed Christianity on Russia. The Russian church was subject to the church in Constantinople but developed as a Russian national church.

- The Baltic nations (Estonia, Latvia and Lithuania) received Christianity through German traders, knights, and monks, as well as through Danish and Swedish kings, from the end of the twelfth century on.

The expansion of Christianity in northern Europe happened slowly from the ninth century on and, unlike in eastern Europe, was not characterized by competition between Rome and Constantinople. Still, Christianity took several centuries until it was firmly established among the people.

- Christianity began to enter Denmark in the first part of the ninth century. However, the important breakthrough came only around 960, when King Harald Bluetooth accepted baptism.

- Further north, both Norway and Sweden became Christian around the year 1000 through the decisions of their kings. Around the same time, Iceland's parliament, which already existed at that early time, also decided that Iceland should adopt the Christian faith.

- Christianity in Finland grew through Swedish influence. However, the conversion of the Laplanders (Sami), who still live in the northernmost parts of Scandinavia, began only much later, around the eighteenth century.

MISSIONARY METHODS

Christianity spread in two main ways, through compulsory Christianization and through monastic mission.

Compulsory Christianization

Force was a significant element in the extension of the Christian church. Compulsory extension included wars for the specific purpose of mission, that is, wars that aimed to subject people to the Christian faith. An example is Charlemagne's conquest of the Saxons in the 770s and 780s and the subsequent imposition of the Catholic faith on them; baptism turned into a sign of submission under the rule of Charlemagne. However, direct missionary wars were the exception. The traditional ambiguity of Christianity toward the use of violence, which persisted into the Middle Ages, had a restraining effect.

Other military conquests happened less directly for the purpose of mission but similarly contributed to the compulsory expansion of Christianity—for example, when the head of a conquered nation converted to Christianity and his subjects were forced to follow. Successful conquest thus built the basis for subsequent mission. Subjection to the victorious political force led to subjection to the supposedly stronger God; political loyalty required religious loyalty. An example of such a practice was the king of Denmark, Harald Bluetooth, who, according to some accounts, underwent baptism after being defeated by the German King Otto I. In practice, it is difficult to distinguish when military conquests happened for the purpose of extending the power of Christianity and when this was simply a by-product. A milder form of coerced Christianization happened through material incentives dispensed to converts or material sanctions imposed on non-Christians.

Religious coercion is based on the assumption, common among most traditional societies, that a community needs a unified faith for social cohesion. New political boundaries thus naturally require new religious boundaries. A theological basis for extension by coercion can be traced back to Augustine's theological arguments in the conflict with the Donatists and with Pelagius: Augustine defended some use of force to compel heretics to the orthodox faith, citing the parable of the great banquet in Luke 14, where the master told the servant to "compel them to come in" (14:23 NIV).[3]

---

3. Augustine, Letter 93: Augustine to Vincentius (408 CE), *NPNF* 1/1:383. See also above, ch. 6. The missiologist David Bosch regards Luke 14:23 as *the* paradigmatic missionary text for the medieval period (*Transforming Mission*, 236).

Augustine intended to apply this forced persuasion only to schismatic and erroneous beliefs. As such, to him it was not persecution but application of church discipline. However, as a consequence, Pope Gregory the Great (590–604), one of the most important and influential popes of the first millennium, moved Christianity to a place where the defense of Christendom and its extension appeared often the same. It is obviously a small step from applying coercion in defending against heresy to extending the tactic to convert pagans.

Furthermore, in his conflict with the Donatists, Augustine emphasized that baptism was effective simply by the act itself (a position in Latin called *ex opere operato*), independent of the quality of the one performing it; against the Pelagians, he stressed that baptism, applied to erase the guilt of original sin, could not be erased (Latin: *character indelibilis*). As such, baptism became a primary means of mission, effective even where coerced because it supposedly led to behavioral change. The goal of missionaries was to win, by whatever means, the consent of pagans to be baptized. Coerced Christianization rests on the belief that baptism grants salvation and that any kind of suffering in this world is reasonable if seen in the light of avoiding eternal condemnation.

The Monastic Movement's Implicit and Explicit Missionary Dimension

A more creative and specific, and possibly more important, channel through which Christianity spread in the early medieval period was the monastic movement, with hermits and monks setting up monasteries all over Europe.

How did those monks, who had withdrawn from society to live in purity and separation from the world, become such important agents of mission?

Monastic communities, even though not created for the purpose of mission, had an implicit missionary dimension because of their lifestyle:

- Monks were held in high esteem as expressions of uncompromising Christian life: they were poor and worked hard.
- Their agricultural achievements impressed the people and gave them substantial help: it was the monks' labor that brought back cultivation in lands that had been devastated by the Germanic invasions.

- Monasteries were centers of culture and education: the invasions had swept away the old tradition of learning, except in the monasteries, where it was maintained.
- Monasteries became centers of social and diaconical activity, caring for the poor and the suffering: in times of turmoil, people were grateful for the help they received.

Overall, in lifestyle and social engagement, the monastic movement showed extraordinary resilience and recuperative power against the waves of invasions and the looting and banditry that ensued.

But monasticism had also an explicit missionary dimension: Many monasteries were established in remote frontier areas, where people had previously had little contact with Christianity. Hermits began by constructing permanent buildings and cultivating the land. Monastic settlements turned into a visible sign, a preliminary realization, of a world ruled by the love of God, and they became a missionary base for the further extension of the Christian faith into pagan areas.

Two Forms of Missionary Monasticism: Irish Monks and Benedictine Monks

During this early time, two forms of missionary monasticism can be distinguished: As part of their discipline of penance and the quest for their own salvation, Irish monks deliberately chose a lifestyle of ascetic homelessness and peregrination. They journeyed throughout Europe and relinquished any permanent abode. On their journeys they would help those whom they encountered, and they erected small worship places before moving on. The Irish monks, who operated independent of Rome, were thus missional as a result of this ascetic, nomadic lifestyle. Most famous were Columba (521-97), who spread Christianity in Scotland, and Columbanus (543-615), who founded many monasteries (which then turned into bases for the further spread of Christianity) across Europe, particularly in France, Switzerland, and northern Italy.

Benedictine monks, on the other hand, were driven not so much by the desire for personal perfection as by the direct goal of spreading the Christian faith. Pope Gregory the Great, himself originally a Benedictine monk, was the first to conceive of a planned "foreign mission": He sent the Roman abbot Augustine (not the famous Augustine of two hundred years earlier) and forty Benedictine monks from Italy to the British Isles to spread the Christian faith among the Anglo-Saxons. This form of monastic mission kept a strong connection with Rome and took a critical view of the more independent Irish missionaries. The Anglo-Saxon church linked to Rome became the dominant church in the British Isles, but the independent traditions continued to exist.

A century later, Anglo-Saxon missionaries became an important point of origin for the mission to Germany. Most famous was Boniface (c. 675–754), sometimes called the apostle to Germany, who in the eighth century propagated the Christian faith in the Eastern Frankish Empire, in Bavaria, Hesse, and Thuringia.

An important way of transmitting the Christian faith was through teaching: Christian missionaries usually addressed crowds rather than individuals, because religious faith was understood as a communal matter rather than an individual decision. Personal instruction was confined to community leaders, kings, or princes, who would be able to further influence the people. The teaching included instruction in the various aspects of the Christian salvation narrative (such as the origins of the universe and mankind, the fall into sin, the coming of Christ as redeemer) and elements of more polemic and propagandist nature directed against pagan worship—the superiority of the Christian God over all others, his power and justice, and the material rewards that Christians would have.

Missionaries preached to the people in their native languages and were often the first to codify these languages. Their linguistic contributions are, similar to missionaries in modern times, significant.

CHRISTIAN INCULTURATION IN EUROPE

Population groups migrating into western Europe brought their own cultural heritage. Early medieval Christianization in Europe succeeded in large part because the church absorbed many elements of traditional faith and pagan culture, and successfully connected local myths and stories with the Christian message.

In the process of inculturation during the early medieval period, various patterns complemented each other, again not unlike modern mission movements: Christianity was introduced partly in radical opposition to traditional culture, partly in harmony with it, and partly in compromise, absorbing traditional elements and thoroughly transforming them.

Destruction of Pagan Religion

Christian expansion was often accompanied by destruction of pagan religion and culture; the intention was not just to demolish pagan structures but to show that the gods of the pagans were powerless to avenge this insult and therefore demonstrate the superiority of the Christian God. The most famous and legendary act of destruction was when Boniface felled the sacred oak of Thor, a Germanic pagan god, in the heartlands of Germany and used the oak wood to build a church.

The Felling of Donar's Oak

The felling of a large oak dedicated to a Germanic pagan god would, in contemporary evangelical language, be called "power evangelism." This story is a good example of how Christianity overcame traditional pagan allegiances and how, by using the wood of the oak to build a church, it integrated objects of pagan religion into Christianity.

The narrator is Willibald (c. 700–c. 787), himself an Anglo-Saxon missionary to Germany and a younger coworker of Boniface. He was ordained as priest and consecrated as bishop by Boniface.

> Now at that time many of the Hessians, brought under the Catholic faith and confirmed by the grace of the sevenfold spirit, received the laying on of hands; others indeed, not yet strengthened in soul, refused to accept in their entirety the lessons of the inviolate faith. Moreover some were wont secretly, some openly, to sacrifice to trees and springs . . . while others, with sounder minds, abandoned all the profanations of heathenism . . . With the advice and counsel of these last, the saint [i.e., Boniface] attempted, in the place called Gaesmere, while the servants of God stood by his side, to fell a certain oak of extraordinary size, which is called, by an old name of the pagans, the Oak of Jupiter [this is Robinson's translation; in fact, it was a tree believed to belong to the German god Donar]. And when in the strength of his steadfast heart he had cut the lower notch, there was present a great multitude of pagans, who in their souls were earnestly cursing the enemy of their gods. But when the fore side of the tree was notched only a little, suddenly the oak's vast bulk, driven by a blast from above, crashed to the ground, shivering its crown of branches as it fell; and, as if by the gracious compensation of the Most High, it was also burst into four parts, and four trunks of huge size, equal in length, were seen, unwrought by the brethren who stood by. At this sight the pagans who before had cursed now, on the contrary, believed, and blessed the Lord, and put away their former reviling. Then moreover the most holy bishop, after

> taking counsel with the brethren, built from the timber of the tree a wooden oratory, and dedicated it in honor of Saint Peter the apostle.

Source: Robinson, *Life of Saint Boniface*, by Willibald, 62–64.

Transformation of Popular Religion

Christianity spread significantly by absorbing elements of traditional faith. An example of such absorption was the conversion of pagan temples into Christian churches. The church thus made use of the sacredness of a location, redirecting it into the Christian faith. This principle of missionary inculturation was outlined in a letter from Pope Gregory to Abbot Mellitus, a missionary to the Anglo-Saxons:

> I have long been considering in my own mind concerning the matter of the English people; to wit, that the temples of the idols in that nation ought not to be destroyed; but let the idols that are in them be destroyed; let water be consecrated and sprinkled in the said temples, let altars be erected, and relics placed there. For if those temples are well built, it is requisite that they be converted from the worship of devils to the service of the true God; that the nation, seeing that their temples are not destroyed, may remove error from their hearts, and knowing and adoring the true God, may the more freely resort to the places to which they have been accustomed. And because they are used to slaughter many oxen in sacrifice to devils, some solemnity must be given them in exchange for this, as that . . . they should . . . celebrate the solemnity with religious feasting, and no more offer animals to the Devil, but kill cattle and glorify God in their feast.[4]

In the process of absorbing elements of traditional faith, Christianity reinterpreted and redefined pagan symbols and introduced them in the symbolic, liturgical, and artistic expressions of the church: pagan festivals were reinterpreted and turned into Christian festivals; lesser pagan powers were turned into angelic or saintly intermediaries, introduced to bridge the gap between God and the world, and were called on for daily matters like toothaches or a sick child for which God was regarded as too remote to be bothered with. These practices allowed pagan polytheism to survive within the Christian monotheist framework. The vibrant medieval spirituality, with

---

4. Bede's *Ecclesiastical History of England*, bk. I, ch. 30, 64; see also Hen, "Converting the Barbarian West," 36.

its veneration of saints and a variety of locally observed cults, had its roots in this transformation of popular religion. The process of inculturation in northern and western Europe was thus similar to the way Christianity had become the official religion of the Roman Empire.

Something similar can be observed regarding behavioral conduct: As people in great numbers became Christians, they did not fundamentally—or at least not immediately—change their patterns of behavior. Rather, their traditional behavior was reshaped, redecorated with Christian elements, and gradually transformed. For example, warriors were transformed into knights bound to a code of conduct including gallantry, service to others, and Christian virtues. Similarly, classical warfare was redefined within a Christian framework and at least partly (though often only in theory) transformed, with gratuitous violence rejected.

Christianization of Paganism or Paganization of Christianity?

This inculturation processes can be described as baptizing traditional religious practices and behavior. The religious interests and expectations linked to specific localities or times were absorbed, reinterpreted, given new direction, and partly transformed. Yet, at the same time pagan elements continued to exist in the underground of Christian faith life and spirituality. With the medieval church so different from the church of the first two centuries, critics say that the pagan elements of the invading cultures were virtually reshaping Christianity and giving it a completely new outlook. In other words, many people who had shifted their allegiance to Christianity underwent only an incomplete conversion. They continued to worship stones, trees, springs, and old gods, and maintained the cult of the dead by conducting memorial banquets at their ancestors' tombs. They saw these traditional religious practices as additional "insurance." The church tried to slowly eradicate these habits or to offer Christian alternatives with similar functions.

Whether the church was successful and whether it was persistent enough in its effort may be debated. However, it may exactly have been this generosity of the medieval inculturation process, giving traditional religious practices some continuing right of existence, that allowed Christianity to be so successful in setting roots in medieval Europe and, over the long term, in transforming European societies. The crucial question thus remains: Was the result indeed Christianization of paganism, or rather a paganization of Christianity? In short, how to distinguish successful inculturation from syncretism?

For Further Reading

Evans, Gillian Rosemary. *The Church in the Early Middle Ages.* I. B. Tauris History of the Christian Church. London: I. B. Tauris, 2007.

Hen, Yitzhak. "Converting the Barbarian West." In *Medieval Christianity,* edited by Daniel Bornstein, 29–52. People's History of Christianity 4. Minneapolis: Fortress, 2010.

Jenkins, Philip. *The Lost History of Christianity: The Thousand-Year Golden Age of the Church in the Middle East, Africa, and Asia—and How It Died.* New York: HarperOne, 2008.

Kreider, Alan. "Changing Patterns of Conversion in the West." In *The Origins of Christendom in the West,* edited by Alan Kreider, 3–46. Edinburgh: T&T Clark, 2001.

MacMullen, Ramsay. *Christianity and Paganism in the Fourth to Eight Centuries.* New Haven: Yale University Press, 1997.

———. "Christianity Shaped through Its Mission." In *The Origins of Christendom in the West,* edited by Alan Kreider, 97–117. Edinburgh: T&T Clark, 2001.

Learning Activities

1) Review key elements of this chapter by answering the following questions:

    - What ethnic group triggered the period of tribal invasions of Europe? Where did they come from?
    - Name different ethnic groups that invaded Europe in the fourth and fifth centuries.
    - When did the Roman Empire end?
    - What time and event may be regarded as the beginning of the history of western Europe? Why?
    - What are reasons for the shift of Christianity's center from the East to the West?
    - What are the differences between Irish and Benedictine mission?
    - Name four famous missionaries of the medieval age.
    - How did the church react to the Germanic invaders in the fourth and fifth century?

2) To probe your understanding of what we have learned about this period, to deepen the understanding of its significance, and to apply it to your present experience, discuss the following questions:

    - What was the social role of the church in Europe during the time of the Germanic invasions?

- From what we have learned so far, why did the Roman Church gain such power and prestige in the early medieval period?
- How did different parts of the church work together in the expansion of Christianity?
- How did monasticism contribute to the spread of Christianity?
- Discuss the missionary methods of Christian expansion in early medieval times: What were their strengths? Weaknesses? Compare with mission in your own context.
- Try to understand the compulsory Christianization of the medieval era: What was the theological rationale behind it? Can you find positive elements in this forced Christianization?
- Discuss the different patterns of inculturation of Christian faith in Europe: What were their strengths and weaknesses?
- How do you make theological sense of the fact that Christianity in this period was not only growing but also disappearing?

Chapter 9

Papal History
The Growth of Papal Power

THE LAST CHAPTER TOLD the story of how Christianity spread through Europe and how the center of gravity of world Christianity shifted to the West. This chapter also looks at world Christianity's shift toward the West, but from a different angle: the institution of the church and, in particular, the institution of the papacy. The diverse followers of the resurrected Christ initially moved toward several regionally unified power centers and then toward an increasingly unified and centralized leadership; in other words, the successors of a simple fisherman who had died the cruel death of a martyr became powerful ecclesial and eventually political rulers. This is a story of power politics, of competing claims for primacy between different centers of Christianity and different patriarchs; even more fundamentally, it is the story of a conflict between religious and political leaders, culminating in the dramatic events of the cold winter of 1076–77, when a king had to kneel in penitence before the pope to ask for forgiveness and readmission to the church.

The chapter briefly reviews the development of Christian leadership in the first centuries and describes how the church in Rome gained importance. We will see how the Roman church leader, at quite an early stage, was already arguing for the primacy of the bishop of Rome. By the fifth century, under the turmoil of the Germanic invasions, the pope gained tremendous status and turned into the *de facto* leader of the Occident. Later, during the early medieval period, the bishops of Rome established the Papal States and began to assume direct political power. A significant part of the background to these power struggles was the long-running dispute between church and state regarding ultimate authority in the occidental world, the so-called investiture controversy.

The chapter asks the following questions:

- How and due to what factors did the papal office grow from being simply the bishop of Rome to the one claiming universal authority?
- Why and how did the pope develop political power beyond his already significant spiritual power?
- How did this increasing ecclesial and papal power—and, more particularly, the outcome of the investiture controversy—influence political developments in western Europe?

THE BACKGROUND: THE RISE OF THE PAPACY IN THE EARLY CHURCH

The single most important factor in the rise of the papacy was the fall of the Western Roman Empire in the fifth century and the subsequent political vacuum. The church and the bishop of Rome stepped into this vacuum, establishing and maintaining order in a time of disorder. However, the first steps toward the universal primacy of the Roman bishop had happened much earlier.

Pre-catholic Times

During the first 150 years of the Christian movement there was no primacy of the bishop of Rome and no united leadership (see ch. 3, especially fig. 3.2). Responsibility for ministry rested on people anointed by the Spirit—apostles and prophets, preachers and teachers. The movement spread by spontaneous mission, with no one in authority directing it.

Soon enough, and already visible in the Pastoral Letters of the New Testament, a more orderly leadership structure emerged—bishops, presbyters, and deacons. At this point, the bishops and deacons were needed only for the administration of external duties. The bishop was simply the first among a group of presbyters. Before long, though, the office turned into a permanent position. Already at that early time, some churches began to assume higher prestige, whether because of their location in a major city or because of their link to specific apostles.

After the Faith Crisis of the Second Century until 300

In response to the challenges in the middle of the second century—defending Christianity against Gnostic and other heretical interpretations—the concepts of a monarchic episcopate and of apostolic succession became popular. Churches began to emphasize their linear connections to the earliest apostles, and the most important congregations began to establish lists of bishops that proved an unbroken chain of apostolic succession since apostolic times. This chain proceeded through the one, monarchic bishop who passed the apostolic connection to those he ordained and to his successor as bishop. "Monarchic episcopate" thus meant the rule of one single person over the affairs of a congregation.

At that time, Rome was still only one of several equally important principal churches. Its gradually growing prestige was based on several factors, including the folowing:

- the importance of Rome as capital of the empire;
- the age, size, and wealth of the congregation;
- Rome's active spiritual and theological contribution to other congregations in times of internal crisis (as seen in the First Letter of Clement);
- the legend of the martyrdom of Peter and Paul in Rome;
- the old claim that Peter and Paul had founded the congregation.

In the middle of the third century, Cyprian, the bishop of Carthage (see ch. 2), emphasized the importance of the church as a visible institution: "There is no salvation outside of the church."[1] Or: "It is not possible to have God as father, if you do not have the church as mother."[2] At the same time, he stressed the bishop as the foundation of the church. However, there was still no idea of the primacy of the bishop of Rome. Cyprian, then, may be seen as the father of episcopalism rather than of papalism.

---

1. Cyprian, Epistle LXXII, 21 (*ANF* 5:384).
2. Cyprian, *On the Unity of the Church* 6 (*ANF* 5:423).

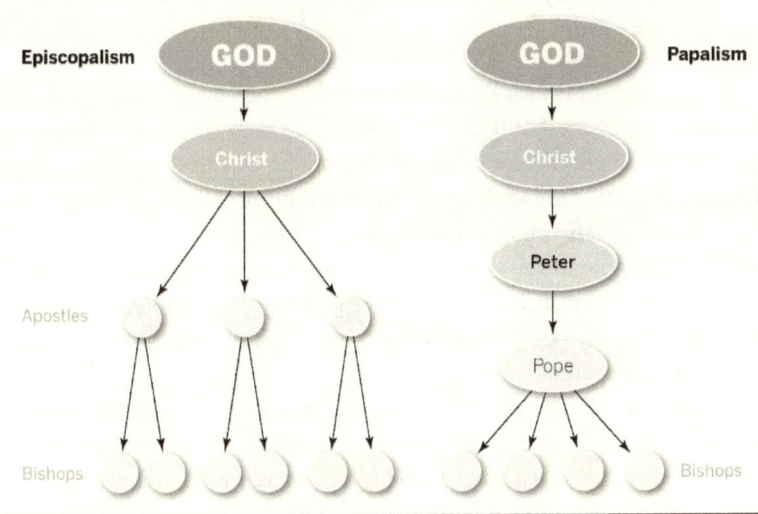

Fig. 9.1: Different leadership models: Episcopalism vs. papalism

THE DEVELOPMENT OF PAPAL AUTHORITY FROM THE FOURTH TO THE SIXTH CENTURY

During early medieval times, the institution of the papacy took important steps toward papal primacy. It will be helpful to distinguish between

(1) claims of primacy, and

(2) the realization of primacy;

and between two aspects of papal primacy:

(1) ecclesial, meaning the relationship of Rome to the rest of Christianity; and

(2) political, meaning the relationship of the supreme church leader to the supreme political leader, that is, the relationship between the pope and the emperor.

What Factors Played a Role in the Rise of the Papacy in the Fourth Century?

First, from earliest times, Rome had played an important role as preserver of orthodoxy. In the Trinitarian debates of the early fourth century, Rome successfully supported the victorious Nicene party and thus effectively established its own credentials as a pillar of orthodox belief.

Second, when Constantine moved the capital of the Roman Empire to Constantinople around the year 330, the bishop of Rome became the most important authority in the western part of the empire, increasingly overshadowing the political authority of the emperor or his representative, the exarch in Ravenna.

Third, as the catholic church under Constantine was increasingly organized in correspondence to the empire's political structure, a hierarchical ecclesial organization emerged, with bishops overseeing the churches of one district, metropolitans leading the church of a whole province, and patriarchs governing the few most important centers. In terms of church administration, the only long-term candidates for the supreme head of the church were Rome or Constantinople. In theological terms, the competition was between Rome, Constantinople, and Alexandria. The two other patriarchates, Antioch and Jerusalem, never had the same influence. Fourth, Rome had one crucial advantage over Constantinople—its greater independence in relation to the emperor.

Finally, the veneration of Saint Peter was already popular around that time, having been tolerated or even encouraged by the church. Rome's prestige was closely linked to the prestige of this apostle.

Overall, during the fourth century the papacy did not yet claim universal primacy. It aimed only to establish Rome as supreme patriarchate of the West, thus claiming and developing primacy for the West.

How Did the Concept of Universal Primacy Develop in the Fifth Century?

The period of the fifth century saw substantial advances in ecclesial and political aspects, that is, in Rome's relationship to the other centers of authority and in its relationship to the emperor. The most important contribution toward universal papal primacy came through a pope who was not only extraordinarily powerful and skilled in political diplomacy, but who also understood the intricacies of theological debates: Pope Leo I, who was pope during the crucial years 440–61.

Leo I can be regarded as the first pope to clearly express a claim for universal papal primacy. While developing this claim, he at the same time needed to consolidate what had already been gained—the reality of Roman primacy in the West—and reassert his authority against regional bishops who, while acknowledging Leo's spiritual authority, might not necessarily accept his administrative or juridical authority in diocesan church matters.

Politically, Leo I gained enormous prestige when Attila, having met with Leo, withdrew from his threat to move toward Rome. The reasons for Attila's withdrawal are not known, and it is not clear whether the pope's intervention actually played much of a role, but Leo I benefited from appearing to be the savior of Rome and Italy. Only a short time later, Leo I was unable to keep the Vandals from entering Rome and sacking it, but he skillfully negotiated with them and averted some of the harm and ransacking that was common in such attacks. In the turmoil that followed, the church—led of course by Leo—also helped maintain order.

The popes after Leo I could not always maintain the same authority, but the institution continued to develop, and the supremacy of the pope over the political sphere grew as well. Pope Gelasius I (492–96) taught that God had provided two ruling authorities in the world, monarchs and bishops, but that the burden of the priests was even greater and that the emperor was subject to the pope in matters of faith.[3] Pope Symmachus (498–514) developed this idea further and held that the pope was beyond judgment by any secular power.

Theologically and ecclesially, Leo I established the basis for the primacy of the Roman bishop by stressing Matthew 16:18, Luke 22:32, and John 21:15–17:

> "And I tell you that you are Peter, and on this rock I will build my church, and the gates of Hades will not overcome it."
> (Matt 16:18 NIV)

> "But I have prayed for you, Simon, that your faith may not fail. And when you have turned back, strengthen your brothers."
> (Luke 22:32 NIV)

> When they had finished eating, Jesus said to Simon Peter, "Simon son of John, do you love me more than these?" "Yes, Lord," he said, "you know that I love you." Jesus said, "Feed my lambs." Again Jesus said, "Simon son of John, do you love me?" He answered, "Yes, Lord, you know that I love you." Jesus said, "Take care of my sheep." The third time he said to him, "Simon,

---

3. Burns, *Medieval Political Thought*, 288–89.

son of John, do you love me?" Peter was hurt because Jesus asked him the third time, "Do you love me?" He said, "Lord, you know all things; you know that I love you." Jesus said, "Feed my sheep." (John 21:15-17 NIV)

Leo said that Jesus had made Peter and his successors the foundation for the whole church. This claim of universal authority was significantly advanced when, during the christological debates in Chalcedon, Leo's position, proposed in a document called the *Tome*, became the recognized orthodox christological definition. This middle position of the bishop of Rome between Nestorians and Monophysites (see ch. 7) was perhaps the biggest boost to the authority of Rome.

During the period of Pope Symmachus in the early sixth century, documents emerged that further supported papal authority. One of these documents recounted the legend of how Pope Sylvester I (314-35) had actually healed, converted, and baptized the Emperor Constantine. These documents were later found to be forged, though they had already achieved their intended effect—strengthening the papacy.

The fifth century had brought clear advances for ecclesial papal supremacy and for the political power of the pope, allowing the bishop of Rome to appear more and more as a religious counterpart to the secular emperor. However, political and ecclesial realities, and of course the popes' opponents, often enough did not support papal authority. In terms of ecclesial relations, the Fourth Ecumenical Council of Chalcedon decided in a subtly formulated and apparently contradictory statement that Constantinople should have equal privileges to imperial Rome and be magnified and ranked second to it: "The 150 most devout bishops apportioned equal prerogatives to the most holy see of new Rome, reasonably judging that the city which is honored by the imperial power and senate . . . should also be elevated to her level in ecclesiastical affairs and take second place after her."[4] This has usually been interpreted as meaning that Rome and Constantinople had equal ecclesial rights, but that the bishop of Rome had honorary primacy. In terms of political relations, though, the emperor frequently intervened in papal elections and thus demonstrated that ultimate power lay with him rather than with the church.

---

4. Council of Chalcedon, Canon 28, in Tanner, *Decrees of the Ecumenical Councils*, 1:100.

THE ROMAN CHURCH ASSUMES SECULAR POWER

Gregory I (590–604) was, with Leo I, probably the most important pope of the first millennium. He stood at the beginning of a development that added a further aspect to the complex power politics of the papacy: the acquisition of land and secular power in the Italian Peninsula. Soon enough, the power of the Roman bishop would encompass not only (*a*) Rome's position in the universal church and (*b*) the pope's relationship to the emperor, but also (*c*) the pope's secular rule of a country. Gregory I did not yet go that far, but the beginnings of this development can be seen in his time.

How Did the Pope Begin to Assume Political Power in the Sixth Century?

Gregory I became pope in the midst of a political and social crisis in Rome: the invasion of the Lombards, a Germanic tribe who conquered large parts of the peninsula. At the same time, an epidemic broke out in Rome, and a flood had destroyed much of the stored food. Realizing that no help could be expected from the political government in Constantinople or from its representative, the exarch in Ravenna, Gregory took up the challenge and began to organize the distribution of food and the rebuilding of aqueducts to provide sanitation, and, most importantly, he entered into negotiations with the Lombards. His successful peace negotiations happened independently of the political government in Constantinople or Ravenna. Gregory was not driven as much by political interests as by actual pastoral care for the suffering people in and around Rome. But his direct political intervention became a precedent for papal independence from political authorities in political negotiations. His independent diplomacy on behalf of Rome turned Gregory I into the *de facto* ruler of the city and the surrounding area. This actual political position built the basis for what later became known as "Saint Peter's Patrimony."

Besides laying the groundwork for the church's assumption of direct political power and its own territorial rights, Gregory successfully expanded Rome's status over the occidental church by sending Benedictine missionaries to Britain and by intervening in church matters in North Africa and in the Frankish territories.

POPES AND EMPERORS IN WESTERN EUROPE FROM THE SEVENTH TO THE TENTH CENTURY

As the churches in the western and in the eastern part of the Roman Empire increasingly drifted apart (see ch. 10), papal primacy was more concerned with developing the political aspect of papal power—that is, Rome's relationship to the emperor—than the ecclesial aspect, its relationship to the worldwide church. Regarding the latter, Rome would naturally claim universal primacy and Constantinople would just as naturally reject it, or accept it only as a primacy of equals without any administrative, judicial, or effective theological superiority. Thus, the church's internal power relations did not change much from the seventh to tenth centuries, but significant developments happened in the relationship between pope and emperor.

The Popes Switch Allegiance to Western Political Powers

During the rapid advances of the Islamic Empire, it became increasingly clear that the Byzantine emperor was unable to provide political and military protection to the heartlands of western Europe. In fact, it was a Frankish leader, Charles Martel, who stopped the expansion of Islam in 732. The church in Rome thus realized that it should rely on the protection of a political power in the West rather than on what was nominally still the Roman Empire's government, in Constantinople. From this time on, Rome began to look for support from the Frankish kings.

In 753, Pope Stephen III (752–57) crossed the Alps to visit the church in the Frankish territories, making him the first Roman bishop to do so. He crowned Pippin, the son of Charles Martel, as king, and thus gave sacral legitimacy to Pippin's ousting of the previous rulers. Pippin's son Charlemagne, who became emperor after the death of his father, repeated the trip and visited Rome—not as a tourist, but to fight the remaining Lombards in Italy. Some years later, on Christmas Day 800, after Charlemagne had extended the political power of the Franks over most of western Europe, including Rome, Pope Leo III (795–816) crowned Charlemagne "Emperor of the Romans." This act can be seen as one of the most important moments in the history of western Europe. The year 800 may also be regarded as the beginning of a specific "western European" history; all earlier history of the West was part of a broader history of the Roman Empire, comprising the whole Mediterranean area.

Whether the coronation of Charlemagne as Roman emperor is to be seen as a demonstration of the ultimate power of the pope to bestow imperial power on a political leader who depends on the pope's blessing and anointing, or whether, quite to the contrary, the emperor actually used the pope to give some sacral flavor to political realities, obviously depends on the interpreter's perspective. The fact that Leo III actually kneeled in homage to the new Western emperor[5]—something that should never happen again—points to the real power relations at work.

The Development of the Popes' Territorial Power: The Foundation of the Papal States

When the Lombards conquered Ravenna and expelled the exarch (Constantinople's representative), the bishop of Rome appealed to Pippin for help. A non-Italian political power, Pippin, thus intervened on behalf of the papacy and defeated the Lombards and their king, Aistulf. Significantly, though, after his victory Pippin did not return the lands (taken from the Lombards) to the original ruler, the emperor of Constantinople, but instead gave them to the pope to be administered by him. This transfer of ownership is known as the "Donation of Pippin" (754), and it became the foundation of the Papal States in central Italy. This direct political (administrative) power over a significant territorial entity increased the prestige and power of the church. It also meant that Rome was now territorially cut off from Constantinople. Yet the problem of this donation was that it still was a political leader who gave it and not, as later popes wanted to see it, the pope granting land to political rulers.

Later that century, Pippin's donation was recorded in a document that presented the event as happening as a result of Constantine's conversion, thus giving it higher authority. Through the centuries it was known as the "Constantinian Donation," until a fifteenth-century humanist exposed it as a forgery. We should note, however, that forgery was at that time not necessarily malicious but was rather a way to give proper dignity to something that deserved it.

Decline in Papal Authority in the Ninth and Tenth Centuries

The ninth and tenth centuries were a period of decline in papal authority, with only a short intervening period in which the church regained some power. Popes succeeded each other quickly and the election of popes depended on power plays among rich families in Rome or on the intervention

---

5. MacCulloch, *Christianity*, 349.

of the king. The pattern was simple: The more powerful the king or emperor, the more the pope was subject to political power. And, vice versa, the rise of papal power in the eleventh century coincided with a period of weakened political authority. The situation was largely the same with dukes or lords ruling over smaller territories. Feudal lords often extended their power when a king's centralizing power was weakened.

The church's understanding of church-state relations diverged strongly from that of the political rulers. While the church asked only for protection, the kings saw themselves as the ultimate authority of a territory, including the church. Charlemagne, for example, liked to compare himself to David, a theocratic king, and the pope to Moses, whose duty was merely to pray with raised hands during the battle.

Political rulers found a multitude of ways to control ecclesial affairs. They introduced laws regarding ecclesial affairs or they themselves imposed and collected tithes; they weakened central papal authority by strengthening episcopal authority and by subjecting monasteries to episcopal authority; and they appointed allies or extended family members as bishops and abbots. A particularly effective way of controlling church affairs was investing bishops and abbots with worldly, political and juridical authority to rule a territory and then donating large parcels of land to them to ensure their loyalty. Thus, senior clerics turned into vassals of the king; they were required to contribute to the king's court and the royal army and to swear an oath of allegiance to the king. This oath of allegiance was a common practice, from the time of the German king Otto the Great (936–73) until the end of the eighteenth century. A further effect of this strategy was that bishops became very busy with political affairs and were unable to pursue their ecclesial responsibilities.

The political rulers not only controlled the ecclesial authorities, they also influenced internal church matters by unifying the liturgy, by promoting preaching and moral teaching, and by providing education for the clergy and promoting canonical life (the spiritual life of the clergy of a main church). They made Sunday a day of rest and regular worship attendance compulsory; they supported magnificent church buildings to show evidence of their devotion. Finally, they regarded themselves as protectors of the church's faith and claimed authority to make crucial decisions in dogmatic debates.

The only period during the ninth and tenth centuries in which the papacy recovered something of its earlier strength and acted as a significant counterweight to secular power was during the papacy of Nicholas I (858–67). Nicholas used the decay of Carolingian power and the subsequent power struggles to strengthen his own papal power and authority.

He successfully played the kingmaker among the factions competing for leadership of the Carolingian dynasty and thus assumed authority above the petty power struggles of political life.

PAPAL REFORM AND CONFRONTATION BETWEEN POPE AND EMPEROR: THE INVESTITURE CONTROVERSY OF THE ELEVENTH AND TWELFTH CENTURIES

Toward the end of the tenth century, the church began to assume tremendous power. It was from this point on that the Catholic Church increasingly turned into a papal church. The source of this power did not initially come from the church hierarchy but from the monastic Christian movement.

The Reform Movement of Cluny

In the year 910, a small group of monks withdrew to a remote area of Burgundy where they were given land and funds by William I, Duke of Aquitaine (western France) to establish the monastery of Cluny. The donation was unusual in its time because it came with no strings attached, except the request to pray for the duke and his family. The vision of the monks was that, in Cluny, the kingdom of God should begin and that their incessant worship should reflect the heavenly glory. It was from this center of worship and incessant prayer that the renewal of the church began.

The Cluny reform program was first a restoration of monastic life. The Cluny community emphasized strict monastic discipline and obedience to the abbot according to the original Benedictine rule. It established a network with subsidiary houses under the supervision of the abbot of Cluny, thus building an alternative spiritual power that, over the long term, strengthened the institution of the church. The Cluny monks reformed the monastic economy and protected monastic property from secular authorities. They submitted themselves directly to the pope, free from episcopal authority and, even more important, from local powers, that is, they had no need to swear allegiance to worldly rulers. The boldness of their vision found visual expression in the church that they built: in its final form, it was for several centuries the largest building in the West, until the construction of St. Peter's Basilica in Rome in the sixteenth century.

From the eleventh century on, Cluny's reform program went beyond simply the restoration of monastic life and turned into an ecclesial and political reform, extending to the church as a whole and to the relationship between church and state. In this reform, several long-serving abbots of Cluny played a significant role, among them Odilo (994–1049) and Hugo (1049–1109). This ecclesial and political reform movement aimed at subjecting the whole church under the pope. It provided an important impulse for the increased authority of the papacy and for the popes' insistence on independence from political rulers. The Cluny reform movement called for liberation of the church from all interference by secular authorities; it rejected the buying and selling of ecclesiastical posts, a practice that (with reference to the story in Acts 8) was called simony, and it likewise rejected any secular or lay investiture, that is, the appointment of bishops, abbots, and priests by nobles or kings. The movement pushed for all clerics, not only monastics, to adhere to strict clerical discipline. It was also during this time that the call for celibacy of all clerics grew louder. By preventing clergy from getting married, the church prevented them from passing on church property to their descendants. This celibacy also set them apart from laypeople. In the Second Lateran Council (1139), the church for the first time officially declared clerical marriages invalid; the repeated calls for celibacy give evidence of how much resistance the idea had to overcome.

The Gregorian Reform Movement and the Struggle for the Independence of the Church

The political and ecclesial reform ideas of Cluny began to bear fruit in the middle of the eleventh century. This was the peak of the investiture controversy, a conflict between political and religious governments about who had the power to appoint bishops and abbots. In the background was the question of who had ultimate power in a territory or, eventually, in the world.

The main protagonists in this fascinating story would be the young King Henry IV and Pope Gregory VII (1073–85). The father of Henry IV, Henry III (1039–56), a powerful German king and Emperor of the Holy Roman Empire, had been influenced by the Cluny reform movement and had supported the struggle of the church against simony. However, he still claimed the right to appoint popes and did so several times by deposing claimants to the papacy and appointing bishops of his own choice as popes. One of the popes Henry III nominated was Pope Leo IX (1049–54). Leo IX contributed significantly to the reform of the church by convening regular annual synods, by visiting the churches in Italy, France, and Germany, and by introducing a universal church organization—the collegium of cardinals, which would be responsible for the election of the pope.

Gregory VII's Concept of Papal Authority

The text below is part of the so-called *Dictatus papae*, through which Pope Gregory VII stated his concept of papal power. It is a summary of how the pope understood his relationship with the bishops and with the political powers. The text was probably written shortly after the death of Gregory, but it fully reflects his views, recognizable by his actions. The eleventh dictum below was the first distinct claim of the exclusive right of the bishop of Rome to the title of pope, once applied to all bishops,[6] and the common title for all priests in the Greek Church. It is also the title for the head of the Coptic Church.

1. *That the Roman Church was founded by God alone.*
2. *That the Roman bishop alone is properly called universal.*
3. *That he alone has the power to depose bishops and reinstate them.*
4. *That his legate, though of inferior rank, takes precedence of all bishops in council, and may give sentence of deposition against them.*
5. *That the Pope has the power to depose [bishops] in their absence.*
6. *That we should not even stay in the same house with those who are excommunicated by him.*
8. *That he alone may use the imperial insignia.*
9. *That the Pope is the only person whose feet are kissed by all princes.*
11. *That the name which he bears belongs to him alone.*
12. *That he has the power to depose emperors.*
13. *That he may, if necessity require, transfer bishops from one see to another.*
16. *That no general synod may be called without his consent.*
17. *That no action of a synod, and no book, may be considered canonical without his authority.*
18. *That his decree can be annulled by no one, and that he alone may annul the decrees of any one.*
19. *That he can be judged by no man.*
20. *That no one shall dare to condemn a person who appeals to the apostolic see.*
22. *That the Roman Church has never erred, nor ever, by the testimony of Scripture, shall err, to all eternity.*

---

6. Robinson, *Readings in European History*, 1:274.

26. That no one can be considered Catholic who does not agree with the Roman Church.
27. That he [the pope] has the power to absolve the subjects of unjust rulers from their oath of fidelity.

Source: Ogg, *Source Book of Medieval History*, 262–64.

An important coworker of Leo IX was Hildebrand, a monk from Cluny. Hildebrand became papal administrator during the papacy of Leo IX; he played an important role in successive papal elections and was eventually himself chosen as pope, assuming the name of Gregory VII. When Emperor Henry III died, his six-year-old son ascended the throne as Henry IV. Benefiting from the political power vacuum, since the young ruler was not yet able to fully assume power, the church began to strengthen its position. It rejected the strong influence of German kings and the appointment of popes through the king. To emphasize the independence of the church from secular power, a church council (1059) determined that the election of the pope had to happen through the collegium of cardinals.

When Gregory VII was elected as pope in the year 1073, he continued to enforce the ecclesial and political reform program that he had learned at Cluny. He stressed that the pope was the head of the universal church and also the highest ruler in the world. The relation of pope and king, he said, is like sun and moon: the kings receive their light from the pope. The pope is thus entitled to free the subjects of a king from their obedience to that ruler, and this is exactly what Gregory VII did in his conflict with Henry IV.

In 1075, Gregory VII convened a synod that prohibited lay investiture. This was a revolutionary step, as it meant that all bishops and abbots who had previously been appointed by a king or nobleman, and given regional political authority and property, were freed from their oath of loyalty to the king. However, Henry IV insisted on the traditional rights of a king and continued to appoint bishops. When Gregory VII reacted angrily, Henry IV did what his father had done thirty years earlier: he deposed the pope. But times had changed. When two bishops sent by Henry IV arrived in Rome to announce that the pope had been deposed, they encountered such a storm of outrage that Gregory VII himself had to call for calm. He then proceeded to excommunicate and depose Henry IV, thereby freeing all of Henry IV's subjects from their oath of loyalty.

Of course, whether the king's subjects would recognize the pope's excommunication of the king did not so much depend on the authority of the pope but on political circumstances. In this case, though, the opponents of Henry IV used the excommunication as an opportunity to move against the king. Henry IV realized that if he wanted to keep the throne, he had to ask the pope for absolution and readmission to the church. He thus undertook a procession of penance to Canossa (1077) to beg the pope for a revocation of the ban against him. After much hesitation, Gregory VII granted him absolution and Henry IV was readmitted to the church.

Canossa did not end the question of whether the political or the religious government had the ultimate authority in a community; this question has continued to shape the politics of western Europe until the present day, with different periods offering different solutions. Instead, Canossa stands for the most dramatic peak in the relationship between pope and king. For German kings and for the prestige of secular power it was a low point, yet the shocking humiliation of a political ruler by the pope had a long-term effect—subsequent political rulers became determined to organize the church on a national level and integrate it into the nation-state.

Gregory VII's Account of Henry IV's Penance at Canossa

King Henry's pilgrimage of repentance to receive papal absolution was the most dramatic expression of the long conflict between spiritual and temporal power. Henry IV had been deposed by Gregory VII and feared that some territorial leaders would use the excommunication to move against him. He therefore felt compelled to seek absolution.

The text below offers Pope Gregory VII's description of the events in Canossa. It reveals something of the pope's reluctance to reverse the excommunication of the king.

> *Before he [King Henry IV] entered Italy he had sent us suppliant messages, offering to render satisfaction, in all respects, to God, St. Peter, and ourselves. He also renewed his promise that he would be perfectly obedient in the matter of amending his life if only he might win from us the favor of absolution and of the apostolic benediction.*
>
> *When, after many delays and after much consultation we had, through all the envoys who passed between us, severely reprimanded him for his offenses, he at length came of his own accord, accompanied by a few followers, with no hostility or arrogance in his bearing, to the town of Canossa, where we were tarrying. And there, laying aside all the trappings of royalty, he stood in wretchedness, barefooted and clad in woolen, for three days before the gate of the castle, and implored with profuse weeping the aid and consolation of the apostolic mercy, until he had moved all who saw or heard of it to such pity and depth of compassion that they interceded for him with many prayers and tears and wondered at the unaccustomed hardness of our heart; some*

even protested that we were displaying not the seriousness of the apostolic displeasure but the cruelty of tyrannical ferocity.

At last, overcome by his persistent remorse and by the earnest entreaties of those with us, we loosed the chain of anathema and received him into the favor of our fellowship and into the lap of the holy mother Church.

Source: Purinton, *Christianity and Its Judaic Heritage*, 333–34.

The Concordat of Worms

The investiture controversy distinguished between different forms of investiture: the investiture of the ring as a symbol of a senior cleric's marriage to the church, the investiture of the crosier (like a shepherd's staff) as a symbol of both power over the diocese and property rights to the church building, and the investiture with the scepter as a symbol for the church's worldly property and political authority. Some years after Canossa, Pope Calixtus II and the German king Henry V made an agreement (concordat) in Worms (1122) that intended to settle the investiture controversy. Henry V agreed to abstain from investiture with the ring and the crosier but maintained the right of investiture with the scepter, thus acknowledging the king's right to transfer political leadership to a bishop. This agreement can indeed be regarded as a victory for the church, for since the time of the Carolingians in the eighth century, kings and emperors had always maintained the right to appoint bishops and invest power in them. Now the only remaining power of the king was to invest the bishop with his political power.

THE PEAK OF PAPAL POWER: THE POPE AS LEADER OF THE WEST IN THE TWELFTH AND THIRTEENTH CENTURIES

It was another political vacuum in the German empire that brought a further increase in the power of the church in its relationship to the state. After the death of King Henry VI, his son Frederick II, who was only three years old, became king. He was to become one of the most powerful European rulers of the medieval time, but being so young, his ascension to the throne created a power vacuum, from which Pope Innocent III was able to benefit.

The Papacy of Innocent III (1198–1216)

Pope Innocent III was one of the most powerful popes ever. He successfully demonstrated the dominance of the pope over political rulers by compelling them to obedience in political and moral matters. He restated the previous Gregorian principles—that the pope rules over secular rulers and that they receive their power through him. He described his office as not only a representative of St. Peter but as a representative of Christ (*vicarius Christi*), who was believed to hold kingship over the world.

Innocent III acted successfully both in political and ecclesial matters. Politically, he presented himself as the one who had ultimate power over the election of kings and the emperor. In a famous papal decree, *Per venerabilem* (1202), Innocent III explained that the right of German princes to elect their king had been transferred to them by the pope when, at the time of Charlemagne, he transferred the papal recognition of the emperor from the Greeks to the Franks. The pope, according to Innocent III, had the responsibility to investigate whether the one elected by the German princes was worthy, and only then would the pope crown him. In cases of disputed elections, the pope was to be the ultimate arbiter and to decide based on the qualifications of the candidates. Operating under these principles, Innocent III successfully intervened in various political conflicts and in the competing power claims of different European dynasties. He extended his direct political power in central and southern Italy and Sicily. He deposed King John of England (1166–1216) by excommunicating him and later returning him to power as his vassal.

His call for the Fourth Crusade (1202–4; see chs. 10 and 12), leading to the conquest of Constantinople and the establishment of a Latin empire in Constantinople (1204–61), may be seen as belonging to either the political or the ecclesial realm. The dream of subjecting the Eastern Orthodox Church to the authority of the pope seemed close to realization. But in fact the conquest of Constantinople profoundly alienated the Orthodox Church for centuries to come.

In ecclesial matters, Innocent III vigorously opposed heretics. He successfully suppressed heretical groups, particularly Cathars (see ch. 11) in southern France. In 1215, following the conciliar tradition of the early church, he convened the important Fourth Lateran Council. This was the council of the Roman Catholic Church that codified the doctrine of transubstantiation and made important decisions on episcopal inquisition and church reform.

The papacy of Innocent III was a peak of papal power, but his increased claim of political power undermined his spiritual authority. A growing number of Christian sects rejected the papal church and began to regard the pope as the Antichrist. Although Innocent III's successors were in general unable to maintain the same level of power, these later popes continued in the same vein—acting as undisputed and absolute rulers of the church, strengthening the central authority of the church and intervening in political affairs.

Papal Absolutism

The power of the papacy continued to develop in several directions: The pope became the ultimate *source of the law of the church*, as a unified canonical law for the whole Catholic Church gradually developed from the twelfth century on. But even more, the pope became the *supreme judge* of the church. Innocent III and his successors reinforced the long tradition of Rome's claim to being the ultimate arbiter in all church matters. *Church administration was centralized* to an extent unthinkable in earlier times. The bishops, who until that time had retained a high level of independence from the pope, became increasingly subject to papal influence and authority. A typical example was the election of bishops, which originally had been the responsibility of the clergy of a cathedral. In the process of growing centralization, Innocent III and his successors introduced several channels to influence the election of bishops—the right to scrutinize and confirm each election, for example. Under the condition of medieval transport and communication, direct government of the whole church by the pope was not possible and would develop only in modern times. Yet the basic framework for the absolute rule of the pope was certainly set in this period.

The popes also continued to claim supreme political power, as for instance in the papacy of Pope Boniface VIII (1294–1303), who issued the papal bull *Unam sanctam* (1302). This document reiterated the earlier statement of Cyprian that there is no salvation outside the Catholic Church (*extra ecclesiam nulla salus*) and that it is "necessary to salvation for every human creature to be subject to the Roman pontiff"[7]; however, his claim already stood in stark contrast to the political reality.

---

7. Pope Boniface VIII, *Unam sanctam*, 1302, in Bettenson, *Documents of the Christian Church*, 116.

Pre-Catholic time (until around 150)	No primacy of the bishop of Rome and no united leadership
After the faith crisis in the 2nd century (2nd and 3rd century)	No primacy of Rome, but *monarchic* episcopal leadership and idea of apostolic succession
4th century	Rome's claim for *primacy in the West* after the establishment of Constantinople
5th century	First *claims of universal papal primacy* and an early realization through the christological debates during the time of Pope Leo I (440-61)
6th to 8th century	Development of *worldly power* of the pope starting with Gregory I; foundation of the Papal States in the 8th century
11th to 12th century	Papal reform and confrontation between the pope and the emperor: The investiture controversy, the claim of universal papal power, and the vision of the *pope as universal monarch;*
13th century	Growing gap between claim and reality: the pope behaving like the ruler of the world

Fig. 9.2: Summary: Seven steps in the development of papal power

ASSESSING THE OUTCOME OF THE INVESTITURE CONFLICT

Although many modern people have little sympathy for the medieval papacy and its gradual rise in power, because it seems to contradict the humility of the one the church claims to follow, a critical assessment should take also note of the lasting positive results of the investiture conflict.

First, the church seems to have reduced, at least partly, secular influence on its internal affairs. The church may thus be seen as winner in the investiture controversy. This freedom of religion should be seen as a positive achievement, compared to most traditional societies where political rulers commonly intervene in religious matters based on their claim of ultimate political and possibly even sacral authority.

Second, the church's claim of ultimate authority, including political matters, had both an equalizing and a critical effect: when a religious body like the church extends its authority over kings and noblemen, it emphasizes that these secular rulers are subject to the same moral principles and the same discipline as their subjects. At the same time the church reaffirmed its basic caveat regarding all political claims of ultimate authority. This prepared the ground for citizens' critical attitude toward political authorities. Leaders and laws are ultimately subject to a higher spiritual authority.

Third, the humiliation of kings by the popes and the papal accumulation of power boosted secular rulers' suspicion of the church and strengthened political rulers in their intent to limit papal power. Secular rulers in this period learned that the political sphere also needs to be protected from ecclesial interference. This political resolve ultimately laid the groundwork for European secularization as a differentiation of spheres of life. Although secularization caused Christianity to lose authority and is thus often interpreted negatively as the church losing influence and as Christian values losing relevance in public life, it also contributed to the development of highly treasured values in public life—democracy, freedom of expression, and human rights. As much as religious institutions demanded freedom from political intervention, political institutions likewise needed independence from religious intervention. Many historians regard the medieval investiture conflict as the root of European secularization and of European political development: democratic development ultimately needs a non-sacral view of political rulers. In other words, dictatorship always goes together with at least some degree of sacralization of political power.

Fourth, the precarious balance of power between religious and political powers through the subsequent history of Europe, with both limiting each other and inhibiting a one-sided hegemony, led Europe on a course where no single entity was able to gain overwhelming imperial power. Of course, during some periods of European history, some rulers were able to unite large parts of Europe within one empire. Mostly, though, Europe developed as a variety of small states. This apparent disunity and diversity, seen by some as a disadvantage, was actually one reason—there are of course others (e.g., geography)—why Europe did not develop as one large and united Christian empire. The relative smallness of European states eventually encouraged people's participation in political affairs: large political entities are rather disempowering, as seen in the history of large empires and even large democratic institutions like the European Union or the United States.

Fifth, the peak of papal power may be regarded as the beginning of its decline, for two reasons. On the one hand, it was difficult to maintain such an accumulation of power over longer periods of time. On the other hand, the accumulation of political and economic power undermined the church's spiritual authority. Unfettered papal absolutism allowed growing corruption at the papal court and among many senior clerics.

For Further Reading

Blumenthal, Uta-Renate. *The Investiture Controversy: Church and Monarchy from the Ninth to the Twelfth Century.* Philadelphia: University of Pennsylvania Press, 1988.
Brown, Peter. *The Rise of Western Christendom: Triumph and Diversity, A.D. 200–1000.* 2nd ed. Malden, MA: Blackwell, 2003.
Morris, Colin. *The Papal Monarchy: The Western Church from 1050–1250.* Oxford: Clarendon, 1989.
Ullmann, Walter. *A Short History of the Papacy in the Middle Ages.* 2nd ed. London: Routledge, 2003.
Whalen, Brett Edward. *The Medieval Papacy.* Basingstoke: Palgrave Macmillan, 2014.

Learning Activities

1) Review key elements of this chapter by answering the following questions:
   - What different aspects of papal primacy, as seen through history, can we distinguish?
   - What were the historical steps in the development of papal power? What was the political context of each of these steps?
   - What was lay investiture? What was simony?
   - What was the Donation of Constantine?
   - Remember four important popes and four emperors/kings between the fifth and the eleventh century.
   - What was the background of the papal state?
   - What theological arguments were used to defend papal power?
   - Through what means did the secular government dominate church life in the medieval period, up until the eleventh century?

2) To probe your understanding of what we have learned about this period, to deepen the understanding of its significance, and to apply it to your present experience, discuss the following questions in small groups:
   - What do you think about the church ruling a territory?
   - Assess the outcome of the investiture controversy: What was the result? Who was the winner?
   - Discuss how the conflict between state and church affected the political development of the West.

CHAPTER 10

The History of a Growing Division
The Churches in East and West Go Separate Ways

THE LAST CHAPTER TOLD the story both of the growing claim of the Roman bishop's primacy over the whole of Christianity and of the moves toward its realization. Unavoidably, this claim led to a confrontation with the only other potential leader of Christianity, the patriarch of Constantinople. Yet, the rift between the churches in the East and in the West goes further back, long before the claims of papal primacy, to the third century. It was rooted in differences of language, philosophical thinking, values, and spiritual emphases.

Against this emerging split, political and ecclesial leaders both East and West sought continuously to unify Christian belief and centralize ecclesial administration. This was the story of the ecumenical councils of the fourth and fifth centuries. However, the solutions found at Ephesus and Chalcedon came at the price of excluding alternative theologies—the non-Chalcedonian christologies of the Nestorians and the Monophysites. Yet, exclusion and suppression never achieved elimination. The alternative interpretations of Christ gradually developed into a variety of churches, among them the Assyrian Church of the East, the Armenians, the Syrian Jacobites, and the Copts. They lingered on *within* the empire, and grew considerably *beyond* the boundaries of the empire, out of reach of the emperor's power to establish unity of faith and eradicate spiritual dissent. These churches are a significant part of the history of the churches in Asia and in Africa. Several attempts to reconcile the Chalcedonian churches with the excluded traditions were in vain, resulting only in the emergence of new conflicts.

This chapter tells the story of a separation *within* Chalcedonian orthodoxy that has remained until today—the separation between the Roman Catholic Church and the Orthodox churches. Since 1054, the two churches have lived in separation, even though their mutual condemnations were annulled in 1965.

The chapter, then, asks the following questions:

- What were the most important factors in this division?
- How did the separation unfold?
- Why was the division so long-lasting?
- How did Eastern Orthodoxy develop in medieval times, that is, after its separation from the West?

We will first follow the major events and periods of this history, focusing on emperors and popes as East and West became alienated from each other. We will then discuss what factors and major theological issues lay behind the division, concluding with a summary of some important developments in the Orthodox tradition in later medieval times.

HISTORICAL STEPS IN THE RIFT BETWEEN EAST AND WEST

The victory of Chalcedon—at the cost of excluding significant parts of the church—had been reached through an alliance of the bishops of Rome and Constantinople. It was not long, though, before the alliance broke down in what was the first schism between Rome and Constantinople, one episode in the long history of their deteriorating relationship. The following section describes seven major periods leading up to the lasting division.

The Acacian Schism, 484–519

After the Council of Chalcedon, Emperor Zeno and Bishop Acacius of Constantinople tried to bring the excommunicated monophysite Christians back into the fold in order to unite the divided church. However, their declaration of unity issued for this purpose, the *Henoticon*, alienated Rome, which insisted that everything necessary had been said already at Chalcedon. To make matters worse, the declaration of unity did not even mention Leo I's *Tome*, which had formed the basis for the Chalcedon compromise. Pope Felix III thus rejected the new formula for reunification and banned Acacius—and was in return banned by him. The Acacian schism was the first official break between the Eastern and Western churches, and it lasted until a new emperor, Justin I, took the throne in 518 and withdrew imperial support for the *Henoticon*, thus ending this particular attempt at reunification.

Imperial pressure on the Chalcedonian declaration remained an issue throughout the sixth century. This also formed the background of the Fifth Ecumenical Council, also known as the Second Council of Constantinople (553). The theologians at the imperial court of Justinian had introduced edicts, the so-called Three Chapters, that condemned several widely recognized theologians of the past—among them most prominently Theodore of Mopsuestia (c. 350–428)—who were seen as having been close to Nestorius. Theodore was clearly dyophysite, that is, Chalcedonian, yet he was regarded as the father of the Antiochenian School, as a teacher of Nestorius, and as an important theologian for the Assyrian Church of the East, which had spread mainly in Persia, outside of the Roman Empire, and which did not recognize the condemnation of Nestorius in Ephesus. With the condemnation of Theodore, the emperor and his theologians hoped to please the miaphysite party and contribute to a reunification of Christianity. The Fifth Ecumenical Council in Constantinople did indeed endorse the Three Chapters and their condemnations.

The Monenergist/Monotheletist Conflict in the Seventh Century

One century later, in 633, history repeated itself when Emperor Heraclius made another attempt to reunite the two major Christian factions in his empire, the Chalcedonians and the Monophysites. He supported Patriarch Sergius of Constantinople, who introduced a formula to reconcile the Monophysites, suggesting that although Christ had two natures, he only had one activity (energy) and one will. These are, respectively, the theories of monenergism and monotheletism (from Greek *thelema*, "will"). It was a well-intended compromise that should have reunited a divided Christianity, and indeed, it was initially welcomed, not least by the Roman Pope Honorius. The compromise also gained the support of many Egyptian Monophysites, who had meanwhile largely developed into the independent, miaphysite Coptic Church (see ch. 7). For some time it seemed as if monotheletism would win the day and remain the valid doctrine, backed by the emperor and the most important patriarchs. Yet, soon enough both Chalcedonians and Monophysites began to criticize the new doctrine as conceding too much ground. The Roman pope Martin I led the opposition in the West and even accepted martyrdom for his conviction—the last pope to die as a martyr, tragically killed by a fellow Christian emperor. No less vocal was the opposition in the Eastern Church, led by the famous theologian Maximus the Confessor (c. 580–662). He met the same end as Pope Martin I.

Eventually, the Sixth Ecumenical Council of Constantinople 680-81, based on a letter from Pope Agatho of Rome, recognized dyotheletism, the doctrine of Christ's two wills—human and divine—and condemned monotheletism. Pope Honorius, who in the early stages of the debate had adopted monotheletism, was posthumously condemned; this is a noteworthy reminder that popes, despite later claims to the contrary, are as fallible as anyone else. The monenergist/monotheletist conflict did not set the churches in the East and in the West against each other, but it deepened the conflict between the bishop of Rome and the combined political-ecclesial government in Constantinople.

The Iconoclastic Controversy of the Eighth and Ninth Centuries

This was also the situation in a new round of conflict that broke out in the eighth century. Again, it was not the two churches against each other, but the church in the West together with important parts of the church in the East jointly opposing an imperial policy—the prohibition of icon veneration.

Throughout the first few centuries of the church, the veneration of icons had strongly expanded. Parallel to this, concerns about idolatry in Christian worship had grown. Did not the second of the Ten Commandments clearly prohibit any physical representation? This critical attitude toward the use of images seemed to be validated by the growth of Islam, which radically rejected images. Emperor Leo III (717–41) was the first emperor to implement so-called iconoclast policies (i.e., destroying religious icons) and to forbid the use of icons in the church. His son Emperor Constantine V (741–75) continued this by convening a church council in Constantinople in 754 to condemn the worship of icons.

Yet, the veneration of icons was deeply rooted in the practice of the church, and resistance to these iconoclast policies arose both in the East and in the West. Both Pope Gregory II (715–31) and Pope Gregory III (731–41) supported the veneration of icons. The capital city, Constantinople, was itself divided between iconoclasts and so-called iconodules, that is, supporters of icon veneration. The use of icons was particularly embedded in the spiritual practice of monastic communities, and many monks secretly kept icons during times of prohibition. Icons were also treasured in many families, with mothers hiding icons and passing on the tradition of veneration to their children. The most vocal theological support for icons came from John of Damascus, who argued that the Old Testament's prohibition of icons had been valid only until Christ. Icons are a window to God, he said, a mystical access to His glory, illuminating the ultimately unknowable God. Since God had become man, we should not object to representing him in images. The debate received further doctrinal clarification with John's differentiation of *veneration* (*dulia* or *proskynesis*) of icons, which was allowed, and *worship* (*latreia*), which belonged only to God.

It was only during the rule of Empress Irene (780–802) that the church, through the Seventh Ecumenical Council at Nicaea in 787, officially recognized the veneration of icons in worship. Yet, the story did not end there—the struggle lasted another half a century, as another iconoclast ruler, Emperor Leo V, prohibited the use of icons, and Theodore, the abbot of the monastery of Stoudios, led the defense of icons. The final iconodule victory eventually came with Empress Theodora, who ordered a restoration of the icons in 843. Since then, the first Sunday of Lent has been one of the most important festive days of the Eastern Church, commemorating this "triumph of orthodoxy."

Originally, iconoclasm was not a major theological problem between East and West—it was much more an issue in the Eastern Church, with iconoclast Byzantine emperors against iconodule monks. However, the conflict eventually affected East-West relations by increasing the animosity between the Byzantine emperors and the Roman popes.

The Photian Schism of 867

The Photian schism was a mutual excommunication by Patriarch Photios of Constantinople and Pope Nicholas I of Rome, a result of the two leaders' competing power claims over missionary endeavors in central and eastern Europe. The immediate background was Rome's criticism of Photios' deposing of the previous patriarch, Ignatios, and Photios' criticism of Rome's tampering with the wording of the Nicene Creed (see below).

The schism did not last long. Pope Nicholas I soon died and Rome came under political pressure from advancing Islamic forces in southern Italy; both factors rendered the division between Rome and Constantinople irrelevant. However, the schism gave a taste of what was to come.

The Schism of 1054

The schism of 1054, which lasted formally until 1965, came as a result of what appears today to be a minor theological issue—the Western church's introduction of unleavened bread in the Eucharist. At that time, Rome had increasingly adopted the doctrine of transubstantiation, the theory that Jesus Christ was bodily present in the bread and wine of the Eucharist. It was thus important to use a kind of bread that did not crumble, because crumbs falling to the ground would dishonor the body of Christ. Pope Leo IX sent Cardinal Humbert, a representative of the Cluniac reform movement, to Constantinople to deal with the dispute. However, Humbert was not interested in reconciliation. He came from the southern Italian region of Sicily, an area where the Roman and Orthodox churches lived in constant tension, and he had been deeply alienated by how the Byzantine emperor exercised his authority over the church. He did not hide his contempt for the Eastern tradition and rudely attacked the patriarch of Constantinople, a communicative strategy clearly at odds with reconciliation. The visit of Humbert culminated in his entry into the Hagia Sophia, where worship was in full swing; he placed the already-prepared papal declaration, excommunicating Patriarch Michael Cerularius, on the altar table and walked out. The reverse excommunication of the pope, by the Constantinopolitan patriarch, naturally followed.

No one would have thought this mutual excommunication could last nine hundred years. But two important reasons caused it to be so long-lasting: first, it was an expression of an increasingly deep mutual alienation; second, subsequent events further exacerbated the animosity.

On the Primacy of the Roman Pontiff

The mutual excommunication of Pope Leo IX and Patriarch Michael Cerularius, in 1054, was the last straw in the break between the Eastern and the Western church. The pope's letter to the patriarch, portions of which have been reproduced below, was one of the events leading to this excommunication. It states strongly the pope's position on his primacy. Whether the letter was ever sent is still a question of debate among scholars. Some suggest that another, slightly softer letter, *Scripta tuae* (from January 1054), was instead dispatched.

> Chap. 5 ... *You are said to have condemned publicly in a strange presumption and incredible boldness the Apostolic and Latin Church, neither heard nor refuted, for the reason chiefly that it dared to celebrate the commemoration*

of the passion of the Lord from the Azymes [i.e., unleavened bread]. Behold your incautious reprehension, behold your evil boasting, when "you put your mouth into heaven. When your tongue passing on to the earth" [Ps. 72:9], by human arguments and conjectures attempts to uproot and overturn the ancient faith....

Chap. 7 ... The holy Church built upon a rock, that is Christ, and upon Peter or Cephas, the son of John who first was called Simon, because by the gates of Hell, that is, by the disputations of heretics which lead the vain to destruction, it would never be overcome; thus Truth itself promises, through whom are true, whatsoever things are true: "The gates of hell will not prevail against it" [Matt 16: 18]. The same Son declares that He obtained the effect of this promise from the Father by prayers, by saying to Peter: "Simon, behold Satan etc." [Luke 22:31]. Therefore, will there be anyone so foolish as to dare to regard His prayer as in anyway vain whose being willing is being able? By the See of the chief of the Apostles, namely by the Roman Church, through the same Peter, as well as through his successors, have not the comments of all the heretics been disapproved, rejected, and overcome, and the hearts of the brethren in the faith of Peter which so far neither has failed, nor up to the end will fail, been strengthened?

Chap. 11. By passing a preceding judgment on the great See, concerning which it is not permitted any man to pass judgment, you have received anathema from all the Fathers of all the venerable Councils....

Chap. 32 ... As the hinge while remaining immovable opens and closes the door, so Peter and his successors have free judgment over all the Church, since no one should remove their status because "the highest See is judged by no one."

Source: Leo IX, Epistle *In terra pax hominibus* to Michael Cerularius and to Leo of Achrida, September 2, 1053, in Denzinger, *Sources of Catholic Dogma*, 142–43.

The Crusades and the Breakdown of Relations between East and West

In fact, even after the schism there was a limited coexistence between the Roman Catholic and the Eastern Orthodox churches. Large numbers of Orthodox Christians continued to live under Roman rule and were partly allowed to maintain their Orthodox rite and liturgy. The irretrievable breakdown in East-West relations came only with the Crusades.

The First Crusade in 1099 led to the conquest of Jerusalem and Antioch (see more on this in ch. 12). When the Crusaders, led by a representative of the pope in Rome, appointed Latin patriarchs for the existing patriarchies of Antioch and Jerusalem, they directly ignored the current titular patriarchs, who had been waiting in Constantinople. Worse affronts were to come: during the Fourth Crusade in 1203-4, the Crusaders conquered Constantinople and similarly appointed a Latin patriarch there, thus reestablishing church unity by means of military power and subjugation. Although this episode lasted only until 1261, when the Byzantine army recaptured Constantinople, it left a sense of deep violation among Orthodox Christians for centuries to come. The Byzantine Empire remained irreparably weakened until its eventual fall in 1453.

Failed Reunification

The following centuries brought several attempts at overcoming the division. The most important, the Council of Ferrara/Florence, happened in 1438-39, when growing political and military pressure from the Turkish Ottomans caused the Byzantine emperor and the leaders of the Orthodox Church to seek a reunion with Western Christianity in order to jointly repel the Turkish threat. The pope, for his part, was equally weakened due to the challenge arising from conciliarism (see ch. 12). He was interested in ending the schism in order to strengthen his own position, and he seemed willing to enter into an open discussion of the contentious issues, so a council was held.

Yet, the short-lived union brought by the Council of Ferrara/Florence was to no avail. It had come about by various factors, none of them giving the union any durability. First, the council was held on Roman turf, favoring the hosts; second, the leading figures of the Orthodox party had turned to the Roman side, partly attracted by being consecrated as Roman cardinals, partly impressed by the humanist spirit of Florence; third, the pope regained some strength when the conciliar movement elected a counter-pope, thus causing a new schism and triggering a public backlash against the equally schism-prone conciliar party.

The eventual lack of significant concessions from the Western side made it impossible for Byzantine Christians back home to accept the union. Furthermore, the much-beleaguered Byzantine Church was hardly able to speak on behalf of the whole of Orthodox Christianity, as its center of gravity had moved northward. A few years later, the long history of the Christian Byzantine Empire came to an end. Meanwhile, Western Christianity was moving toward the division of the Reformation, and this new rift pushed any reunification with Orthodox Christianity into the background.

	Event	Opponents	Issues at stake
Step 1 5th / 6th century	Acacian schism	Pope of Rome against emperor and Patriarch of Constantinople	Suggested formula of reunion with Monophysites, the *Henoticon*
Step 2 7th century	Monenergist and monotheletist controversy	Pope of Rome against emperor and Patriarch of Constantinople	Suggested formula of reunion with Monophysites: Had Christ one (divine) will and energy or at the same time a divine and human will?
Step 3 8th century	Iconoclastic controversy	Western church and parts of the Eastern church against emperors of Constantinople	Should the veneration of icons be allowed?
Step 4 9th century	Photian schism	Pope of Rome against Patriarch of Constantinople	Competition in the missionary field and conflict about changes of the creed (*filioque* clause) in the Western church
Step 5 11th century	Great schism	Pope of Rome against Patriarch of Constantinople	Use of unleavened bread in the Eucharist and on-going animosity due to the *filioque*
Step 6 13th century	Crusaders' conquest of Constantinople	Western military powers against church and society of Constantinople	Subjugation of Eastern church and church unity through military means
Step 7 15th century	Failed reunion of Ferrara / Florence	Joint Western political and religious leaders against the Byzantine church led by a weakened emperor	Many contentious issues, most importantly the *filioque* clause and the power of the papacy

Fig. 10.1: Seven steps in the conflict between Roman Catholicism and Eastern Orthodoxy

FACTORS IN THE RIFT BETWEEN THE CHURCHES IN THE EAST AND IN THE WEST

Theologically, there was never any fundamental division between the Roman Catholic and Orthodox churches. Instead, different theological cultures as well as shifts in the broader political configuration both contributed to a growing gap between the two churches.

Political Factors

Most important among the political shifts was the emergence of new alliances. The failure of the emperor of Constantinople to protect the Western part of the empire from the Germanic invasions prompted Rome to seek political support elsewhere, entering into a political alliance with the Frankish kings and thus moving away from Constantinople. Frankish rule eventually replaced the previous Roman Empire, which had been centered in Constantinople. The separation from Constantinople and the establishment of a new political alliance in the West affected ecclesial relations. This led to growing competition, with the pope (the highest authority in the West) on one side and the Byzantine emperor and the patriarch of Constantinople on the other. The competition could be felt both in theological disputes and in the rivalry for political and ecclesial influence, for example, in central and eastern Europe.

Theological Factors

Theological differences did play a role, but, often, they became divisive only due to political and ecclesial factors.

Theological developments increasingly revealed different theological cultures (see ch. 7), even though core concerns were similar. For both churches, the crucial question was how people are saved, yet their respective answers used different soteriological frameworks. The church in the East put more emphasis on metaphysical and ontological categories. It saw redemption as a process in which humans, by means of a pedagogical progression, a spiritual learning process, were taken up into the divine, culminating in *theosis*, a process of divinization and of growing community in the fellowship of the Holy Trinity. This is not to be mistaken for humans (ontologically) becoming God but should be understood simply as human participation in the divine nature (2 Pet 1:4). In contrast, the Western theological tradition emphasized legal categories—how to reconcile the destroyed relationship between God and man and how to offer necessary satisfaction for humanity's sin. It thus emphasized the cross and the substitutionary death of Christ.

The continuing christological discussions after the Council of Chalcedon, as well as the various attempts at finding a solution, caused constant conflict. With the Nestorian and the Monophysite parties out, the remaining orthodox party, headed by Rome and Constantinople, was not fundamentally divided. However, the ongoing division in the church prompted Chalcedonian (i.e., "orthodox") Christians to suggest occasional compromises with the non-Chalcedonians. But such suggestions often resulted only in antagonizing factions of the Chalcedonians' own party.

A major conflict was the Trinitarian debate about the Western church's addition of the word *Filioque* ("and from the Son") into the article on the Holy Spirit in the Nicene Creed. The added word expressed the belief that the Spirit proceeded from the Father *and* the Son (against the original wording that saw the Spirit as proceeding only from the Father). The wording about the origin of the Spirit (i.e., "from the Father *and* the Son") was intended to emphasize Christ's equality with the Father. Whether this was meant simply as a single origin, that is, that the Spirit proceeded *through* Christ, or in fact pointed to a double origin, remained a subject of much debate. The changed wording of the creed was first introduced in Spain in 589, supposedly to counter any remaining Arian beliefs that denied Christ's full divinity. It thus responded to a specific regional issue. It was later supported by Charlemagne, gradually became common practice in the West, was adopted by various popes and, eventually, was officially recognized by the Roman Catholic Church in 1014 as part of the Nicene Creed. Theologically, the increased emphasis on Christ's divinity was not a problem for the church in the East. The crucial point of conflict around the *Filioque* was instead one of power—illegitimate papal interference in a conciliar decision, that is, adding something to a creed without the consent of an ecumenical council. The pope thus implied that his authority was above that of such a council.

Ecclesial, Liturgical, and Cultural Factors

The churches in East and West moved apart not only politically and theologically but also in their church polity and in some liturgical and ecclesial practices. Also, the cultural differences between East and West further deepened when the Roman Church expanded among the Germanic peoples of northern Europe.

Church polity: While the church in the West took a path of increasing competition with secular power, the Eastern Orthodox Church readily subordinated the sacral to the secular and accepted political rulers' authority over church matters. This so-called *caesaro-papist* tradition alienated Roman Catholics, who struggled for independence from secular authority. This different church polity remains visible even today, with Eastern Orthodox churches often lacking critical distance and submitting readily to monarchic or authoritarian governments. The emergence in Eastern Orthodoxy of autocephalous churches, that is, independent churches with a patriarch or other primate for each autonomous church, exacerbated the strong alliance between church and throne. Furthermore, leaders of autonomous national churches naturally defended the national interests of their respective countries. In contrast, Roman Catholicism gradually increased the central power of the Roman bishop and developed as a transnational institution. While competing national, regional, or territorial interests were indeed effective underneath the surface of institutional unity in the West, the church as a whole took an international direction. When nationalist movements emerged in later times—in the nineteenth century, as a late fruit of Enlightenment—they stood in conflict with the internationalism of Roman Catholicism.

Eucharist: While the medieval Catholic Church tried to clarify how the change of the eucharistic bread and wine into the body and blood of Jesus Christ was possible, the Orthodox Church refrained from any such speculation about how such a change happens, instead emphasizing the mysterious character of the Eucharist. This was less a theological difference than a difference in theological and philosophical culture.

Icons: Although originally the iconoclast controversy of the eighth and ninth centuries did not divide Eastern and Western Christianity, the two sides gradually developed different iconographies and different understandings of the use of icons in worship. Visual representation in the Catholic Church is naturalistic and often three-dimensional, and its purpose is to educate believers or simply to decorate church buildings. In times of widespread illiteracy, visual representation served as a Bible of the poor (Latin: *Biblia pauperum*). In contrast, icons in the Orthodox tradition reflect the mysterious character of divine events: they represent persons in glorified, transfigured, and grace-filled form, avoiding the naturalism of Catholic iconography. Orthodox icons do not serve educational purposes but are an integral part of Orthodox spirituality and are intended to lead believers to the glory of God.

Different liturgical and ecclesial cultures: A rather minor area of divergence was the development of the priesthood. From early on, the Western church insisted that higher clergy should be celibate. By the eleventh century, compulsory celibacy of all priests had become a major policy of the Roman Catholic Church (see ch. 9). In contrast, Eastern Orthodoxy maintained marriage as option for ordinary clergy, though not for bishops. A growing alienation between the different traditions was also visible in different liturgical practices—for example, the use of leavened (Orthodox) or unleavened (Catholic) bread in the Eucharist, and the Orthodox Church's distribution of the bread and wine to the faithful in contrast to the Catholic Church's distribution of only the bread. Reserving the wine for the clergy was a sign of the increased veneration of the eucharistic elements in the Roman tradition.

THE EASTERN CHURCH AFTER 1054 UNTIL THE POLITICAL END OF CONSTANTINOPLE

From the eleventh century until the fall of Constantinople in the fifteenth century, two important developments—one political and the other theological—shaped Orthodox Christianity.

Political Developments: Orthodoxy Moving North

During the ninth century, Vikings (or Norsemen, later called Russians) from the north of Europe had begun to migrate south through the vast lands of present-day Russia to the lands north of the Black Sea, present-day Ukraine. Their advance had put political and military pressure on the Byzantine Empire. Constantinople responded by initiating religious contacts, a plan proposed by Patriarch Photios and aimed at taming the invaders. In 988, these mission efforts, coupled with growing economic ties and gradual integration of the invading culture into the Greek and Bulgarian cultures, led the Russian prince Vladimir of Kiev to be converted to Christianity and to subsequently adopt elements of Byzantine culture. This year is usually regarded as the beginning of Russian Orthodox Christianity. In the thirteenth century, when Kiev came under attack from the westward-advancing Mongols, the center of Christianity in the land of Russia moved to Novgorod and from there to Moscow.

Parallel to this extension of Orthodox Christianity toward the north, political and military pressure—from Islamic rulers, from Western crusading armies, and from continuing territorial encroachment by outside forces—weakened the Byzantine emperor for good. Although it regained power over the imperial throne in 1261, the empire's political unity was never fully restored. In the absence of central Byzantine power, territorial leaders gained independence from the empire and established their own states with largely independent autocephalous national churches. Initially, these churches would still accept the authority of and have their leader appointed by the Orthodox patriarch in Constantinople. However, the continuous erosion of Byzantine power, a broad opposition to the Ferrara/Florence reunion agreement accepted by the politically weakened Constantinople, and ultimately the fall of Constantinople in 1453 undermined the authority of the patriarch of Constantinople.

After the end of the Byzantine Empire, Moscow was ready to step into the vacuum and gradually claim leadership over Orthodoxy. Half a century later, around 1510, the term *Third Rome* was coined to give expression to

Moscow's leadership.[1] A logical consequence of this process came in 1547: the then-political ruler of Moscow, Grand Prince Ivan IV (known as "the Terrible") would be crowned as Tsar (a word derived from the name Caesar), thus inheriting the Roman and Carolingian (Frankish) imperial traditions.

Moscow as the Third Rome

The idea of a third Rome emerged in the middle of the fifteenth century and was first claimed by Novgorod in 1490, where the term *Third Rome* was used for the first time. The idea of Moscow as the third Rome became more widespread from the early sixteenth century on. It first appeared in a letter from the monk Filofei to the Russian Grand Prince Vassilij and Ivan the Terrible, an extract of which is given below. From the late seventeenth century on, the Russian church had to give up this idea; in a 1667 council of the Russian Church in Moscow it submitted theologically and canonically to the Greek Church. However, the idea of inheriting a long European tradition—and realizing it as the third Rome, on a higher level than the two previous ones—still smolders in the imagination of some politicians.

> *I would like to say a few words about the existing Orthodox empire of our most illustrious, exalted ruler. He is the only emperor on all the earth over the Christians, the governor of the holy, divine throne of the holy, ecumenical, apostolic church which in place of the churches of Rome and Constantinople is in the city of Moscow, protected by God, in the holy and glorious Uspenskij Church of the most pure Mother of God. It alone shines over all the earth more radiantly than the sun. For know well, those who love Christ and those who love God, that all Christian empires will perish and give way to the one kingdom of our ruler, in accord with the books of the prophet, which is the Russian empire. For two Romes have fallen, but the third stands, and there will never be a fourth.*

Source: van den Bercken, *Holy Russia and Christian Europe*, 146.

---

1. In a letter by the monk Filofei to the Grand Prince of Moscow Vasilij III; see van den Bercken, *Holy Russia and Christian Europe*, 146. Rather de-emphasizing the theory of Moscow as Third Rome and critical of its importance is Meyendorff, "Was There Ever a Third Rome?," in *Rome, Constantinople, Moscow*, 131–48.

Theological Developments: Monasticism and Hesychasm

While theology in the West further developed in more scholastic and legal ways—for example, using philosophical categories to interpret the change of bread and wine into the body and blood of Jesus Christ, or using legal categories to explain the death of Christ as atonement for original sin—Orthodox theology continued to develop in a more mystical direction that refrained from such terminological precision and that stressed the mysterious character of salvific events. Most important theologians of the Orthodox tradition came from the monastic tradition, where they were deeply immersed in the monasteries' spiritual life. Monasticism did play a crucial role in the West, but for the Orthodox church it was comparatively more important in shaping theology, spirituality, and church life.

Orthodox theology drew from the mystical tradition of early Christianity, which had found expression in the writings of Dionysius the Areopagite (see chs. 11 and 13). Famous theologians of the Orthodox tradition were Maximus the Confessor (c. 580–662), a monk deeply influenced by Dionysius; John Climacus (or John of the Ladder), in the seventh century, from St. Catherine's Monastery in the Sinai; John of Damascus (c. 675–749), who contributed important theological arguments in the iconoclastic controversy; Symeon the New Theologian (949–1022), whose emphasis (in writing and preaching) on personal spiritual experience brought him into open conflict with church authorities; and Gregory Palamas (1296–1359), who came from Mount Athos, the most important center of monastic spirituality in Eastern Orthodoxy.

Gregory became known as an important defender of *hesychasm* (from Greek *hesychazō*, "to keep still"), a tradition based on ideas he had received from the monastic community of Mount Athos and theologians like John Climacus and Symeon the New Theologian. Hesychasm was a contemplative movement within Eastern Orthodoxy based on psychophysical techniques, including silent prayer, breath control, specific physical postures, and the repetitive recitation of the "Jesus Prayer": "Lord Jesus Christ, Son of God, have mercy on me, a sinner." The goal of these spiritual exercises was to rid the mind of all distracting thoughts and to induce a vision of divine light similar to the one that enveloped Jesus on the Mount of Transfiguration, Mount Tabor.[2] Hence, hesychast practitioners were also called Taborites.

The growth of the hesychast movement sparked a major controversy in late medieval Orthodox Christianity. Barlaam, an Orthodox monk from Calabria, criticized hesychast techniques because he denied the possibility

---

2. Krausmüller, "Rise of Hesychasm," 101–4.

of access to the glory of God through mystical practices. He insisted that God was essentially unknowable and that the Holy Spirit was part of God's essence or innermost being. In response to Barlaam's accusation of heresy, Gregory defended the hesychast movement by distinguishing the transcendent and unknowable God from the divine energies, which the mystic seeker can access. The controversy was decided in favor of hesychasm, and the movement continued to influence Orthodox Christianity in Russia and elsewhere.

Orthodox Christianity maintained its distinctive path throughout the centuries and through political ups and downs, keeping its connectedness to the patristic era and continuing a tradition where mysticism and theology, that is, personal experience of the divine and the teaching of the church, were deeply entangled. Mysticism was regarded as "the perfecting and crown of all theology: as theology *par excellence*."[3]

For Further Reading

Chadwick, Henry. *The Making of a Rift in the Church: From Apostolic Times until the Council of Florence*. Oxford: Oxford University Press, 2003.
Hussey, Joan Mervyn. *The Orthodox Church in the Byzantine Empire*. Oxford: Oxford University Press, 2010.
Krausmüller, Dirk. "The Rise of Hesychasm." In *The Cambridge History of Christianity*, vol. 5, *Eastern Christianity*, edited by Michael Angold, 101–26. Cambridge: Cambridge University Press, 2008.
Louth, Andrew. *Greek East and Latin West: The Church, AD 681–1071*. Crestwood, NY: St. Vladimir's Seminary Press, 2007.
Meyendorff, John. *Byzantine Theology: Historical Trends and Doctrinal Themes*. New York: Fordham University Press, 1979.
———. *Rome, Constantinople, Moscow: Historical and Theological Studies*. Crestwood, NY: St. Vladimir's Seminary Press, 1996.
Runciman, Stephen. *The Byzantine Theocracy*. Cambridge: Cambridge University Press, 1977.

Learning Activities

1) Review key elements of this chapter by answering the following questions:
    - What were the core differences between the Roman Catholic Church and the Orthodox Churches?
    - What is their relationship today?

---

3. Lossky, *Mystical Theology*, 9.

- o What was the iconoclastic debate about?
- o What was the *Filioque* debate about?
- o Name five important theologians of the Orthodox Church in the medieval time.

2) To probe your understanding of what we have learned about this period, to deepen the understanding of its significance, and to apply it to your present experience, discuss the following questions:

- o Discuss the schism between the Eastern and the Western Church. Was it "necessary"?
- o What are the differences in visual representation in the Catholic and in the Orthodox tradition? What do you think about visual representation of the divine?
- o What was the crucial difference in the political theologies of Eastern Orthodoxy and Roman Catholicism? Recall recent political developments where different political theologies have been visible.
- o What was the hesychast controversy about? What basic theological convictions clashed in this controversy?

Chapter 11

The History of "the Other Church"
Revivals, Reform, and Alternative Faith Expressions in Medieval Times

MEDIEVAL CHRISTIANITY IS OFTEN seen as a dull period when the church was subject to the power of authoritarian rulers, both ecclesial and political. However, the story of a church driven by political forces and by the growing power of ecclesial leaders, as told particularly in chapter 9, is only one part of the whole, as this chapter will show. Here we read about another kind of church: the church as a movement, an alternative community. For lack of a better term, we call it simply "the other church." This other church stands not in exclusive opposition to the powerful church. Rather, the Christian movement has, since the time of Jesus, been a movement that oscillates between emancipation and hegemony, between empowerment of the disempowered and the power of the establishment, or, as the title of this book suggests, between pilgrims and popes.[1] Yet, the strength of this movement was that these two aspects remained related to each other: on the one hand, the powerful church could never completely escape its own beginnings, the call that those in power shall be humbled and the oppressed shall find liberation; on the other, the church as an emancipatory movement would remain mostly loyal to at least the idea of the one catholic church.

In other words, this alternative Christian faith movement consists, now as then, of Christians who move beyond the given boundaries of church life

---

1. See similarly the expression "Church of Power and Church of Piety," in Stark, *God's Battalions*, 102.

and critically accompany the institutionally established church. It comprises different theological and spiritual traditions, mostly radical ones. It partly rejects the institutional church, partly stands in contrast or opposition to it, and partly remains subject to it while maintaining its differences. The alternative church's relationship to the established church in medieval times should thus not be seen in black-and-white terms, because Christians often had multiple affiliations. They could equally participate in the church's standard faith practices and show loyalty to the institutional hierarchy while at the same time supporting more radical forms of devotion. Various movements and alternative forms of Christianity appeared spontaneously: as the enthusiastic reaction of a crowd to a charismatic preacher, or sometimes as the conversion of a charismatic individual who then attracted followers. Some of these movements began to spread beyond the initial enthusiasm, turned into an itinerant movement, occasionally survived, and, if so, often went through a process of institutionalization themselves.

Was this other church "the church of the people" or the church of a spiritual elite? Again this would be an oversimplification of the complex realities of people's beliefs, for ordinary people actively participated both in the established church—sharing in the ambivalences of power, partly supporting and partly objecting—and in alternative faith movements. The people's spiritual lives were subject to the same dialectic of institutionalization and protest as was Christianity overall.

The story of this alternative Christian faith movement shows something of the tremendous vitality of medieval Christianity. During the early history of Christianity, when the Christian community still stood outside and in critical opposition to the social mainstream, Christianity was itself mainly an alternative social movement. Christians did not turn their criticism against the church but were absorbed by establishing congregational life and engaging in mission. Later, as Christianity became the official religion of the state and a core pillar of society, monastic Christianity emerged as the most important alternative faith practice. The monastic movement also remained the main expression of the "other church" during early medieval times. However, from the eleventh century on, a multitude of new faith practices and theological ideas began to appear. Reform and protest movements emerged in parallel to the growing power of the church and in criticism of a church that had adapted too much to the patterns of the world. In addition, the late eleventh century (and after) brought broader Christian revivals that triggered a variety of new faith expressions.

For the medieval period, we can observe three distinct paths of historical development. Either alternative Christian faith movements were, after a period of critical opposition, reabsorbed into the church, thus becoming part of the establishment and assuming status, wealth, and power; or, they became more radical and more firm in their rejection of what they regarded as a corrupt institutional church and therefore were condemned by the established church as heretical counter-churches. Finally, some groups were successful in this difficult balancing act and continued to coexist in loyalty and critical opposition to the establishment. This was partly the case with the monastic reform and mendicant movements. Yet even then, groups maintaining such independence could turn into an alternative tool of church government and an alternative power source for the papacy, outside the diocesan network.

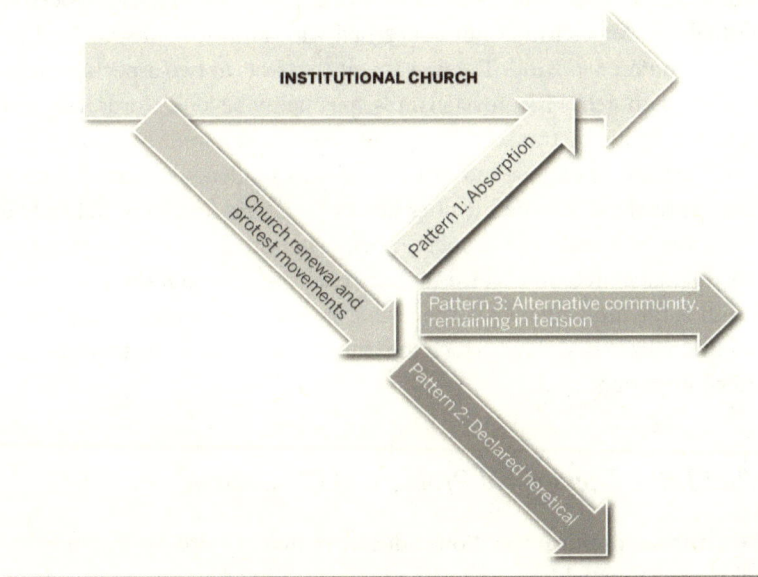

Fig. 11.1: *The basic pattern of development of the other church in medieval Catholicism*

This chapter, then, tells the stories of medieval reform, of protest movements and of faith communities among the socially disempowered: mystics and monks, militants and mendicants, and reformers and revivalists. The chapter addresses the following questions:

- What were distinctive forms and expressions of alternative Christian faith movements?
- What theologies did these alternative Christian groups promote, and what theological challenges did they encounter?

- How did the relationship between the institutionally established church and alternative Christian communities develop?

CHRISTIAN MYSTICISM

Mysticism has always been one aspect of Christianity and, as such, does not belong to only one period. However, it was during the medieval period that some of the most famous Christian mystics emerged and that Christian mysticism was strongly influenced by Neo-Platonism.

Christian mysticism, like mysticism in general, is a tradition that regards the experience of immediacy with God as the central goal of a person's spiritual life. Mysticism is not concerned with knowledge *about* God but longs for union *with* God. The movement contrasts in two aspects with the established church: First, mysticism is spirituality beyond words, connecting to the divine by transcending mere verbal expression. As such, mysticism is critical of dogma and of Christianity's tendency to codify faith in exact expressions of belief. It does accept dogmatic formulas, but only as expressions of a quest of the soul. Priority is given to the movement of the soul; dogmatic precision is of secondary relevance. Second, since the center of faith is the individual soul, the visible church community—even less an institutionalized body, into which the church had increasingly turned—is of limited importance.

What Is the Theological Problem of Christian Mysticism?

The Christian mystical tradition is deeply rooted in Platonist tradition and philosophy, from which it inherits a basic problem. Underlying the idea of immediacy with God is the conviction of man's essentially spiritual nature: the human soul is essentially related to God. Having a soul means being able to participate in the realm of eternal truth, the realm of God; some early theologians such as Origen, who was strongly influenced by Plato, saw the soul—as did Plato himself—as preexistent and immortal.

In contrast, some theologians were and are fundamentally critical of the idea of the soul's kinship with the divine and, as a consequence, they are critical of Christian mysticism.[2] They stress that human beings are part of the created world and thus fundamentally separated from God. The gap between God and the world has been overcome only in Christ; it cannot be overcome by human spiritual practice. Others maintain that the mystical

---

2. See as an example the statement quoted in Fremantle, *Protestant Mystics*, vii.

union with God can be understood as a union mediated through Christ, a union through the Word, a contemplation of the *logos*. As such, Christian mysticism does not require the questionable assumption of the soul's kinship with the divine. It can be based simply on the possibility of relating to the divine through Christ. Something of this dichotomy can be seen in the Hesychast controversy between Gregory Palamas and Barlaam (see ch. 10). It became more of an argument in the later Protestant tradition and it partly explains why mysticism has been less developed within Protestant Christianity. Within modern-day Protestantism the different views reappear in the dichotomy between Evangelical and Pentecostal-charismatic Christians.

The Historical Development of Christian Mysticism

The first important Christian mystic was Dionysius the Areopagite (whom we will meet again in ch. 13), living around 500, who merged the Neo-Platonist philosophy of the late ancient world with oriental Christianity. Critics regard his mysticism as barely more Christian than pagan and Neo-Platonist, as leading Christian faith to a pantheistic confluence of the soul and the divine. Some later mystics, including Hugo of St. Victor (1097-1141), revived the mysticism of Dionysius Areopagita; Bonaventura (1221-74), a scholastic theologian, was similarly influenced by the Areopagite. Later important mystics are Meister Eckhart (c. 1260-1327) and John Tauler (c. 1300-1361). With mysticism developing mainly outside the institutional framework, many female theologians played an important role, among them Hildegard of Bingen (1098-1179), Mechthild of Magdeburg (c. 1210-c. 1285), Birgitta of Sweden (1303-72), Julian of Norwich (1342-after 1416), Catherine of Siena (1347-80), and others.

MONASTIC REFORM MOVEMENTS: THE EMERGENCE OF NEW MONASTIC ORDERS

Toward the end of the early Christian period and during the whole medieval time, monasteries were part of the "other church." They preserved an ascetic Christian lifestyle and contributed in many ways to society: as centers for education and learning, as diaconical and welfare centers, and as places of refuge and hospitality. More importantly, they remained symbols of an ideal Christian existence. They stood in contrast to secular society and to the established church, which often seemed to have lost the original vision of Christian life and renewal. Toward the end of the eleventh century, as the established church grew in political power, an increasing number of new monastic orders emerged. This process of growth stood in contrast to the growing power of the church, recalling the growth of the ascetic movement in the fourth century, when Christianity became officially permitted. Some of these communities were double monasteries, with one section each for men and for women—though the genders were strictly separated—similar to the earliest Christian monasticism. Some new monastic orders, though, built special convents for women.

Cluny

The earliest of these new orders, founded in 910, was Cluny (see ch. 9). Although the monks of Cluny followed the Benedictine rule, they differed from the Benedictines in two important respects. First, they did not operate as self-sufficient units who provided for their needs by manual labor. Rather, they regarded continuous prayer and worship as their main labor, their contribution to the church and the world. Second, they established a network of Cluniac monasteries that were not independent but were accountable to the abbot of Cluny. The heads of these daughter houses (or priories) met once a year with the abbot of Cluny to deal with matters that had arisen. The whole network of mother and daughter houses can thus be seen as one large community, which, after around two hundred years, included more than a thousand centers. The strength of the Cluniac movement led even some formerly independent Benedictine monasteries to join the community. Cluny, like most other orders, attracted abundant donations that gradually increased the wealth of the monastery, bringing it into conflict with its founding purpose. This growing affluence became a common reason for groups, at Cluny and elsewhere, to move away from the original order.

Cistercians

That is how the Order of the Cistercians was established. In 1098, a group of monks left their Benedictine monastery to set up a new community at Citeaux (Latin: *Cistercium*), Burgundy. They were disappointed with the course that the Cluny movement had taken—they saw it as abandoning the original Benedictine rule—and they wanted to return to a self-sustaining monastic life, combining manual labor with prayer. In 1118, the order was recognized as an independent religious order separate from the Benedictines.

The Cistercians distinguished themselves by strict asceticism and a simple lifestyle that stood in contrast to the growing wealth of Cluny. Their spiritual life was characterized by mysticism, visionary-ecstatic elements, and a strong veneration of the Virgin Mary; the wave of spiritual revival triggered by this new order caused it to spread quickly.

The most important Cistercian monastery was founded at Clairvaux in 1115. It became famous for its first abbot, Bernard of Clairvaux (1090–1153), whom some regard as the most influential person in twelfth-century Europe, as much for his political as for his theological and spiritual contributions. Through him the order of the Cistercians turned into one of the most important religious orders, with a role similar to that of Cluny a century earlier. Bernard's spiritual teaching, which contained charismatic elements such as the gift of tears—modern Pentecostals might call it "the spirit of weeping"—spread beyond the Cistercian order and inspired many Christians. His role in supporting the pope's call for the Second Crusade (see ch. 12) shows how the concerns of alternative Christianity and the institutional church could be mutually reinforcing.

Carthusians

In the same period (the end of the eleventh century), Saint Bruno of Cologne, a remarkable scholar of his time, felt called by God to withdraw from the world and offer his life to prayer and meditation. Together with some followers he established a communal hermitage in a remote mountain valley of the French Alps, La Chartreuse (hence the name). The Order of Carthusians did not follow the Benedictine rule but set a new rule that combined communal monasticism with solitary devotion. They were a community of hermits who spent most of the day in solitude—in their own cells in strict silence. Compared to other religious orders, the Carthusians were stricter and more withdrawn, allowing less contact with the outside. They served simply by prayer, which they undertook on behalf of the church and the world.

Canonical Reform

Some new religious orders may be seen as revival within the existing church structure. This was the case with the canonical reform movement, which aimed at reviving the communal togetherness of the "canon"—the clergy of a cathedral or the community of priests of a larger church—under stricter rules. It introduced a more monastic lifestyle while maintaining the pastoral responsibility of the clergy. The most famous of these canonical reform orders were the Canons Regular of St. Augustine (not to be confused with the Order of St. Augustine) and the Order of Premonstratensians, founded in 1120 in Prémontré, France.

Lay Communities

The ideal of deeper devotion, a faith commitment beyond the ordinary, found further expression in a variety of religious guilds or confraternities of laypeople. In modern language, such groups would simply be called para-church fellowships, gatherings of people with a deeper Christian commitment. These communities were the result of several waves of revivals throughout the high and late medieval period. They contributed to charity—feeding the hungry, caring for the poor and the sick, and (a very important communal service) burying the dead.

A special expression of such lay confraternities was the order of knights, who merged their knightly ideals and practices with ascetic Christian and communitarian life. Their commitments included fighting against infidels, protecting pilgrims going to the Holy Land, and caring for the sick. For this purpose they acquired property and built fortifications in Palestine—for instance, the citadel at Acre in northern Israel. The story of these knights forms part of the story of the Crusades (see ch. 12). The knight orders served directly under the pope, without any other intervening authority. The three most famous groups were the Order of Hospitallers, also called the order of Saint John of Jerusalem and nowadays known as the Maltesian Order; the Order of Knights Templar, founded in 1119 and dissolved in 1312 with much of its property given to the Order of Hospitallers, after playing a crucial role in financial transactions for the Crusaders;[3] and the Teutonic Knights, founded at the end of the twelfth century. These orders continue in various forms today—as part of the "other church," as charities, or sometimes as secretive (and often militant and crusading) arms of the church, similar to groups that emerged in later times like the Catholic lay order Opus Dei.

MENDICANT ORDERS

Toward the end of the twelfth century, a new form of religious order appeared: fraternities (or fellowships) of begging monks. They were inspired to realize a radical form of discipleship by giving away all their property and sharing in Jesus' poverty. They were not unlike other monks and hermits,

---

3. Stark, *God's Battalions*, 177–79.

stressing asceticism and a simple and pure life, but these begging monks did not live apart from the world—they moved among the people. Their purpose was to serve in the community and, in response to the poor level of preaching at the time, to share the word of God as itinerant preachers.

As these movements consolidated, they established their own rules and organizational structures. A significant feature was their direct accountability to the pope—independent from the bishop's authority. The orders' rules stipulated that mendicant monks, both individually and as whole orders, should live without property. This latter point became a contentious issue, as the orders began to attract donations and became more institutionalized. The dilution of their initial radicalism led some groups to set up their own communities, where they tried to uphold the original vision of uncompromising discipleship.

The social context of the emerging mendicant orders was the medieval city, which increasingly attracted an itinerant migrant population and in which ghettos of poor, homeless, and sick people became prevalent. The traditional parish structure was unable to respond to the new needs of these growing cities. At the same time, city dwellers' increasing affluence made it possible for mendicants to survive in this context. Mendicant orders can thus be seen as an adjustment of the church to a new economic and social-political situation.

The two most famous mendicant orders were the Franciscans and the Dominicans.

Francis and the Minor Brothers

Francis (1182–1226) was born in Assisi, central Italy, into a rich family. At the age of twenty-six, he experienced a radical conversion that caused him to give up all his belongings and begin a preaching ministry. His preaching attracted a growing number of followers, and Francis gathered them into a community of poverty and shared goods. The rule of this new community, the order of the minor brothers (*Ordo Fratrum Minorum—OFM*), soon received the approval of Pope Innocent III. Francis and his followers lived a simple life of itinerant preaching, singing, and begging. The movement quickly spread across Italy and beyond, and it became an important missionary force. At an early stage, a woman from Assisi—Clare, supposedly from a wealthy social background—was moved by Francis' teaching and joined the movement. In response to this, Francis arranged a convent for her and other women. That was how the Order of the Poor Clares (also called Clarisses) was founded in 1212, and it was officially recognized by the church in 1253.

Even today, Francis is one of the most inspiring Christian personalities. His faith and his identification with Jesus were so deep that, according to legend, he received the stigmata, the marks of the wounds of the crucifixion, on his hands. In his preaching he emphasized the suffering and poverty of Christ, thus giving comfort to the people in their own suffering and poverty. Modern Christians are stunned by both his poetic and his ecological theology, most vividly and famously articulated in his poem "Canticle of the Sun." In his praise for the wonders of God's creation in this literary work, he expresses tenderness, affection, and relatedness to all parts of creation.

> Be praised, my Lord, with all Your creatures,
> Especially Sir Brother Sun,
>
> By whom You give us the light of day!
> And he is beautiful and radiant with great splendor.
>
> Of You, Most High, he is a symbol!
> Be praised, my Lord, for Sister Moon and the Stars!
>
> In the sky You formed them bright and lovely and fair.
> Be praised, my Lord, for Brother Wind
>
> And for the Air and cloudy and clear and all Weather,
> By which You give sustenance to Your creatures!
>
> Be praised, my Lord, for Sister Water,
> Who is very useful and humble and lovely and chaste!
>
> Be praised, my Lord, for Brother Fire,
> By whom You give us light at night,
>
> And he is beautiful and merry and mighty and strong!
> Be praised, my Lord, for our Sister Mother Earth,
>
> Who sustains and governs us,
> And produces fruits with colorful flowers and leaves![4]

The strict subordination of the Franciscans under the authority of the church made them an attractive ally in the eyes of the official church, causing many popes to support them. At the same time, they gained great popularity for their obvious service among the people.

From 1220, the Franciscans increasingly turned their attention to theological education and produced important scholastic teachers like Alexander of Hales, Duns Scotus, and Bonaventura.

---

4. "Canticle of the Sun," lines 5–22, quoted in Habig, *St. Francis of Assisi*, 130.

Dominic and the Order of Preachers

Dominic of Guzman (1170–1221), from Spain, was inspired to set up his mendicant order by an encounter with the heretic Cathars (see below) while traveling through southern France. He realized that the Cathars' ascetic lifestyle, a sharp contrast to the official clerics' easy life, was a key reason the group attracted so many followers. Therefore, to defend orthodoxy against these heretics, he founded a monastic order that emphasized not just teaching and preaching but also an exemplary ascetic life. Different to the Franciscans, Dominic and his community saw poverty less as a goal in itself and more as a means to counter the influence of heretical movements, thus fighting the Cathars with their own weapon[5] by leading a life of poverty while offering orthodox preaching.

In 1216, Dominic was allowed to found the Order of Preachers (now abbreviated as OP), which went on to produce some of the most famous scholastic teachers, among them Albert the Great and Thomas Aquinas. The Dominicans' focus on teaching and their defense of orthodoxy soon turned them into a major force in the inquisition against heretics. This inquisitional background of the Dominicans has shaped their image up to the present.

Waldes and the Waldensians

The earliest mendicant order was actually founded in 1176; however, it followed a very different course than the Franciscans and Dominicans would later take. Waldes was a rich merchant from Lyon, France. Similar to Francis some thirty years later, he experienced a conversion to the ideal of poverty; he gave away what he possessed, began a life of radical discipleship, and gathered a community of equally committed lay men and women around him. A condition for admission to the community was a clear conversion, the renunciation of the world, and a commitment to apostolic poverty and apostolic ministry.

Yet, different to the preaching and singing of the Franciscans, the Waldensians' zeal and ideas were rejected by the ecclesial hierarchy. They were banned: first, because their proclamation was critical of core medieval Catholic ideas and practices such as purgatory, indulgences, and prayers for the deceased; second, because they discouraged oath-taking and participation in wars and thus undermined crucial elements of medieval society.

However, what made them seem even more dangerous was their strict adherence to the Bible and their unauthorized lay preaching, which made

---

5. Merlo, "Heresy and Dissent," 236.

the movement appear subversive, a threat to the Catholic Church. From the very beginning, Waldes and his followers had indeed set out to translate biblical texts and writings of the church fathers into the vernacular to support their preaching. In fact, Waldes truly cared for orthodoxy, to the extent that he at first sought papal approval. The pope was initially sympathetic and regarded him as generally orthodox but did not allow him to preach. Waldes' insistence on lay preaching eventually went beyond what the institutional church could allow, and in 1184 (and again in 1215), the church officially declared the group heretics. Despite such condemnation and subsequent persecution, the movement quickly spread in northern Italy and southern France and survived in remote valleys of the Alps. It underwent some division, with some offshoots actually gaining papal approval, but they soon disappeared or were absorbed into existing mendicant orders.

The similar and yet so different stories of the Waldensians and the Franciscans show how revivalist reform groups critical of the institutional church could either be reabsorbed as part of the broader church, as a tool of its government, or be dismissed as heretical. The Waldensians, for their part, prefigured central aspects of the Reformers' teaching and may thus be regarded as a *pre-Reformation movement*. Not surprisingly, in the sixteenth century, the Waldensian church did become part of the broader reformation movement.

The Origins of the Humiliati

Even before the Waldensians, other groups aimed at a life of simple poverty, imitating the lives of the apostles. One such group, originating in northern Italy, were the Humiliati, "the humble ones." Committing themselves to personal poverty, communal life, and evangelism, they reacted against the growing materialism of the time. However, like the Waldensians, they defied the restriction on preaching and were excommunicated. Some of them were subsequently readmitted to the church, while others merged with the outlawed Waldensian movement.

The text below is an excerpt from the *Chronicon universale anonymi Laudunensis*, written by an anonymous church chronicler and generally regarded as trustworthy.

> At that time there were certain inhabitants of Lombard [northern Italy] towns who lived at home with their families, chose a peculiar form of religious life, refrained from lies, oaths, and law suits, were satisfied with plain clothing, and presented themselves as upholding the Catholic faith. They approached the pope and besought him to confirm their way of life. This the pope granted

> them, provided that they did all things humbly and decently, but he expressly forbade them to hold private meetings or to presume to preach in public. But spurning the apostolic command, they became disobedient, for which they suffered excommunication. They called themselves Humiliati, because they did not use colored cloth for clothing but restricted themselves to plain dress.

Source: Wakefield and Evans, *Heresies of the High Middle Ages*, 159.

What Was the Significance of the New Monastic and Mendicant Orders for Christianity at Large?

Three aspects may be highlighted. First, the broad movement of new emerging orders shows something of the spiritual vitality of the period from the late eleventh to the early thirteenth century. The new movements built a bridge between popular faith and the belief of the Catholic Church and were part of Christianity's response to a changed social context. They signified new pastoral initiatives that went beyond the traditional congregational capacity of the institutional church. The trajectory of the movements shows the willingness of most groups to submit to the Roman Catholic Church. By supporting these emerging initiatives, the institutional church reaffirmed its own legitimacy. The established church thus benefited from the spiritual and physical energy of the religious and mendicant orders, adapting its ministry and deepening its relationships to new contexts.

Second, the new movements were an opportunity for women to follow a different path from the one imposed on them by patriarchal tradition. The monastic lifestyle was one of the few opportunities for women to pursue academic studies and lead more autonomous lives. Many of those entering women's convents came from aristocratic backgrounds. They turned away from their economic and social privilege and dedicated their life to an ascetic—though more self-determined—life in the convent.

Third, the religious and mendicant orders can be interpreted as instruments of the church, exercising transnational control over national and regional churches. One of the challenges of Roman Catholicism's central government structure had always been integrating regionalist interests and centrifugal forces. The Gregorian reform movement signified tremendous progress in the church's ability to govern a transnational religious body. The emerging monastic and itinerant orders, under the supervision of the pope, allowed the central government to oversee regional affairs through two different networks—the traditional diocesan network and the network of religious orders. This feature remained a powerful tool in the Roman Catholic governing structure in later times.

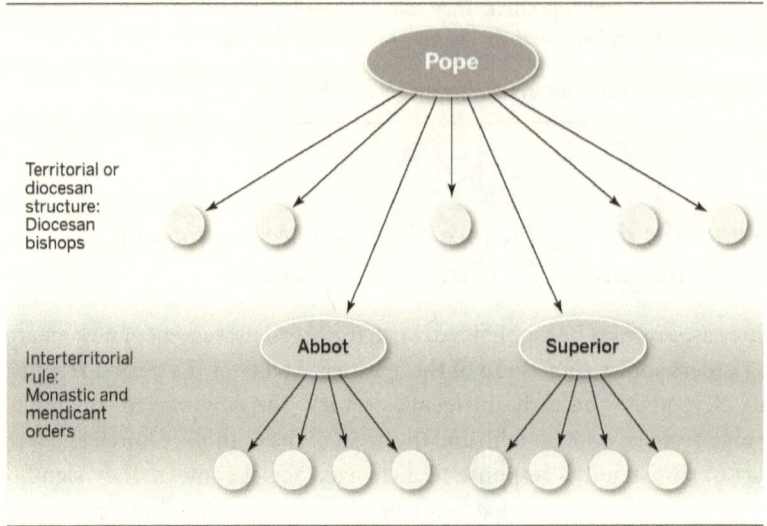

Fig. 11.2: *The dual governance structure of the Catholic Church*

RADICAL AND HERETICAL MOVEMENTS

Heresy was a phenomenon that in earlier medieval times had hardly been a problem, since the majority of people were rural and illiterate, and they displayed heretical behavior only (if at all) by maintaining pagan religious practices—they hardly had the intellectual means to develop or distinguish heterodox faith. In short, "heresy was a matter for educated elites."[6] The early medieval church simply required participation in the basic acts of the church and left doctrinal matters to intellectuals. However, from the eleventh century on, the situation changed. As trade and the economy in parts of Europe expanded, and as urban life produced wealthier, more literate, and more independent-minded citizens, new religious interests and new belief forms emerged. Thus, the high and late medieval period saw a flourishing of alternative Christian faith practices, new theological ideas, and Christian fringe movements. Some of these movements exhibited radical elements in their religious practice that brought them into conflict with the established church, even though their teaching might have been orthodox; such was the

---

6. Merlo, "Heresy and Dissent," 229.

situation of the Waldensians. Other groups taught ideas that went beyond the Christian framework and were condemned as heretical.

The Cathars

The most famous medieval group that was persecuted as heretical was the Cathars. They were also known under various other names: Albigensians, due to their prevalence around the city of Albi in southern France; Bogomiles, after the priest Bogomil from Bulgaria; or Paulicians, relating them to an earlier Christian heretical group. The Cathars were a strongly ascetic movement with a theological tendency toward dualism. It is assumed that they were influenced by Manichaean groups from the Middle East through whom Gnostic beliefs had been preserved and passed on to spiritual groups in eastern Europe.

The Cathars practiced a life of radical poverty and asceticism, of penitence and a willingness to accept martyrdom. Critical of the affluence of the established church, they propagated a simple church, abandoning much of the opulence of traditional church life. Accordingly, they rejected the sacraments and most other rituals. Their only significant ritual was a special initiation ceremony for entering the church. Due to their ascetic radicalism and their convincing lifestyle, the Cathars attracted many followers and, from the eleventh century on, spread throughout many parts of western Europe, particularly in the economically active regions of Flanders, Burgundy, the Rhineland, eastern Spain, northern and southern France, and northern and central Italy. At times, in southern France, they were nearly the dominant form of Christianity.

The Catholic Church responded with brutal suppression—Pope Innocent III moved against them by calling a crusade, thus initiating the cruel Albigensian wars (1209–29). To eradicate the Cathars' heresy, the church established the Inquisition (see also ch. 12), in which the Dominicans played such a central role.

The Teaching of the Cathars according to the Book of the Two Principles

The Cathars posed a significant challenge to the Catholic Church during the high medieval time. They understood themselves clearly as Christians, called themselves "Good Christians," and made ample reference to the Bible. *The Book of the Two Principles* is the most important surviving work of Cathar literature. Its author is not known, but it may have been written around 1240 in northern Italy. Following are parts of the two first sections and of section 13 of the long treatise.

Part 1. On Free Will

[1] Here Begins the Book of the Two Principles. . . . I have made it my purpose to explain our true faith by evidence from the Holy Scriptures and with eminently suitable arguments, invoking to my efforts the aid of the Father, of the Son, and of the Holy Spirit.

[2] On the Two Principles. To the honor of the Most Holy Father, I wish to begin my discussion concerning the two principles by refuting the belief in one Principle, however much this may contradict well-nigh all religious persons. We may commence as follows: Either there is only one First Principle, or there is more than one. If, indeed, there were one and not more, as the unenlightened say, then, of necessity, He would be either good or evil. But surely not evil, since then only evil would proceed from Him and not good, as Christ says in the Gospel of the Blessed Matthew: "And the evil tree bringeth forth evil fruit. A good tree cannot bring forth evil fruit, neither can an evil tree bring forth good fruit."

[13] On the Principle of Evil. Therefore, it behooves us of necessity to confess that there is another principle, one of evil, who works most wickedly against the true God and His creation; and this principle seems to move God against His own creation and the creation against its God, and causes God himself to wish for and desire that which in and of himself He could never wish for at all. Thus it is that through the compulsion of the evil enemy God yearns and is wearied, relents, is burdened, and is served by His own creatures. Whence God says to His people through Isaiah: "But thou hast made me to serve with thy sins, thou hast wearied me with thy iniquities"; and again, "I am weary of bearing them." And Malachi says, "You have wearied the Lord with your words." And David says, "And [he] repented according to the multitude of His mercies." And the Apostle says in his first Epistle to the Corinthians, "For we are God's coadjutors" . . .

And so it appears plainly that this concept of how one may serve God buttresses my argument. For if there were only one First Principle, holy, just, and good, as has been declared of the true Lord God in the foregoing, He would not make Himself sorrowful, sad, or dolorous; neither would He bear pain in himself, nor grow weary or repent, nor be aided by anyone, nor be burdened with the sins of anyone, nor yearn or wish for anything to be done which was delayed in coming to pass, since nothing at all could be done contrary to His will; nor could He be moved by anyone or injured, nor could there be anything which would trouble God, but all things would obey Him from overwhelming necessity.

Source: Wakefield and Evans, *Heresies of the High Middle Ages*, 515–16, 523–24.

Joachim of Fiore and the Expectation of Radical Historical Change

Joachim of Fiore (1132–1202) was a Cistercian monk who lived a generation before Francis of Assisi. He became famous for his *millenarian prophecies* about the expectation of a new age, the "Age of the Spirit." In this age, the hierarchy of the church would be unnecessary and infidels would unite with Christians. His ideas became popular long after his death and inspired groups of followers—partly revolutionary, partly just enthusiastic—who in the thirteenth and fourteenth centuries spread a messianic and millenarian message, vividly described in Norman Cohn's classic account *The Pursuit of the Millennium*. In fact, Joachim's scheme of history as unfolding in three stages had deep long-term influences, particularly in post-Hegelian theories of history, with Auguste Comte or Karl Marx understanding history as proceeding through three stages: theological, metaphysical, and scientific (Comte), or primitive communism, class society, and final communism (Marx).

Following Joachim's teaching, many people expected the third and last era to begin in 1260, a year that became a focal point for medieval revivals. The era of the spirit would inaugurate a time when the church would be restored to its apostolic form. Popular yearning for a radical change in the church, which many perceived as having strayed from the original vision of Jesus Christ, found support in a prophecy that offered a meaningful interpretation of the present turmoil. Joachim's apocalypticism influenced several religious movements of the high and late medieval times such as the Spiritual Franciscans or the flagellants.

The Spiritual Franciscans

The Spiritual Franciscans were radical followers of Francis who were critical of how the church had absorbed the Franciscan movement and were disappointed at how quickly the Franciscan order had moved away from the founding vision of Francis by establishing close relations with the social elite. When the order also softened its stance regarding acquisition of property to allow communal (but not individual) ownership rights, they strongly opposed this change and tried to uphold the strict poverty of the original Franciscan order. As a consequence, the Spiritual Franciscans split from the more moderate Franciscans.

In their opposition to the papacy, they discovered the hitherto little-known ideas of Joachim and spread them together with their own writings, to which they attached Joachim's name. These pseudo-Joachite prophecies proclaimed both a coming Antichrist who would chastise the corrupt and worldly church and a messianic savior who would herald the Age of the Spirit. The messianic expectations of the time were variously projected on political leaders, deceased or alive, like Frederick I Barbarossa, who had perished in the Third Crusade (see ch. 12); Baldwin of Flanders, who was put to death in the aftermath of the Fourth Crusade; or Frederick II, who was seen by some as the emperor of the last days.

The Flagellants

One of the more amazing medieval revivals of the thirteenth and fourteenth centuries was the Flagellants, who moved through wide parts of western Europe. The movement was said to number up to eight hundred thousand and reached the peak of its popularity during the Plague, in the middle of the fourteenth century.

The flagellants practiced a radical form of penance and self-mortification by self-inflicted public whipping. The plague that reached Europe in 1347, known as the Black Death, was interpreted (like earlier social and political crises) as an expression of God's punishment for the church's corruption and its practice of granting absolution through the sale of indulgences. By blaming the church's practice for the present crises, the movement clearly challenged the church hierarchy. Through their publicly celebrated penance, the flagellants hoped to abate God's anger.

The flagellants first appeared in 1259 after a famine in central Italy. They interpreted this crisis with reference to the thought of Joachim of Fiore, that is, as part of the turmoil that would precede the advent of a new era. As the movement became more critical of the church and began to oppose central pillars of Catholic belief, the church hierarchy condemned it, despite its strong popularity. Penitential flagellations are still known today in places like the Philippines.

Beguines and Beghards

The Beguines were medieval groups of women who developed a communitarian life as an alternative to the usual life under male control in the family, the church, and society. Different theories exist about the origin of the name. Parallel to the Beguine movement, ordinary working men gathered in male communities called Beghards.

The Beguine movement began in northern France, the Rhine Valley, and the Low Countries in the early twelfth century. The Beguine communities were in many ways similar to convents, but with three important differences. First, while convents were more for upper-class women and often had high entrance fees, the Beguine communities welcomed women from the lower classes, who of course equally yearned for a more self-determined life. Second, the Beguines engaged in labor for the purpose of economic self-sufficiency and as a religious vocation, or they cared for the needy; in contrast, women in convents spent more time, though not exclusively, in spiritual practice. Third, when Beguines entered the religious community, the so-called beguinage, they dedicated themselves to chastity and charity without being bound by permanent vows. They could leave communal life at any time.

The Beguine communities were an attempt at a self-determined life in the midst of a patriarchal society. Except for the presence of priests and confessors, they lived free from male interference. Some members of Beguine communities developed theological ideas, often of a mystical kind, independent of Catholic teaching. This spiritual and theological independence was one reason why the movement came into conflict with the church hierarchy and was eventually condemned as heretical and suppressed.[7] Another reason may be that the movement became a threat to a male-dominated hierarchy that felt challenged by these dissident and "uncontrolled" independent-minded women.

THE CATHOLIC CHURCH AND THE "OTHER CHURCH"

This has been only a partial description of the multiplicity of revivals, radical commitments to Christian discipleship, attempts to reform the church, and popular faith movements of the medieval era. Some of the protest and reform movements were spirit-driven revivals and can be seen as part of the long charismatic tradition. Others (like the Waldensians) were more "evangelical" and emphasized faithfulness to the Bible.

The list could be extended to include (*a*) the Crusades (see ch. 12), which were not only militant movements directed against the Muslims in Palestine but also expressions of a colorful popular religious culture that brought forth stunning revivals (e.g., the Children's Crusade in 1212); (*b*) the Great Hallelujah (1233), a revivalist peace movement in northern Italy; (*c*) ecstatic dancers in the Rhineland and Holland who, in 1374, during a

---

7. Council of Vienne (1311–12), *Decree on the Errors of the Beghards and the Beguines*.

short period of five months, moved from church to church, performing their acrobatic dances in front of the altar; or (*d*) the late medieval burning of the vanities, when urban Christians in an act of self-purification spontaneously handed over their valuables to be burned.

Overall, the medieval revivals aimed at revitalizing rather than overthrowing the existing religious structure, which of course had the Roman Catholic Church at its center,[8] and the church leadership was usually wise enough to tolerate these alternative faith expressions, knowing that prohibition would hardly be successful and that integration of such religious energies would be better than suppression.

It was different when direct doctrinal questions were at stake. These were raised by groups like the Cathars or the Waldensians; similarly, John Wycliffe (1328–84), John Huss (1369–1415), and others challenged the church not so much through alternative faith practices but through their theological thought. They are to be discussed as predecessors to the Reformation.

For Further Reading

Cohn, Norman. *The Pursuit of the Millennium: Revolutionary Messianism in Medieval and Reformation Europe and Its Bearing on Modern Totalitarian Movements*. New York: Harper & Row, 1961.

Dickson, Gary. "Medieval Revivalism." In *Medieval Christianity*, edited by Daniel Bornstein, 147–78. People's History of Christianity 4. Minneapolis: Fortress, 2010.

Merlo, Grado G. "Heresy and Dissent." In *Medieval Christianity*, edited by Daniel Bornstein, 229–64. People's History of Christianity 4. Minneapolis: Fortress, 2010.

Whalen, Brett Edward. *Dominion of God: Christendom and Apocalypse in the Middle Ages*. Cambridge, MA: Harvard University Press, 2009.

Learning Activities

1) Review key elements of this chapter by answering the following questions:
    - What is mysticism?
    - Why was mysticism part of the "other church"?
    - What changes did the monastic reform movement bring? In other words, in what ways were the monasteries that emerged since the tenth century different from the earlier monastic movement?

---

8. Dickson, "Medieval Revivalism," 175.

- o Describe three monastic reform movements of the high medieval era.
- o Describe two mendicant orders.
- o Describe two heretical movements of the medieval era.

2) To probe your understanding of what we have learned about this period, to deepen the understanding of its significance, and to apply it to your present experience, discuss the following questions in small groups:
   - o What were theological qualities and characteristics of the reform movements? What are their dangers?
   - o Why did many of the renewal, reform, and revival movements emerge from the eleventh century on? In other words, what was the social and historical context of the protest and renewal movements?
   - o In what ways were the religious and mendicant orders and other reform movements used as instruments of papal government, strengthening papal authority? Can you see similarities to today?

CHAPTER 12

Outward Militancy and Inward Divisions in High and Late Medieval Times

THIS CHAPTER WEAVES TOGETHER the stories of the powerful institutional church and of the growing reform and popular faith movements. First comes the story of the Crusades, which combined interests of the established church with popular religiosity: a history on one hand so tragically entrenched in Christianity's missionary drive and on the other hand so fundamentally antagonistic to key principles of the Christian faith. The impacts of this history still reverberate today. Second is the story of how the crusading drive was equally directed against dissent in the heartlands of Europe and led to several waves of inquisition. Yet, this outward and inward militancy could not conceal a growing crisis within the institutional church: Not long after the Gregorian reform movement of the eleventh century had established a basis for a church independent from secular interference, the church became again radically dependent on political authorities—to such an extent that the pope physically moved to France. The ensuing crises and schisms within the Roman Catholic Church revealed an obvious need for thorough reform. One of the late medieval attempts at reforming the institutional church was the conciliar movement, which will take us to the eve of the Reformation.

This chapter addresses the following questions:

- What religious, social, and political motifs and motives generated the Crusades?

- What were the results of the Crusades, and how did they shape the later history of Christianity?
- What were the political factors behind the divided papacy in the late fourteenth and early fifteenth century?
- What was the conciliar movement? Why did it fail to reform the church?

THE CRUSADES

From the late eleventh century on, a new form of Christian encounter with the world emerged: the Crusades. In every century since then, it has shaped the perception of Christianity in the eyes of non-Christians and Christians alike.

What Religious Factors Inspired the Crusaders?

The Crusaders were both driven by personal spiritual motives and encouraged by the church. First, they saw their journey as a form of pilgrimage and as one of many opportunities to show a deeper spiritual commitment during a time when Christian faith had become a matter of course. The Crusades were thus similar to other increasingly popular pilgrimages—to Rome, to Santiago de Compostela in Spain, or to other holy places of Christianity. The Crusades simply extended this idea by going on a pilgrimage to the birthplace of Jesus. Second, the Crusaders found that this special pilgrimage not only served as their own spiritual quest but also contributed to the church by combating the Muslims, who had taken the Holy Land. The Crusades thus provided a dual opportunity, particularly for knightly Crusaders: displaying the moral ideals of knighthood and demonstrating military heroism and bravery while fighting for the church. Third, going on a journey to remote Palestine promised both aristocrats and those from lower social strata an extraordinary spiritual experience. Finally, the official church encouraged the Crusades by rewarding each participant with a full indulgence, that is, a full remission of sins. The offer of such an advantage in attaining salvation attracted many.

What Social and Political Interests Motivated the Different Groups of Crusaders?

Most generally, the Crusades aimed at liberating the Holy Land to make pilgrimages secure. Indeed, Muslim attacks on Christian pilgrims had become more frequent toward the end of the eleventh century, and many pilgrims had risked their lives visiting the Holy Land.[1] The social and political interests that drove ordinary people to support the crusading adventure were different from the motivations of political and ecclesial leaders. For many ordinary people, the Crusades promised not only a spiritually extraordinary experience but also an opportunity for adventure, escaping a largely predestined life at home. Some Crusaders had rather practical reasons for running away, such as family difficulties or judicial problems. The Crusades thus did attract some socially unadjusted people.

Aristocrats and kings were, similar to ordinary people, attracted by the promise of adventure. But more than that, the Crusades were also a welcome opportunity to show their spiritual heroism and enhance their prestige at home. Furthermore, the Crusades channeled their subjects' restive and militant energies away from intramural conflicts in Europe and led them into a campaign that was beneficial both for the church and the aristocrats. One social malady in times of peace was groups of unemployed soldiers who continued as freelance bandits, and the Crusades diverted such groups to foreign lands. The Crusades had still another pacifying effect: joint engagement against an outside enemy distracted European rulers from their local or regional rivalries. In other words, exporting conflict abroad reduced conflicts at home. Many noblemen were also attracted by the hope of finding material treasure in foreign lands. Some aristocratic descendants joined the Crusades because they saw little prospect of inheriting their fathers' positions and stood a greater chance of making a fortune by venturing abroad.

The Crusades were strongly encouraged by the official church, not least because the popes themselves saw possible benefits. Sending the armies of powerful kings and dukes on a crusade enhanced the political authority of the popes: it subjected the secular rulers to the popes' agenda and increased the popes' prestige. In effect, the combined armies of kings and dukes were a papal army, officially led by someone the pope had appointed. This corresponded with the old papal dream of hegemonic leadership over the (occidental) world.

---

1. Riley-Smith, *First Crusaders*, 37–38.

How Did the Crusades Unfold?

Several clearly identifiable crusades happened over a period of around 150 years, from 1095 until the middle of the thirteenth century. The political events that triggered the call to the First Crusade were the Seljuk Turks' westward expansion (starting in the middle of the eleventh century), occupying Jerusalem and advancing toward Constantinople. The Seljuks were a people group from Central Asia. Their empire incorporated Persia, and they replaced the Abbasids, who had ruled Palestine but tolerated pilgrims. The Byzantine Emperor Alexios I had called for Christians to help him against the Seljuks' threat. In response, Pope Urban II, at the Synod of Clermont (1095), called the people to join in a crusade, not only to help those in Constantinople but also to reconquer Jerusalem:

> I, with suppliant prayer—not I, but the Lord—exhort you, heralds of Christ, to persuade all of whatever class, both knights and footmen, both rich and poor, in numerous edicts, to strive to help expel that wicked race from our Christian lands before it is too late. I speak to those present, I send word to those not here; moreover, Christ commands it.[2]

The people gathered at Clermont responded enthusiastically, and many spontaneously offered to go and also to exhort those not present. The First Crusade began in 1096 and succeeded three years later in the conquest of Jerusalem, where the two most important centers of Islamic worship (after Mecca and Medina), the Al-Aqsa Mosque and the Dome of the Rock, built on the site of the former Jewish Temple, were turned into churches. This triple claim—Jewish, Christian, and Muslim—over Jerusalem shows something of the city's conflicted identity. The First Crusade led to the foundation of several small crusader states: the Kingdom of Jerusalem, the Principality of Antioch, the county of Edessa, and the county of Tripoli. Although they had been called initially by the Byzantine emperor, the Western Crusaders showed little respect for the Orthodox Church. They established a Latin patriarch in Jerusalem, ignoring the Byzantines' claim to the city, a claim based on the fact that Jerusalem had been under Byzantine control before it was conquered by the Muslims in 637. This affront might seem insensitive, but it happened at least partly because of the Crusaders' frustration with the Byzantine emperor, who had failed to support the Western powers as

---

2. Excerpted from the Chronicle of Fulcher of Chartres, bk. I, in Peters, *First Crusade*, 53.

promised. Unsure whom to fear more, the Western Crusaders or the Seljuk threat, the emperor remained militarily and politically ambiguous.

An Eyewitness Account of the First Crusade

Fulcher of Chartres was a priest and a scholar who chronicled the First Crusade, which he had joined as a chaplain to Stephen of Blois and Robert of Normandy. Fulcher describes how the crusade brought together people from all parts of Europe, and what they felt when departing or when seeing their loved ones leave.

> *Such, then, was the immense assemblage which set out from the West. Gradually along the march, and from day to day, the army grew by the addition of other armies, coming from every direction and composed of innumerable people. Thus one saw an infinite multitude, speaking different languages and coming from diverse countries. All did not, however, come together into a single army until we had reached the city of Nicaea [May 1097]. What shall I add? The isles of the sea and the kingdoms of the whole earth were moved by God, so that one might believe fulfilled the prophecy of David, who said in his Psalm: "All nations whom Thou hast made shall come and worship before Thee, O Lord, and shall glorify Thy name"...*
>
> *Oh, how great was the grief, how deep the sighs, what weeping, what lamentations among the friends, when the husband left the wife so dear to him, his children also, and all his possessions of any kind, father, mother, brethren, or kindred! And yet in spite of the floods of tears which those who remained shed for their friends about to depart, and in their very presence, the latter did not suffer their courage to fail, and, out of love for the Lord, in no way hesitated to leave all that they held most precious, believing without doubt that they would gain an hundred-fold in receiving the recompense which God has promised to those who love Him.*
>
> *Then the husband confided to his wife the time of his return and assured her that, if he lived, by God's grace he would return to her. He commended her to the Lord, gave her a kiss, and, weeping, promised to return. But the latter, who feared that she would never see him again, overcome with grief, was unable to stand, fell as if lifeless to the ground, and wept over her dear one whom she was losing in life, as if he were already dead. He, then, as if he had no pity (nevertheless he was filled with pity) and was not moved by the grief of his friends (and yet he was secretly moved), departed with a firm purpose. The sadness was for those who remained, and the joy for those who departed. What more can we say? "This is the Lord's doings, and it is marvelous in our eyes."*

Source: Ogg, *Source Book of Medieval History*, 290–91.

In the twelfth and thirteenth centuries, several crusades followed, none as successful as the first. The Second Crusade of 1147–49 was again announced by the pope but led by political leaders. The chief propagandist of this crusade was Bernard of Clairvaux, who was not only a mystic but also a powerful advocate of ecclesial power. The reported miracles that accompanied Bernard's call seemed to validate his request as willed by God. However, the Second Crusade was weakened by open conflicts between the Western Crusaders and the Byzantines, and by divisions between the different parts of the Crusader armies. It ended in a devastating defeat. Most of the Western Crusaders died at the hands of the Turks, and the remaining warriors failed in an ill-advised siege of Damascus, with just a few returning home in disgrace. The end of the Second Crusade undermined the confidence of the Crusaders and restored Muslim confidence.

The Third Crusade of 1189–92 aimed at recapturing Jerusalem, which had been retaken in 1187 by Muslims. The Crusade was led by English, French, and German forces and is notable for the death of the powerful Emperor Frederick I Barbarossa, who drowned when he tried to cross a river on his horse. The crusade ended in partial success but without the recovery of Jerusalem. Instead, Richard the Lionhearted signed a treaty with the Muslim sultan Saladin that allowed Christian pilgrims free access to Jerusalem.

Initially, the Fourth Crusade of 1202–4 aimed at achieving what the Third Crusade had failed to do: take back Jerusalem. Yet, invited by a Constantinopolitan claimant to the throne and the promise of a large payment, the Crusaders changed course, conquered Constantinople, and installed a new emperor, Alexius IV. When Alexius failed to live up to his promise, the Crusaders attacked the city, established a Latin empire in the East and subjected the Orthodox Church to the Church of Rome. This attack against the Orthodox Church was what ultimately destroyed the relationship between the Roman Catholic and the Orthodox Church for centuries to come (see ch. 10).

The Fifth Crusade of 1217–21 aimed at attacking Egypt; the Crusaders hoped to weaken the Muslim stronghold over Palestine. Yet, after some initial gains, it ended in defeat.

The Sixth Crusade of 1228–29 was led by Emperor Frederick II, who had previously been excommunicated by the pope for not keeping his vow to lead a crusade. It ended, without a battle, in a successful agreement that allowed Frederick to gain power over most of Jerusalem while permiting Muslims access to their holy sites. Jerusalem remained Christian until 1244.

The later crusades all ended badly. After the failure of the Seventh Crusade (1248–54), undertaken by the French King Louis IX, people began to lose interest. The Seventh Crusade had been better organized and funded than any previous crusade, yet it ended in defeat: it seemed as if God did not want to grant victory to this enterprise. Eventually, growing popular opposition against the heavy taxes for such costly endeavors brought an end to the Crusades.

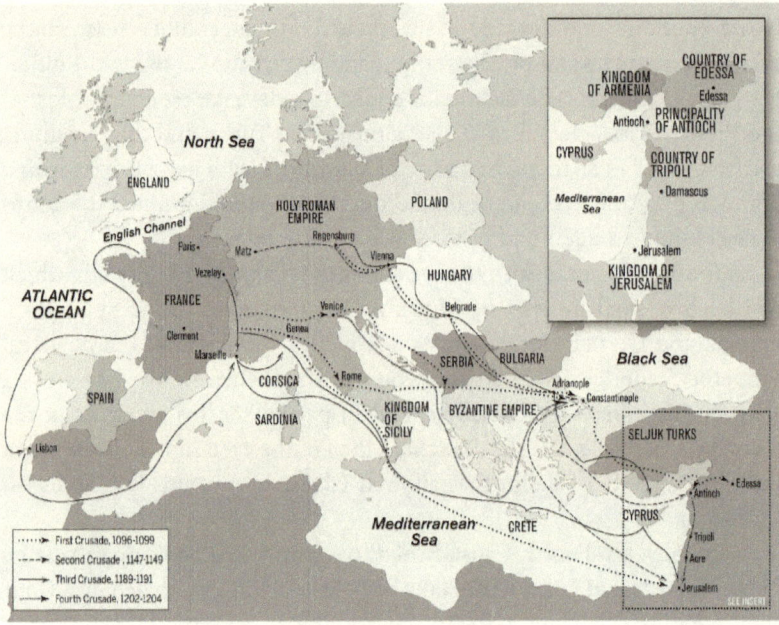

Fig. 12.1: The first Crusades

Besides these crusades, the period also brought some spontaneous movements initiated not by popes and kings but by ordinary people, similarly calling for a pilgrimage to liberate the Holy Land from unbelievers. The most remarkable among these was the Children's Crusade of 1212, which gathered children as young as six (as well as some adults) from all parts of France and led them eastward. Their end is uncertain; some remained in various maritime cities, only a few returned.

The Children's Crusade

The Children's Crusade (1212) was an amazing chapter of medieval revivalism. It was a movement of children from various parts of Europe, most importantly from France, joining a conquering journey to the Holy Land. In France, the crusade was preached by a young peasant boy named Stephen, and in Germany by a boy named Nicholas from Cologne.

The text below is from the Chronicle of Cologne, an anonymous document that records the history of kings and emperors from the sixth to the early thirteenth century.

> *In this year occurred an outstanding thing and one much to be marveled at, for it is unheard of throughout the ages. About the time of Easter and Pentecost, without anyone having preached or called for it and prompted by I know not what spirit, many thousands of boys, ranging in age from six years to full maturity, left the plows or carts which they were driving, the flocks which they were pasturing, and anything else which they were doing. This they did despite the wishes of their parents, relatives, and friends who sought to make them draw back. Suddenly one ran after another to take the cross. Thus, by groups of twenty, or fifty, or a hundred, they put up banners and began to journey to Jerusalem. They were asked by many people on whose advice or at whose urging they had set out upon this path. They were asked especially since only a few years ago many kings, a great many dukes, and innumerable people in powerful companies had gone there and had returned with the business unfinished. The present groups, moreover, were still of tender years and were neither strong enough nor powerful enough to do anything. Everyone, therefore, accounted them foolish and imprudent for trying to do this. They briefly replied that they were equal to the Divine will in this matter and that, whatever God might wish to do with them, they would accept it willingly and with humble spirit. They thus made some little progress on their journey. Some were turned back at Metz, others at Piacenza, and others even at Rome. Still others got to Marseilles, but whether they crossed to the Holy Land or what their end was is uncertain. One thing is sure: that of the many thousands who rose up, only very few returned.*

Source: *Chronica Regiae Coloniensis Continuatio prima*, s.a. 1213, MGH SS XXIV 17–18, in Brundage, *The Crusades*, 213.

From the early beginnings, the Crusades aimed not just at Muslims in the Orient but also at Muslims and other non-Christians, particularly Jews, within Europe. The most important of these European crusades was the *Reconquista* in Spain, a slow recovery of Muslim-occupied territory on the Iberian Peninsula. The process had already begun late in the eighth century, but it was elevated to the status of a crusade in the twelfth century and thus received greater spiritual significance. The reconquest progressed quickly, and by 1250 only the small kingdom of Granada in the south of Spain remained Islamic. The process finally ended in the fateful year 1492—the year of Columbus' voyage of discovery—with the expulsion or forced conversion of the remaining Muslims and Jews. Spanish Catholicism has retained something of the crusading spirit inherited from this period.

Jews had been living across Europe for centuries, and they had been the occasional target of popular wrath; the Crusades brought renewed vigor to this persecution. The most infamous attack against Jews happened during the First Crusade, when several groups of German Crusaders committed a series of massacres in the Rhine Valley. Indeed, the Crusades triggered a string of pogroms against the Jews and are an integral part of the tragic history of anti-Judaism in Europe. It is, however, important to note that many bishops attempted to protect the Jews, even putting their own lives in peril.[3]

What Were the Direct Political Results and Long-Term Impacts of the Crusades?

Politically, the Crusades were a failure. They either failed to achieve the initial goal—"liberating" Jerusalem and the Holy Land—or were successful only in the short term, and they were unable to halt the advance of Islam. In fact, instead of helping the Eastern Empire (as originally intended), the Crusades hastened its demise. After the First Crusade, the papacy largely lost control of the crusading movement and the Crusades became instruments of national policy.

The long-term impacts are more difficult to assess, but the Western attacks did foster a perception of the West as a threat. Modern Islamist rhetoric—and other rhetoric critical of the West's expansionism—often points to the Crusades. Of course, whether such rhetoric reflects a genuine feeling of the people or rather tries actively to portray the West as a threat is a matter for debate. The Muslim world's sense of being overpowered by the West may have more to do with more recent (nineteenth- and twentieth-century) political developments. In fact, before the end of the nineteenth century, Muslims had not shown much of an interest in the Crusades.[4] Besides, earlier Muslim conquests were equally militaristic, and Crusaders had some right to claim that they were simply trying to recapture lost territories. Yet, the Crusades did prefigure what would happen in later colonial expansion.

Maybe less an impact of the Crusades than an expression of a deep-rooted motif in European history is the West's obsession with Jerusalem and the Holy Land, which found powerful expression in the Crusades, as Barbara Tuchman has shown impressively in *Bible and Sword*. From the founding myths of England and the medieval tales of King Arthur, through

3. Poliakov, *History of Anti-Semitism*, 1:45.
4. Stark, *God's Battalions*, 246.

the history of pilgrimages to Jerusalem, all the way to nineteenth- and twentieth-century premillennial hopes that a return of the Jews to the Holy Land would hasten the second coming of Christ, European politics have in one way or another been linked to Jerusalem.

What Then Were the Spiritual and Ecclesial Impacts of the Crusades?

First, the Crusades enhanced the authority of the popes: they had called for the Crusades and had appointed the leaders. The Crusades thus were an expression of the rise of papal power. Second, the Crusades deepened the rift between Christians in the East and the West—they caused the Orthodox churches to remain perpetually suspicious of the motives of the Western church. Third, the Crusades led to increased mistrust and animosity between Christians and Muslims and beyond. Fourth, the Crusades also influenced the perception of mission. Still today, outsiders' perceptions of Christianity and of Christian mission bear the shadow of the Crusades. That some Christian groups and movements voluntarily adopt names including the word *crusade* further strengthens this perception. Fifth, the crusading spirit influenced monasticism and led to the emergence of a new ideal of Christian existence: the monastic warrior. Finally, the crusading ideal was reapplied to conflicts within the Christian heartland in Europe—combating heresies, dealing with schismatic or political opponents, and attacking religious minorities such as the Cathars, Beghards, and Beguines.

Yet, the Crusades also had positive side effects, unintended as they may have been. Most important was the encounter with the philosophical and scientific traditions preserved in the Muslim and Jewish worlds, which led to a widening of knowledge. It was through these encounters that the Occident learned more about Aristotle (see ch. 13). The direct encounter with Palestine also led to a rediscovery of the historical narratives of the Bible and the humanity of Jesus, which inspired biblical scholarship.

THE INQUISITION

The Inquisition can be understood as a refined application of the crusading spirit in the service of suppressing heresies within the Christian heartlands of Europe: a form of warfare, a *crusade turned inward*, to detect heretical beliefs. It began with the fight against the Cathars, known as the Albigensian Crusade (1209-29; see ch. 11). When the campaign against the

Cathars ended, the church remained suspicious that many believers would secretly follow their teaching. To combat this, a special ecclesial tribunal known as the Inquisition was established.

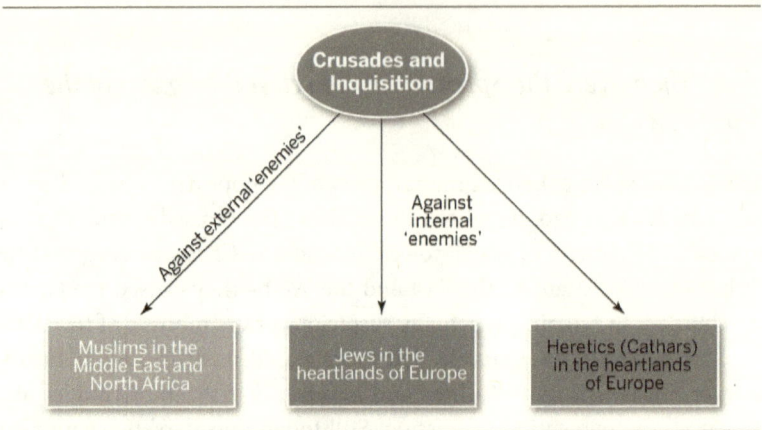

Fig. 12.2: The targets of the Crusades and the Inquisition

The first wave was called for by Pope Innocent III (1198–1216) and became a standing institution of the church in 1232 during the papacy of Gregory IX. The Inquisition was directly accountable to the pope but effectively directed by local bishops and often carried out by Dominican monks; it was marked by severe questioning, draconian punishment, and a lack of rights for the accused. It should be noted that, though the inquisitorial methods were unfair and violent, they were not worse than the common judicial standards of the day. In the thirteenth century the church urged the political government to introduce secular laws against the heretics.

The second wave of the Inquisition began in the late fifteenth century and became infamous when it was revived in Spain and turned against Jews and Muslims. The rationale was similar to that of the first wave: after the forced conversion of many Muslims and Jews in the final stages of the reconquest of Spain, the church suspected many of them of simply having yielded to the pressure to convert while still secretly holding to their old beliefs. The Inquisition thus aimed at detecting pseudo-converts, or crypto-Jews and crypto-Muslims. Most famous among the Spanish inquisitors of that period was the Dominican Grand Inquisitor, Thomas de Torquemada (1420–98), who served in the position from 1483 until his death. He was the inspiration for the famous parable of the Grand Inquisitor in Dostoevsky's classic *The Brothers Karamazov*.

The third wave of the Inquisition began in sixteenth-century Italy as part of the Counter-Reformation. After this third wave it faded away and, in 1908, was eventually redesigned by Pope Pius X as the Congregation of the Holy Office. In 1966, it was converted into a theological advisory committee of the papal curia in matters of doctrine.

THE BABYLONIAN CAPTIVITY OF THE CHURCH (1305–77) AND THE DIVIDED PAPACY (1378–1415)

By the middle of the thirteenth century, the German empire had dissolved into small independent territories. Parallel to this decay, the French monarchy became the dominant power, though partly contained by England. Despite the achievements of the Gregorian reform movement, the papacy soon fell under the influence of different political rulers. With the rise of France as the hegemonic power in Europe, the papacy became increasingly dependent on the French kings.

Boniface VIII (1294–1303) was the medieval pope who arguably went the furthest in claiming absolute ecclesial power. He declared that all political and spiritual power in the world was under the pope's authority and that all kings were subject to the pope. This view brought Boniface into regular conflict with political rulers, most significantly with King Philip IV of France. After the death of Boniface VIII and the short-lived papacy of Boniface's successor, the new pope, Clement V, decided to remain in his home country of France. He moved his residency to Avignon, where the next six popes, all French, lived as well. This period in exile—visibly in dependence on and in captivity to the French hegemonic power—is called the Babylonian Exile of the Church.

Eventually, after sixty-eight years of residence in Avignon, the papacy moved back to Rome. Two main motives influenced this decision: First, people in Rome and elsewhere were increasingly vocal in calling for such a return. The Romans wanted to resume the tradition of the Roman papacy, and they were supported by popular mystics like Catherine of Siena and Birgitta of Sweden. Second, the pope's return was necessary to stabilize the Papal State against growing threats from warring factions in Italy.

However, the story did not end there. The pope's return to Rome triggered a split of the church into two papal churches, one with its center in Rome and the other still in Avignon. This situation became known as the Great Western Schism and lasted from 1378 to 1417. The followers of the two papal camps split along traditional political alliances. Obedient to the papacy in Avignon were France and its allies, Sardinia, Sicily, Naples,

Scotland, and some German territories; obedient to Rome were most parts of Germany, middle and northern Italy, and England. The schism was caused not by any significant administrative, doctrinal, or liturgical differences but purely by competing nationalities and individual interests.

The schism seriously undermined the credibility of the church and led to growing calls for radical reform. The Great Western Schism is thus an important part of the background to the Reformation. The question remained, though: What is thorough reform? The following two centuries were largely concerned with trying to find an answer to the question of what church reform meant and how far it should go.

THE CONCILIAR CHURCH REFORM MOVEMENT

One popular answer was to follow the example of the early church in dealing with conflict—calling a general council of the church that, in joint deliberation and prayerful debate, could find a solution to the problems of the church. This suggestion was called conciliarism. There was, however, an impediment: calling a council to resolve the problems of the church would imply that the church council *had* the power to do so; in other words, it would establish the church council as the supreme authority in the church, taking precedence over even the pope. This was why the papacy never really supported the idea.

Conciliarism was promoted by theologians like William of Ockham, Marsilius of Padua, and Pierre d'Ailly and Jean Gerson, two scholars from the University of Paris. Ockham and others stressed that councils should also include laymen, to reflect the church as a community of all believers. Most did not go that far and simply wanted the church to be under clerical rather than papal control. Conciliarism paralleled earlier political developments, as monarchs were forced to relinquish power and yield to commoners' growing political assertiveness. These processes had resulted in constitutional limitations of monarchic power, spelled out in the Magna Carta in England (1215) and realized in the inclusion of commoners in Parliament (1295); similarly, France in 1302 established the Estates-General, an early and partial form of citizens' participation in political decision-making.

Conciliarism in Action: The Councils of Pisa, Constance, Basel, and Florence

To resolve the manifold problems of the church, a council was held in the Italian city of Pisa (1409). It aimed at deposing the two schismatic popes in Rome and Avignon and electing another one to unite the church. However, the unfortunate outcome of Pisa was that a new pope was indeed elected, but when the two existing ones refused to abdicate, it left the church with *three* popes. A new council, intended to resolve the chaotic leadership question, was convened in Constance (1414-18). The council aimed at ending the schism, ridding the church of heresy, reforming the church, and finding ways to overcome inherent corruption and other evils. The first result of the council was that it successfully ended the schism: the pope in Rome resigned, and the other popes were deposed. In the long term, and possibly more important, was the second result—the victory of conciliarism. The council declared itself legitimate and universal, and claimed a higher authority than that of the pope. It was decided that, every ten years from then on, a general council of the church would meet as an organ of the ongoing governance and reform of the church. This decision continued to inspire democratic ecclesial governance in later periods. However, the Roman papacy rejected the validity of the council's decision and later prohibited any appeal (against papal decisions) to such a general council.

Yet, the victory of conciliarism also claimed its victims. The third significant result (besides ending the schism and the declaration of conciliarism) was the eradication of heresy. The Council of Constance condemned as heretical the teaching of the Bohemian reformer John Huss and, after he refused to recant, burned him at the stake. Even progressive reform theologians like Gerson and d'Ailly supported this decision—Huss' refusal to submit to the authority of the council implied that the authority of an individual's reason was higher than that of the church.

The following years saw a power struggle between supporters of conciliarism and supporters of supreme papal rule. It took more than ten years for a general council of the church to convene again, this time in the Swiss city of Basel (1431). The council was called to do several things: heal the revolution in Bohemia that had begun after the death of Huss, implement the idea of a continuous universal council as the highest church authority, and resolve the schism with the Orthodox Church. The Council of Basel was in its beginning the peak of the conciliar movement: the council successfully resisted the pope's pre-emptive attempt to dissolve it and even included representatives of the lower clergy. Yet, the preliminary success and the extension of representation were at the same time a factor in the council's undoing. Even though Europe's political leaders were keen to limit papal power, they were hardly interested in the emergence of this new rival power—the general council as a more or less permanent institution. The monarchic leaders' support for the conciliar movement was, therefore, never more than lukewarm.

After a few months in Basel, the pope used developments in Constantinople (which moved the Orthodox Church to seek reconciliation with Rome) as a pretext to leave Basel and relocate the council to Ferrara, and later to Florence, where a short-lived union with the Orthodox Church was declared (see ch. 10). The council in Basel went on, although with a reduced number of participants. With the papal party withdrawn and a new council convened, Basel's authority was crucially undermined; the initial optimism about finding a new government structure for the church had waned. Besides, the participants in Basel misjudged their actual power and harmed themselves by electing a counter-pope, thus creating a new schism in the church. The relocated Council of Ferrara/Florence (1438–39) signified the decline of conciliarism.

With the end of the council in Florence, the papacy gradually regained some of the strength and authority it had lost during the period from the exile in Avignon through the divided papacy to the councils of Constance and Basel. The idea of conciliarism seemed to have passed. Yet the problems of the church remained, and the calls for reform intensified. It would take more than seventy years for the church to convene another general council. By then it would be too late to heal the profound contradictions that had spread throughout the Western church.

For Further Reading

Limor, Ora. "Christians and Jews." In *The Cambridge History of Christianity*, vol. 4, *Christianity in Western Europe c. 1100–c. 1500*, edited by Miri Rubin and Walter Simons, 135–48. Cambridge: Cambridge University Press, 2009.

Nirenberg, David. "Christendom and Islam." In *The Cambridge History of Christianity*, vol. 4, *Christianity in Western Europe c. 1100–c. 1500*, edited by Miri Rubin and Walter Simons, 149–69. Cambridge University Press 2009.

Pegg, Mark Gregory. *A Most Holy War: The Albigensian Crusade and the Battle for Christendom*. Oxford: Oxford University Press, 2008.

Riley-Smith, Jonathan. *The Crusades: A History*. 2nd ed. New Haven: Yale University Press, 2005.

Stark, Rodney. *God's Battalions: The Case for the Crusades*. New York: HarperOne, 2009.

Thomsett, Michael C. *The Inquisition: A History*. Jefferson, NC: McFarland, 2010.

Tuchman, Barbara. *Bible and Sword: England and Palestine from the Bronze Age to Balfour*. New York: Ballantine, 1984.

Learning Activities

1) Review key elements of this chapter by answering the following questions:
   - What were the Crusades?
   - What factors—ecclesial, political, social, and religious—supported the emergence of the Crusades?
   - What does the term "Babylonian Captivity of the Church" mean?
   - What does the term "Great Western Schism" mean?
   - Name two theologians who developed the concept of conciliarism, and two councils where it played a role.

2) To probe your understanding of what we have learned about this period, to deepen the understanding of its significance, and to apply it to your present experience, discuss the following questions in small groups:
   - What were the successes of the Crusades? What were the failures?
   - Discuss the usefulness of conciliarism as an instrument of church government:
     - What did it mean?
     - What was its ecumenical relevance?
     - What different viewpoints on conciliarism were suggested in the fifteenth century?
     - What were the implicit problems of conciliarism?
   - Discuss how the medieval Catholic Church tried to resolve its structural problems. Compare this with modern totalitarian states' way of dealing with structural problems.

CHAPTER 13

Theological Developments during the Medieval Time

THEOLOGICAL IDEAS ARE NOT simply the fruit of social and political change, as Marxist theory has it; rather, they interrelate dynamically with other areas of life, initiating change and triggering new configurations in the entanglement of society, politics, culture, and intellectual life. In other words, they actively contribute to the course of history. This was also the case with medieval theology, which was one aspect of the medieval history of Christianity. Understanding medieval theological developments is the first step in properly understanding the sixteenth-century Reformation.

Medieval theology begins with Augustine, the bridge from the early church to the later times; throughout the medieval era he remained the single most important teacher in the Western church. Early medieval theology and philosophy remained largely within the framework of earlier Hellenistic philosophy, with Platonism and Neo-Platonism the dominant philosophical schools. This changed in the thirteenth century, when Christian intellectuals rediscovered Aristotle.

Throughout the medieval time, theology and philosophy went hand in hand, with theology as the master and philosophy its maidservant (*ancilla*), a pattern already known in patristic theology.[1] This view reflected a hierarchy—that knowledge of God is higher than rational knowledge. Only toward the end of the medieval period did philosophy develop more independently. Similarly, science was for long periods subordinate to theology.

---

1. See, for instance, Clement of Alexandria, *Stromata* I.5 (*ANF* 2:305).

One may distinguish various forms of medieval theology, most importantly scholastic theology, mystical theology, and popular theology. While popular theology is implicitly present in the various forms of medieval devotional expression, scholasticism and mystical theology were primarily produced in monasteries. Only in later medieval times did the universities emerge and, with them, a new type of university-based theological reflection. Scholasticism was the attempt to present faith and theology with the help of philosophy in a doctrinal system. In contrast, mysticism, usually based on Neo-Platonist philosophy, aimed at leading the individual through a process of growing cognition to union with God.

This chapter addresses the following questions:

- How and through what different periods did medieval theological and philosophical thought develop from the sixth to the fifteenth century?
- What were the most important medieval theological controversies?

The chapter first proposes a periodization of the medieval history of theology, highlighting some of the debates and significant movements of each period; the second section introduces one of the medieval time's most famous debates, the epistemological controversy about the "universals"; and, finally, the third section discusses the late medieval argument between voluntarism and rationalism.

FOUR STAGES OF MEDIEVAL THEOLOGICAL DEVELOPMENT

The First Period: From Augustine until 1000

During the first centuries of the medieval time, western Europe produced little significant theology. Augustine remained the dominant thinker for Western Christianity, but he had scant influence on theology in the East. Meanwhile, theology in the eastern part of Europe developed in continuity with the earlier period, consisting mainly in the reception of earlier Neo-Platonist philosophy. Arguably the most important theologian of the time was Dionysius the Areopagite, an anonymous writer of mystical theology, probably from Syria. He was also called "Pseudo-Dionysius" because he claimed to be Dionysius, the member of the Areopagus council mentioned in Acts 17:34 who, after listening to Paul's preaching, became a Christian. Writing around the year 500 and influenced by Neo-Platonist philosophy, Dionysius developed a negative theology that emphasized the unknowability of God. His theology became known in the West only centuries later, but his influence was far-reaching and all later mystical theology is related, in one way or another, to him.

Dionysius Areopagite on the Church as an Image of the Heavenly Order

In the *Ecclesiastical Hierarchy (De Ecclesiastica Hierarchia)*, Dionysius the Areopagite describes the church as an image of, and as hierarchically graded as, the heavenly order. The text below on the nature of the ecclesiastical hierarchy shows how the church contributes to the process of deification.

> *The nature of the ecclesiastical hierarchy*
>
> *That our hierarchy . . . which is given by God, is God-inspired and divine, a divinely acting knowledge, activity, and completion, we must show from the supernal and most Holy Scriptures to those who through hierarchical secrets and traditions have been initiated into the holy consecration. . . . Jesus, the most divine and most transcendent spirit, the principle and the being and the most divine power of every hierarchy, holiness, and divine operation, brings to the blessed beings superior to us a more bright and at the same time more spiritual light and makes them as far as possible like to His own light. And through our love which tends upward toward Him, by the love of the beautiful which draws us up to Him, He brings together into one our many heterogeneities; that He might perfect them so as to become a uniform and divine life, condition, and activity, He gives us the power of the divine priesthood. In consequence of this honor we arrive at the holy activity of the priesthood, and so we ourselves come near to the beings over us, that we, so far as we are able, approximate to their abiding and unchangeable holy state and so look up to the blessed and divine brilliancy of Jesus, gaze religiously on what is attainable by us to see, and are illuminated by the knowledge of what is seen; and thus we are initiated into the mystic science, and, initiating, we can become light-like and divinely working, complete and completing.*

Source: Ayer, *Source Book for Ancient Church History*, 562–64.

A period of significant theological production in western Europe did occur during the reign of Charlemagne, who gathered important scholars and poets—most importantly the philosopher Alcuin (c. 730–804), from northern England—at his court in an effort to revive the cultural and intellectual life of the Latin world. This period of the eighth century is also called the Carolingian Renaissance. Theological arguments in support of the *Filioque*, the clause "and from the Son" that was added to the Nicene Creed to describe the Holy Spirit's procession not only from the Father but also from the Son (see ch. 10), were an important fruit of this period.

The post-Carolingian time of the ninth century brought a revival of mystical theology triggered by the Irish philosopher John Scotus Eriugena (c. 815–77), who translated the works of Dionysius the Areopagite from Greek into Latin and thus enabled their reception in the intellectual world of western Europe. Another important philosopher of that time was Paschasius Radbertus (c. 785–865), whose thought would lead to the later doctrine of transubstantiation, that is, Christ's real presence in the Eucharist.

The Second Period: Early Scholasticism of the Eleventh and Twelfth Centuries

The eleventh and twelfth centuries brought not only restoration and increased self-confidence to the church but also new, parallel initiatives in theological thought. The most important debate of the time was the controversy over the universals—the discussion about what comes first, generic terms or the particular objects (see below). So-called realist philosophers like Anselm of Canterbury (c. 1033–1109) and William of Champeaux faced off with nominalist philosophers, most important among them Berengar of Tours (c. 999–1088). Anselm was famous not only for his ontological proof of God, which for him was a logical consequence of his realist philosophical position, but also for his soteriological theory of satisfaction, outlined in "Why God Became Man" (in Latin, *Cur deus homo*), which became the dominant medieval Roman Catholic explanation of why Jesus Christ was necessary to save humans. The controversy over the universals was particularly important for the question of Christ's presence in the Eucharist, with the answer offered by the theory of transubstantiation.

Another important theologian of this period was Peter Abelard (c. 1079–1142), who is particularly remembered for his love relationship with Heloise, known to history through their correspondence and through his autobiography, the only autobiography by a medieval philosopher. More important for the history of theology is the alternative answer he offered to the controversy over the universals. His sharp debating skills and his critical writing earned him numerous enemies. Toward the end of his life, his ideas were condemned by a church council. Another important theologian of this period was Peter the Lombard (c. 1096–1164). Although he was not as creative as Anselm or Abelard, his writings became for many centuries the essential teaching of the church, and later theologians commonly developed their thought by commenting on his writings.

The Third Period: The Peak of Scholasticism, from the Middle of the Twelfth to the Thirteenth Century

The peak of papal power in the thirteenth century was paralleled by a peak in theological scholarship, with three important developments that influenced theological production.

First, contact with philosophers from the Islamic world—as a consequence of the Crusades—led to a rediscovery of the full Aristotelian system of philosophy and significant impulses for a new view of the relationship between grace and nature. Before then, Western theology had known only partially about Aristotle, with much of that knowledge coming through quotations in the works of other philosophers. Theology had followed mainly the philosophy of Plato, with Aristotle regarded as Plato's ignoble student. Important thinkers influencing Christianity were the Persian philosopher, astronomer, and physician Avicenna (c. 980–1037), from Bukhara in present-day Uzbekistan; the Andalusian thinker Averroës (1126–98), who was similarly to Avicenna learned in all areas of knowledge; and Moses Maimonides (1135–1204), the most significant Jewish philosopher of the medieval period.

Second, the increasingly wealthy and independent-minded medieval cities began to finance their own centers of higher learning or universities. Until then, theological learning and cultural production had happened through monks at monasteries and, later, in schools attached to important cathedrals. These emerging independent schools were modeled after the institutions of higher education of the Muslim world, such as the famous Al-Azhar school in Cairo. These schools were still clearly Christian schools, but the crucial difference was that they were not under the control of the church and were not financed by the church. The first such independent learning center was the University of Bologna, founded in 1088. Soon, similar centers of independent learning and research were established in other parts of western Europe—Paris in 1150, Oxford in 1167, Cambridge in 1209, and Salamanca, Spain, in 1218, to name a few.

Third, members of mendicant orders, Franciscans and Dominicans, took up teaching positions in the newly founded universities and thus created a significant link between the church authorities and the unrestricted learning that happened at the universities. The great theologians of this period all came from the Dominican or Franciscan orders—the Dominicans Albertus Magnus or Albert the Great (c. 1193–1280) from southern Germany and Thomas Aquinas (1225–74), still the most important Roman Catholic teacher after Augustine; and the Franciscans Bonaventura (1221–74) and

Duns Scotus (c. 1270–1308), founder of the school of Scotists and a strong opponent to Thomas' soteriology.

The Fourth Period: Late Medieval Theology in the Fourteenth and Fifteenth Centuries

The last period of medieval scholastic theology saw growing doctrinal plurality and a diversity of traditions, which provided an important background for the theological debates of the Reformation. The most important schools were the older but still influential *via antiqua* (Latin for "the old way"), the emerging *via moderna* ("the modern way"), and the *via Augustiniana moderna* ("the modern Augustinian school"). These schools continued the earlier debate between realists and nominalists but carried it from the field of epistemology (theories of knowledge) to the field of soteriology: at stake was the question of whether God could have chosen another way to save humankind. Possibly the most famous theologian of this time was the Franciscan William of Ockham (c. 1280–1349), who strictly separated faith and reason. The philosophy of this period laid the groundwork for the theology of the Reformation and the later philosophy of the Enlightenment. Ockham, who belonged to the *via moderna*, stood in opposition to Thomas' harmonization of faith and reason.

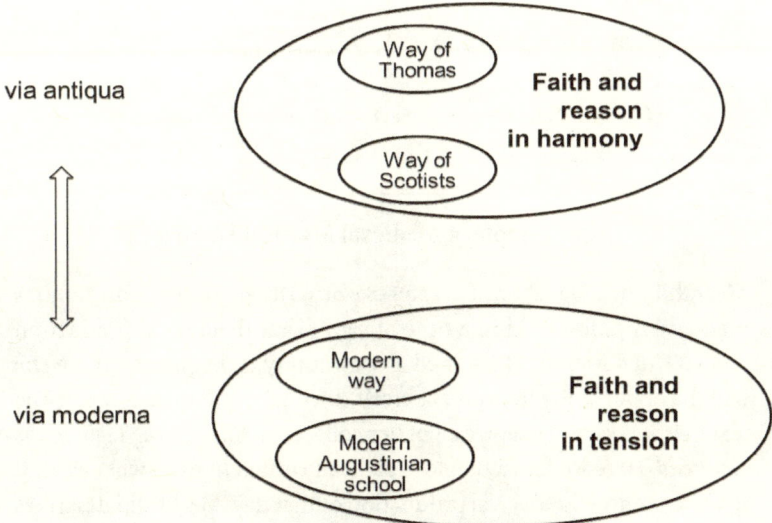

Fig. 13.1: Medieval concepts of faith and reason

All the while, mysticism continued to flourish (see also above, ch. 11), experiencing a revival through independent mystics and members of various religious orders. Many of the famous mystics in this period were women. Mysticism boomed particularly in Germany, where the Beguine Mechthild of Magdeburg (1210–85) had already prepared the ground for its subsequent growth in the thirteenth and fourteenth centuries. Famous mystical theologians were the German Dominicans Meister Eckhart (c. 1260–1327) and John Tauler (c. 1300–1361), as well as Catherine of Siena (1347–80), Julian of Norwich (c. 1342–1416), and Thomas of Kempen (1380–1471), who wrote one of the most famous devotional books in Christian history, *The Imitation of Christ*.

	Theological and philosophical events and movements	Important theologians	Core controversies
400 to 1000	• Neo-Platonist Mysticism • Carolingian Renaissance • Post-Carolingian theological production and revival of mysticism in the West	• (Pseudo-) Dyonisius the Areopagite • Alcuin • John Scotus Eriugena • Radbertus	• Debate about the filioque
1000 to 1150	• Ontological and cosmological proof of God • Realism • Nominalism	• Berengar of Tours • Anselm • Abelard • Peter Lombardus	• Controversy about the transubstantiation • Controversy about the universals
1150 to 1300	• Rediscovery of the full Aristotle • Development of universities • Dominicans and Franciscans entering university teaching	• Albertus Magnus • Thomas Aquinas • Duns Scotus	• Controversy between rationalism and voluntarism
1300 to 1500	• Voluntarism • Via moderna • Revival of mysticism	• William of Occam • Meister Eckhardt • Catherine of Siena • Thomas of Kempen	• Controversy between rationalism and voluntarism

Fig. 13.2: Four periods of medieval theological development

An Example of Medieval Mystical Writing

Mechthild of Magdeburg (c. 1208–82 or 94), one of the most famous medieval mystics, lived in a time of significant theological production and spiritual revival. She joined a community of Beguines, where she had the opportunity to express herself spiritually and theologically. The text below is part of chapter 44 of her collection *The Flowing Light of the Godhead*. Here we find a theology radically different from what we find in the common theological production of that day. Mechthild describes her visions of her soul's encounter with the Lord in, one may say, deeply erotic language, thus reflecting a tremendous spiritual and psychological intimacy.

Then the bride of all delights goes to the Fairest of lovers in the secret chamber of the invisible Godhead. There she finds the bed and the abode of love prepared by God in a manner beyond what is human. Our Lord speaks:

"Stay, Lady Soul."

"What do you bid me, Lord?"

"Take off your clothes."

"Lord, what will happen to me then?"

"Lady Soul, you are so utterly formed to my nature
That not the slightest thing can be between you and me.
Never was an angel so glorious
That to him was granted for one hour
What is given to you for eternity.
And so you must cast off from you
Both fear and shame and all external virtues.
Rather, those alone that you carry within yourself
Shall you foster forever.
These are your noble longing
And your boundless desire.
These I shall fulfill forever
With my limitless lavishness."

"Lord, now I am a naked soul
And you in yourself are a well-adorned God.
Our shared lot is eternal life
Without death."

Then a blessed stillness
That both desire comes over them.
He surrenders himself to her,
And she surrenders herself to him.
What happens to her then—she knows—
And that is fine with me.
But this cannot last long.
When two lovers meet secretly,
They must often part from one another inseparably.

Dear friend of God, I have written for you this path of love. May God infuse it into your heart! Amen.

Source: Mechthild of Magdeburg, *Flowing Light of the Godhead*, 61–62.

THE CONTROVERSY ABOUT THE UNIVERSALS

Medieval theology inherited from Greek philosophy the question of how ideas or generic terms (the names of things) relate to the individual objects. Plato had answered this question by giving higher dignity to *ideas* because they were eternal and unchanging, while the individual *objects* were subject to constant change. When some theologians began to question this view, a controversy about the "universals" emerged.

What Was the Controversy About?

The starting point of the controversy lay in several Platonist principles:

(a) *The general is of higher being or of higher status than the particular.*

(b) *Names or ideas are real*, and more so than the individual transient objects; in other words, truth, true being, and reality are to be found in the general rather than in the individual transient objects. *The more general a name or an idea, the more real it is.*

(c) *Logical relationships are also ontological relationships*; in other words, the relationships of general names to each other and to particular objects designated by such names parallel a relationship of "being," an ontological order of the world.

> As an example: a particular apple surely has some reality, but this reality is a transient one. After the apple is eaten, nothing of it is left. Yet, the name (or the idea) "apple" remains even after the particular apple has disappeared. It still exists and is not subject to transience. It thus has, according to the traditional Platonist view, a higher level of truth. Now, one may imagine that at some point in history, all apples and apple trees disappear. Yet, the idea of an apple would still survive. It could be found in books or in pictures or stories about apples. The *idea* of the apple is independent of the particular fruit; it thus has higher dignity and is of a higher level of truth. Now, we may further imagine both that people completely forget that something like apples ever existed and that all stories about apples are forgotten. With the disappearance of apples, the term *apple* may also fall into disuse. The idea of the apple may thus also be subject to transience. Yet apples belong to the even broader category of fruits and to the again broader category of living things, both of which continue to exist even when all apples have disappeared.

> However, even these may be imagined at some point in time to cease in their existence. Yet even then something remains, be it time as such, or the origin of time and being. This eternal origin is thus of higher being than all the transient beings.

As the second principle above stresses, the universals are real: they are substances (things; in Latin, *res*) that are more original and, we could say, more real than the particular objects. They create and originate the particular beings. This position is called realism because it emphasized that the reality of the things/substances precedes the particular objects. A common short form to understand this position is universals before individuals (in Latin, *universalia ante rem*). The most important representative of realism was Anselm, the archbishop of Canterbury. Anselm became famous for applying this theory to the question of God's existence and using it as a proof for God.

How Did the Controversy over the Universals Lead to Anselm's Proof of God?

One of the principles of realism we have been discussing is the theory that the more general an idea or a term, the more real it is. Anselm theorized that if God was believed to be of the highest universality, the highest ontological level, this necessarily includes God's reality. To be the most universal being includes being the most real (Latin: *ens realissimum*). In other words, in the order of reality, the most general name, the one that includes everything in its being, is also the truest. There is a clear link between the highest truth and the highest being—because if the highest truth lacked being, a truth could be imagined that would be of even higher being, namely, a truth that also *included* its being. The highest reality necessarily also includes its *existence*. This is proof of why God as highest being must also exist. The ontological proof of God thus deduces God's existence from the idea of God: The idea of the most perfect and highest being must necessarily include its existence.

Anselm's ontological attempt to prove God was different from the traditional cosmological proof of God, which had been known already in the philosophy of Aristotle. The cosmological proof found evidence of God instead in the existence of created beings: because beings exist, we must assume the existence of a first and highest being, the unmoved mover, which caused these secondary beings to exist and from which they derive their existence.

While Anselm's ontological proof of God appears as mere tautology, and while attempts to prove God may ring hollow and futile to our modern ears, we need to remember that these proofs came not from a lack of faith but rather from a desire for intellectual self-assurance, for a reconciliation of reason with faith—faith seeking understanding (Latin: *fides quaerens intellectum*). The basis of such intellectual queries was always the revelation received through faith. Proof of God was not supposed to replace faith.

From Where Did Criticism of Realism Arise?

Realism was criticized most strongly for two of its tenets. First was the idea that the more general the ideas (or universals, names, generic terms), the truer and higher they are. This led to an ontologically graded worldview that saw all beings in an order of descent from God. This concept of an ontological pyramid, proceeding from the general to the particular, carried the inherent danger of pantheism, with lower beings still seeming to partake in God's being, simply not in fullness. Pantheism is thus an inherent possibility of all concepts of realism—and the problem of pantheism is that it blurs the strict separation between God and the world that is fundamental to monotheistic faiths.

A second, related concern was that realism's emphasis on the general devalued the particular. This stood in contrast to the Christian tradition, which valued the particular and the individual because each particular being was believed to reflect the creative power of God. As a consequence, it also denied the fundamental equality of all creatures as being part of God's creation. Aloof and abstract generalization did not go together with faith in a God who was equally related to each individual human being and who was involved in the changes of history.

Nominalist Criticism of Realism

Such criticism of realism found expression in an alternative philosophical tradition called nominalism. Nominalism claims that the universals or the common names are not real substances (or beings) but simply names of physical bodies. Actual reality belongs to the particular beings. In other words, universals are summarizing names derived from the individual beings. They come logically and ontologically after the particular objects (in Latin, *universalia post rem*).

Behind the nominalist philosophy stands the philosophy of Aristotle. He taught that reality emerges through form being imprinted on matter, thus giving more value to the physical world than did the philosophy of Plato. An inherent danger of nominalism is sensualism, a doctrine that developed much later, but mentioned here because of its affinity to nominalism; it taught that reality belonged only to what is perceptible by human senses and that knowledge of reality could only be gained by sensory experience.

Representatives of nominalism include Berengar of Tours; Roscellin, about whom little is known; and, in the later period, William of Ockham, who renewed nominalist thought in a new context. The controversy has been popularized through a highly readable mystery novel, *The Name of the Rose*, by the Italian author Umberto Eco.

What Is the Relevance of the Controversy?

What may to some appear as a very abstract debate of little practical relevance had for medieval theology great significance, particularly in the doctrine of transubstantiation. Realism supported the doctrine of transubstantiation, stating that, when the Eucharist is conducted, the change in the elements affects not their appearance but their invisible substance (the idea, name, or inner being of bread and wine). This substance is of higher reality and thus is the truly real being. What remains the same are only the so-called accidents, that is, the visible attributes of the bread and wine. Change happens underneath this apparently unchanged bread and wine in their invisible substance, which is the true being. In contrast, nominalists like Berengar of Tours denied the possibility that the substance of bread and wine in the Eucharist could be changed into the body and blood of Christ while maintaining their previous outward appearance because, he said, the substance (idea or name) of bread and wine is in fact derived from the particular and visibly physical bread and wine.

Alternative Voices in the Controversy

Another solution to the controversy about what is real came from Abelard. He agreed with nominalists that the universals arise in the process of thinking: names are the results of intellectual summaries that subsume similar things under the same word or category. Yet, they still have a relation to absolute reality. He thus suggested that the universals first existed in God, as concepts in God's mind, before creation. As such, they are before the physical being (Latin: *universalia ante rem*). Secondly, universals exist *within* the things when they participate as individual beings in the same kinds and categories (Latin: *universalia in re*). The individual carries in it certain essential elements that it shares with other individual beings. This second position is also called indifferentism: the real similarities are those that are *indifferent* (i.e., not different) in all the individuals. In this way, the category inhabits the kind indifferently, and the kind inhabits the exemplar indifferently. Finally, the universals exist as processes of human reason, through comparing observations when human reason obtains concepts and universal ideas of physical reality (Latin: *universalia post rem*). In other words, the universals are *ante rem* in regard to God's process of creation, *in re* in regard to nature, and *post rem* in regard to human knowledge. Abelard's philosophy is sometimes called *conceptualism*.

Abelard's position stands historically and systematically between realism and nominalism.

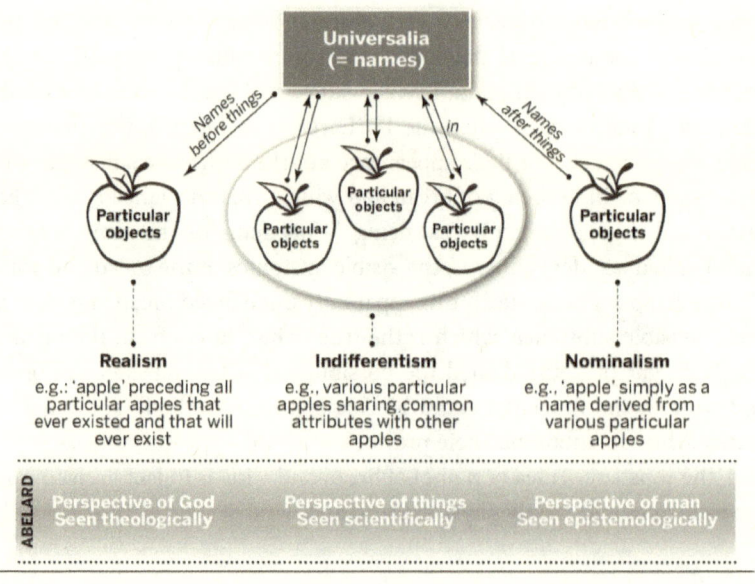

Fig. 13.3: *Different positions in the controversy about the universals*

THE CONTROVERSY BETWEEN RATIONALISM AND VOLUNTARISM

From the late thirteenth century on, medieval theological reflection took new directions. The increased study of Aristotle had caused science to develop more independently from theology; in the controversy about the universals, nominalism had brought a stronger emphasis on the individual and the particular. This led the traditional harmony between God and human reason—or between the religious and the scientific, which had shaped Western philosophy ever since the patristic era—to gradually dissolve.

The Overall Movement of Thought: Separation— Harmonization—Renewed Separation

We remember that Plato had introduced a radical dualism between ideas and matter in the intellectual history of the Occident. However, this dualism softened already in Plato's later works, when he spoke of (*a*) god as the highest being and (*b*) of a chain of being that extends from god through the lower ideas to the material reality. It was this idea that was further developed in Neo-Platonism and that understood all of reality hierarchically. This dissolution of Plato's dualism was the basis of the patristic harmonization of God and reason: the two do not stand in contrast, but knowledge of God is higher than knowledge of reason because God is the highest idea. (A different dissolution of the original dualism between the world of ideas and the world of matter was suggested by Aristotle: He resolved Plato's dualism in his concept of reality by explaining that reality originated in immaterial forms, something like Plato's ideas, imprinting themselves on matter.)

In the thirteenth century, the Aristotelian train of thought was resumed in scholastic teaching. The Dominican theologians Albert and Thomas applied it to the relationship between nature and religion, or between philosophy and theology, explaining that what is known through reason does not stand in contrast but in subjection to what is revealed by God; knowledge of God is not against reason but higher than reason. With this, Albert and Thomas created the basic pattern of thought that has shaped the teaching of the Roman Catholic Church: faith is not opposed to reason but is above it. Faith and reason stand in harmony, in which faith supersedes reason.[2] The teaching of the church is not *against* the teaching of philosophy but surpasses it. Grace is not against nature but above nature, perfecting and completing nature.[3]

---

2. See for instance Thomas, *Commentary on Boethius'* De Trinitate II.3: "What is divinely taught to us by faith cannot be contrary to what we are endowed with by nature."

3. Thomas, *Summa* Ia q. 1 a. 8 ad. 2, which states one of the most basic principles of Roman Catholic theology: Grace does not destroy nature but perfects it (*gratia non tollit naturam sed perficit*). Thomas, *Summa*, 13.

This great harmonization gave way to a renewed separation, which emerged from the teaching of Duns Scotus and Ockham. These Franciscan theologians held that the realm of grace is known through revelation and nothing else. They stressed two points equally: that human reason is unable to grasp the mysteries of the immaterial and divine world; and that rational knowledge is focused only on the material world and unable to access the divine world. This separation between the world of revelation and the material world, or between the otherness of God and the world governed by reason, opened a gap between philosophy and theology, defining philosophy more in worldly terms. The relationship between reason and faith was turned into one of tension. This development paralleled the increased emphasis on the individual and the particular, as seen in nominalist thought.

These developments also found reflection in the field of psychology and anthropology, particularly in the debate about whether reason or human will should take priority.

How Did the Controversy about the Priority of Reason vis-à-vis the Priority of Human Will Unfold?

Most parts of medieval philosophy followed a principle first formulated by Socrates, namely, that the human will naturally follows what it recognizes as good. Virtue is based on understanding and can be nurtured and cultivated by teaching. Or, in shortest form: sin is a form of error. This moral principle remained widely accepted throughout the centuries. During the medieval time, Thomas and the Dominican theologians taught that the human will is guided by the knowledge of what is good. The human will necessarily turns to what it understands as good and thus shows its dependence on knowledge. This view may be called rationalism. It regards reason as superior to will—human reason recognizes what is good and guides the human will accordingly.

On the other side stood Franciscan theologians like Duns Scotus and Ockham, who rediscovered in Augustine's writings a philosophy that strongly emphasized the activity of the will in our mental processes. Augustine taught that the different aspects of a personality—will, sensual perception, and reason—are deeply entangled and that the ultimate goal of human life is a perfect peace, to be found in the perfect vision of God, a state where humans are free from will and desire and find perfect rest in God's glory. Yet, he also taught that the human will was a driving power in the process of human recognition.[4] It is this thought that Scotus and Ockham

---

4. Augustine's voluntarist principles are spelled out particularly in his *On the Trinity*, bk. 11 (*NPNF* 1/3:144–54).

rediscovered in their opposition to Thomism. They explained that, in the process of knowledge, we receive many perceptions. However, only those perceptions on which the human will focuses a person's attention, those that the human will actually chooses, become distinct. In other words, the will drives reason. This position was called voluntarism.

What Was the Theological Relevance of This Anthropological Debate?

Initially, the discussion about the relative priority of will and reason referred to the process of human cognition, but it also found reflection in contrasting understandings of God. The rationalism of Thomas regarded the will of God as a function of God's intellect. This meant, as in the theological understanding of creation, that God creates only what he in his wisdom recognizes as good. In creation God expresses and realizes his own inner being, which is good and reasonable.

Voluntarism criticized this rationalist understanding of God because it seems to limit God's freedom and omnipotence; it makes God appear to depend on something else, namely, what is good. Voluntarist theology instead maintained that God is radically free in his will—he created the world not because it was good, but out of His free will, in an act of pure grace.

How Did the Debate Affect Ethics?

Both sides agreed that the moral law was God's law; however, they disagreed about the foundations of the moral law. Thomas taught that God had established the moral law because it was good and because He recognized it as such. What is good is a consequence of God's wisdom. The moral good is rationally intelligible, and reason and virtue are thus connected. This tradition shaped Roman Catholic moral teaching through the centuries and is reflected in its teaching on *natural law*, the teaching that the higher moral law and the laws given in nature stand in a relationship of continuity. For example, Christian marital laws or family laws do not stand in contrast to nature; they are based on nature or, possibly, they perfect what is already given by nature. Conversely, what is against nature is also against God's law.

On the other side of the argument, voluntarist theologians instead held that something is good only because God wanted it to be good. In his unlimited almightiness God could have defined something else as good.

Nothing as such is sin; it is only God's moral law that causes something to be sin. The consequences of these theological and ethical controversies were played out in the field of soteriology, which brings us to the eve of the Reformation, where the soteriological questions of course played a key role.

What Is the Soteriological Significance of the Controversy?

The question about whether reason or the will takes priority in God's activity had an immediate impact on the question of justification. Is the way God justifies human beings *necessary*, as, for example, Anselm had suggested? Or could God have chosen another way? In the thirteenth century, theologians largely believed that justification involved created habits of grace and that justification happened by humans being elevated to a different state of grace. Such a created habit of grace appeared natural and necessary for our justification. This view of justification is also called *intrinsic*, that is, given by the nature of being. In contrast, opponents of this view suggested that God was radically free and could have opted for an alternative way of justification. As a consequence, various voluntarist theologians of the fourteenth century taught that it was not so much a created (intrinsic) habit of grace in us, but only *God's acceptance of us*, that caused our justification. This is also called the *extrinsic* view of justification. These two conflicting understandings of salvation—intrinsic and extrinsic—foreshadowed the later clash, during the Reformation, between Roman Catholic and Protestant soteriologies.

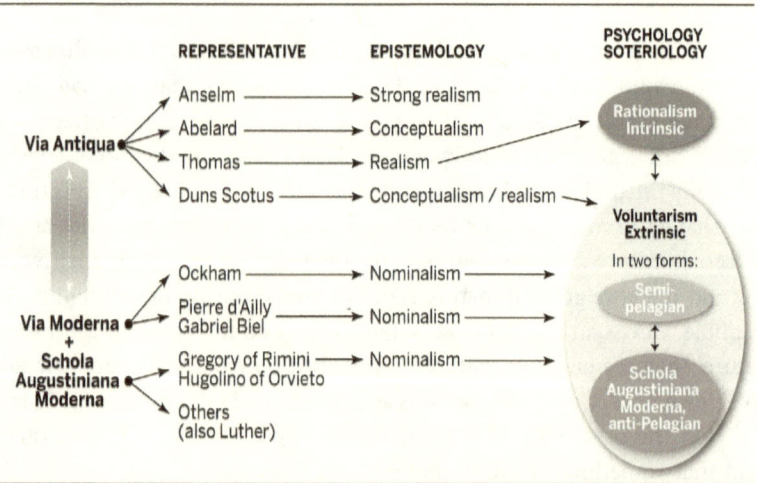

Fig. 13.4: An overview of medieval movements of theology and philosophy

What Did This Controversy Signify for the Intellectual History of the West?

The antagonism between reason and will that emerged during the late medieval period may be seen as the resurgence of an antagonism between its two sources: the biblical tradition and the Greek tradition. In fact, the intellectual history of the West can be read—at least partly—as the changing relationship of these two sources.

The trajectory of occidental thought started from an early reconciliation and interpenetration of the two traditions, beginning with patristic theology and culminating in the theology of Thomas, which then gave way to renewed separation. Ever since the early patristic theology, the two currents had been in harmony, but now, in the late medieval time, the tension between the two sources reemerged. We may call it the tension between Aristotle and Augustine.

Accordingly, the theology of the Protestant Reformers may be understood as calling for a return not only to Scripture—famously expressed in the slogan *sola scriptura*—but also to the voluntarist theology of Augustine, which meant a dissolution of the harmony between faith and reason. This separation and differentiation in theological reflection happened as reason and scientific reflection increasingly gained independence and found liberation from the church's tutelage. Parallel to this process of separation between faith and reason, an analogous process likewise became visible in society: the differentiation of independent political and spiritual spheres, which was a late fruit of the conflict between spiritual and temporal power that had previously been expressed in the investiture controversy.

For Further Reading

Eco, Umberto. *The Name of the Rose*. Translated by William Weaver. London: Vintage, 2004.

McGrath, Alister E. *The Intellectual Origins of the European Reformation*. 2nd ed. Malden, MA: Blackwell, 2004.

Smith, Lesley. "The Theological Framework." In *The Cambridge History of Christianity*, vol. 4, *Christianity in Western Europe c. 1100–c. 1500*, edited by Miri Rubin and Walter Simons, 75–88. Cambridge: Cambridge University Press, 2009.

Stark, Rodney. *The Victory of Reason: How Christianity Led to Freedom, Capitalism, and Western Success*. New York: Random House, 2006.

Van Nieuwenhove, Rik. *An Introduction to Medieval Theology*. Cambridge: Cambridge University Press, 2012.

Learning Activities

1) Review key elements of this chapter by answering the following questions:
    - o Discuss the history of theology through the medieval period: what non-theological factors influenced the theological developments?
    - o Name two theologians from each of the four periods of medieval theology.
    - o What are the theological implications of realism and nominalism? How do you personally understand the universals?
    - o What are the particular theological implications of the rationalist and voluntarist understandings of God?

2) To probe your understanding of what we have learned about this period, to deepen the understanding of its significance, and to apply it to your present experience, discuss the following questions:
    - o How do you understand the relationship between faith and reason?
    - o What can Christians in a modern Asian context gain from these medieval philosophical discussions?

Epilogue

Faith, God-Talk, and Historical Studies[1]

THE STUDY OF THE history of Christianity combines at least three different aspects. Firstly and most simply, it aims at giving an account of what has been, where we as Christians come from. Secondly, addressing people from various traditions, it seeks to critically examine different spiritual and theological traditions and identities within a context of denominational diversity. Thirdly, the study of the history of Christianity is part of the spiritual training of believers; it reveals the basically dialectic pattern of our faith and contributes to theological depth and spiritual formation.

GOD—A QUESTION OR AN ANSWER?

What is faith? Faith is a movement of trusting surrender and of finding existential ground despite the groundlessness of our existence. It is a sense of being at home in a context of alienation, a trust in the meaning and purpose of life although we cannot prove it. It is relying on God's guidance in a reality beyond our control; and it is engaging with a broken world even though we are part of this brokenness and have only limited understanding and ability. This is a first and very simple approach to faith.

In a more philosophical way, we may say: faith is, in simple form, *the art of keeping the question open and of joyfully surrendering to this openness.*

---

1. Revised version of an article first published in Xing Fu Zeng et al., eds., Ren yan wo wei shui fu? Lu Long Guang yuan zhang rong xiu jinian wen zhe, Xiang gang: Jidujiaowenshu chu ban she (人言我為誰乎？盧龍光院長榮休紀念文集，香港：基督教文書出版社), 2014, 15-34.

The question means the questions of our being: Why are we at all? Why are we the way we are? Where do we come from? What is the purpose of our life? Where do we go? What is right? All these questions are unanswerable. They point beyond our reality, beyond any immanent answer from within our own lives. They imply a perspective and position that offers an answer from outside our own reality, overlooking the whole of our life and being. Yet we ask these questions from the perspective and position of our finiteness.

By implying a point beyond our limited being, the said questions point beyond us to a reality often summarized in one word: God. God is a simple yet powerful and life-transforming word that stands for a reality and a power that cannot further be described; it stands for the transcendent ground of our life, for the "beyond in the midst of our life."[2] Hence, faith is always a double movement. Faith on one side is ready to accept the impossibility of finding firm existential ground or definitive answers to basic questions. On the other side, faith defies this paralyzing lack of firm ground and engages in a world beyond understanding. In other words, faith actively defends the transcendence of God and opposes any attempt to forcefully answer unanswerable existential questions, while willingly stepping into a radical practice of love despite lacking firm ground. These two sides are like the two sides of the hidden and revealed God.

The problem of Christian faith expression, in individual *and* corporate forms of faith, is both that we are in a constant danger of appropriating the One we refer to and of turning the mystery of our being into an answer. The word "God" is used lightly, as if we knew what it stands for. From a word that stands for the big question, it is turned into an answer that fills in the gaps of our understanding and knowledge. This is a natural process, as we get used to talking about God. And this is, at the same time, where we as Christians once again fashion ourselves a golden calf. We give answers and claim to do so rightfully, based on the assumption that we have a privileged access to God through Jesus Christ and that, based on this special grasp of God, we are capable of assuming the transcendent position from which answers to the questions of life emerge. This turns a relationship into ownership. It dissolves the alien-ness of God into revelation and familiarity. Instead of being a community that celebrates the open questions, Christianity presents itself as the community that gives answers.

This is where theology and ultimately also pastoral practice come into play. Both have the purpose of leading Christians back to the openness of our existence, as we faithfully surrender to the mystery of our being. Both

---

2. Bonhoeffer, *Letters and Papers from Prison*, 124.

theology and pastoral practice have the same purpose—theology achieves it through critical reflection while pastoral practice achieves it through preaching and pastoral care. That purpose is to liquefy Christian faith where it is petrified, to counteract the defining tendency of the faith community, and to lead our faith back to its mysterious origin while at the same time nurturing trust and a sense of being at home.

DOING THEOLOGY TO UPHOLD THE MYSTERY

This religious tendency to appropriate and petrify what can never be owned and understood, a tendency often supported by church leaders and theologians, is countered by simultaneous theological reflection and pastoral practice. This dialectic between appropriation and critical reopening of the question that lies at the ground of our spiritual journey runs throughout church history and has always inspired theologians. It is in response to this dialectic tension—between the claim of religious knowledge and our inability to know—that Paul Tillich vindicates doubt, because at least there is "faith in every serious doubt, namely the faith in the truth as such, even if the only truth we can express is our lack of truth."[3] Tillich describes this counter-movement against all petrification, this liquefaction, as the ground of Protestantism. It is the Protestant principle that keeps Protestantism from turning any specific historical *Gestalt*, any form of its own, into an idol. The "Protestant Principle cannot admit any identification of grace with a visible reality, not even with the church on its visible side."[4] Christianity is final "because it has the power of criticizing and transforming each of its historical manifestations."[5] Ultimately, the tension between the religious tendency to offer answers and the encounter with the mysterious God who transcends all answers can, with reference to Tillich's autobiographical sketch, be described as standing "on the boundary" between home and an alien land.[6]

The twentieth-century theologian who perhaps most strongly expressed this tension and dialectic was Karl Barth. He described the paradoxical situation of Christian theology as follows: "*As ministers* we ought to speak of God. We are human, however, and so we cannot speak of God. We ought therefore to recognize both *our obligation and our inability*, and by that very recognition give God the glory."[7] He critically reminds the church-

---

3. Tillich, *Protestant Era*, xiv.
4. Ibid., xxi.
5. Ibid., xxii.
6. Tillich, "On the Boundary," 67–72.
7. Barth, "Word of God," 186.

es that people don't need ministers "to help them with the appurtenances of their daily life. They look after those things without advice from us and with more wisdom than we usually credit them with. But they are aware that their daily life and all the questions which are factors in it are affected by a great What? Why? Whence? Whither? which stands like a minus sign before the whole parenthesis and changes to a new question all the questions inside—even those which may already have been answered."[8]

This tension within our faith was discovered long before the last century; it is what inspired Martin Luther along his spiritual and theological path. For Luther, theology was a constant struggle, as Ebeling has pointed out most clearly: "The dominant point of view in Luther is that of the conflict, which he makes as acute as possible, treating it, as one might almost think, with a delight in paradox."[9] In the faith life and theological reflection of Luther, we can discover a constant tension and dialectic between the revealed God (*deus revelatus*) and the hidden God (*deus absconditus*), between the revealed word (*verbum revelatum*) and the alien word (*verbum alienum*), and eventually between gospel and law. Luther pointed out that law and gospel are to be discerned but not to be separated, that they are both Word of God, and that they are not to be identified with the Old and New Testaments, respectively, but that they are two different ways in which God has revealed himself. Earlier traditions of Christianity describe this same dialectic of our faith as a dialectic movement of positive and negative theology, of word and silence, of defining and hiding, of kataphatic and apophatic. It is the basic breathing movement of our faith where, by worshiping God, we affirm and speak of God while, at the same time, we are brought back to humble silence before our creator, acknowledging our powerlessness when facing the suffering of an unredeemed creation and the limits of our wisdom when facing the unanswerable questions of life.

Theological education is a process of learning the language of such faith in tension. It is a special training in communicating faith and interaction within the faith community, daring to speak of God while constantly avoiding confinement of the One to whom it refers. Theological education understood as such language training is a training in the awareness of where our faith language has appropriated the mysterious God and claimed ownership over God. Theological training should, above all else, equip Christian leaders with the power to discern when faith turns into triumphalism or arrogant assuredness and where it ignores the open questions and the still-unredeemed suffering. Theological formation molds our faith and intellect

---

8. Ibid., 187.
9. Ebeling, *Luther*, 143–44.

to become attentive to areas where religious faith language turns into hegemonic expression, where it defines truth and establishes orthodoxy in place of mystery, and where it imposes uniformity that conceals the conflicts of which we are part.

FROM RELIGIOUS EXPERIENCE TO TRADITION

Church history may, on the basis of such an understanding of faith and theology, be described as a theological discipline that follows a historical and dialectical movement: the appropriations and definitions of truth; and their counterpart, the acts of tearing the question open again. Church history thus follows a *dialectic trajectory* from religious experience to tradition and back to renewed religious experience—similar to the tension between word and silence described above.

Indeed, all religious faith has its roots in a primary faith experience, an immediate and overwhelming awareness of standing before the mysterious reality of God. Rudolf Otto described this experience as the experience of the sacred, an experience deeply ambivalent, both frightening and fascinating, a *mysterium tremendum et fascinans*, an experience that is radically different from all ordinary life and that, due to its overwhelming power, evokes fear but equally appears fascinating because it appears so merciful and gracious. Throughout the history of religions, different traditions have been inspired by particular and outstanding primary faith experiences of so-called religious virtuosi (Weber)—mystics, teachers, founders of religious traditions—in short, people who claim or appear to have had direct experiences of divine reality in a unique and personal way that is significant for the broader community. In contrast to these religious virtuosi, ordinary people may have had only fleeting or secondary religious experiences that are derivative of the experiences of the religious virtuosi, reflecting their primary breakthroughs. Even though these ordinary people may similarly have experienced spiritual peak moments, they understand them only by relating them to the previous religious experiences of the virtuosi. Yet, whatever the reputation of the individual, whenever such primary and apparently self-authenticating religious experiences are communicated, it happens by means of language and symbolic expressions that are understandable to ordinary people. In this regard, the difference between religious virtuosi and ordinary people is simply that the former *create new meaning* in existing language and symbols to communicate their experiences, while the latter make use of the former's language and symbols when communicating or interpreting their own religious experiences. Both religious virtuosi (even when creatively renewing language) and ordinary believers rely on existing words, symbols, or frameworks of understanding. If religious virtuosi created a totally new language, they would not be understood anymore. The paradox of religious language is that it has to make use of an ordinary and existing framework of understanding, even as primary religious experiences breach the reality of ordinary life.[10]

As language communicating religious experiences is codified and handed down to later generations, it turns into *tradition*. Tradition is a repeated use of language that has in the past communicated religious experience beyond the immediacy of the moment and that has the power to cause a renewal of such experience. Tradition is as necessary for those who have had a primary religious experience (in order to sustain it over time) as for those who have not (in order to access it). Tradition embeds religious experience in a practice, language, and a belief system that is increasingly standardized and that thus forfeits the immediacy of the primary religious experience. The original charismatic experience turns into religious bureaucracy. As the faith community further grows and matures, "God" turns into a familiar word that loses its alien character. God is domesticated and integrated in the belief and practice of the faith community. Faith turns into belief.[11] Many scholars of church history see this shift in the middle of the second century of the Christian era, when Christianity developed a creed, a canon, and formal doctrines to defend the correct interpretation of Jesus Christ against alternative interpretations. This process transformed "what was essentially a Spirit-guided movement of faith into a 'belief-demarcated' confederation."[12] A careful reading of church history shows that the shift from a Spirit-guided faith movement to a belief system is not something that solely belongs to the past and that is reversed today as we experience a resurgence of faith.[13] Rather, the shift from faith to belief and the resurgence of faith are again part of a dialectic history where the two—faith and belief—have always stood and continue to stand in tension.

WHAT DRIVES THE HISTORY OF CHRISTIANITY?

The study of church history is an attempt to trace this dialectic. It helps us understand how the many conflicts, which cause many people to regard church history as a rather dark story, are actually expressions of this simple

---

10. See overall Berger, *Heretical Imperative*, 32–54.
11. Cox, *Secular City*, 73–84.
12. Cox, *Future of Faith*, 83.
13. Ibid., 213.

breathing movement (see above) of defining and delimiting. A student of church history may discover a basic pattern in the multitude and apparent randomness of historical events, foremost a *dialectic movement of institutionalization and protest*, of petrification and revival, of charisma turning into bureaucracy and of new charismatic experiences arising.

In simple form, the story is the following: As churches grow, the need arises to clarify their institutional structures and to codify their belief. In this process, spiritual immediacy gets lost. Instead of communicating and facilitating spiritual experience, the churches become obstacles to the immediate encounter with God. The church becomes static and more concerned with its own institutional existence than with bringing people closer to God.

Various factors drive the process of institutionalization. First, most churches regard growth as a natural process or even as a form of God's blessing; in fact, most people would naturally measure the success of a church by the number of its members and agree that the stronger the church, the higher its impact and the wider the dispersion of the gospel. Further, generational change often goes together with a loss of zeal and increased bureaucratization. Another factor is the upward social mobility that often results from a devout and more ascetic life and in turn leads to material prosperity and subsequently to increasing this-worldliness.[14] Yet, against a church that has become too institutional, too static, and too self-centered, protest movements arise, trying to regain a more immediate (literally, i.e., unmediated) spiritual experience and relationship with God. Such countercultural Christians, fringe groups, prophetic voices, and charismatic experts leave the bureaucratic church in protest, or they silently set up their own alternative communities where primacy and primordial obedience are thought to be again given to God rather than to the church. Soon enough, though, they themselves start to attract followers and to grow, and the "alternative" movement itself becomes subject to the same institutionalizing forces.

A brief look into the history of Christianity may provide some examples. The reform movement initiated by Jesus soon enough (most strongly when encountering doctrinal challenges from Gnostics and Marcionites in the middle of the second century) turned into a catholic church that harmonized the different faith forms and that defined the limits of acceptable doctrine. At the same time, the Montanist movement emerged as an implicit protest against the Jesus-followers' increasing loss of apocalyptic expectation. Later, when Constantine and subsequent Roman emperors turned Christian faith into a state religion, the monastic movement offered an alternative spiritual experience. Against the power of the medieval church,

---

14. Niebuhr, *Social Sources of Denominationalism*, 54.

various reform and protest movements arose and were partly absorbed into the church, partly dismissed as heresy. The Protestant reformations were movements that tried to regain spiritual immediacy and that rejected the ecclesially mediated form of salvation offered by the medieval Catholic Church. The development of the Lutheran movement shows particularly well the dialectic of institutionalization and protest: within only a few decades, the movement initiated by Luther turned into so-called Lutheran orthodoxy, which was primarily concerned with the right definition of doctrine and with a defense of Luther's heritage against the challenges from Calvinists, Zwinglians, and Radical Reformers, as well as from the Roman Catholic tradition. The revivalist movements since the late seventeenth century—Pietism, Methodism, the Great Awakening, the Evangelical Awakening around the turn of the eighteenth to the nineteenth century, and the Holiness Revival as well as the Pentecostal awakening and the later revivals in the early twentieth century—can all be interpreted within the framework of a dialectic between institutionalization and protest. The two poles stand for a certain tension: on one hand, the need for *a mediator* to communicate, channel, and safeguard a tradition of religious experience; on the other, many spiritual seekers' quest for an *unmediated religious experience*.

The dialectic tension between institutionalization and protest is not the only pattern that helps us find meaning in the multitude of historical events. Another dialectic movement is the movement between an emphasis on the word and an emphasis on the spirit. The *dialectic of word and spirit* is of a different category than the one of institutionalization/protest and does not match it, although institutionalization quite often emphasizes the codified word, while an emphasis on the spirit often appears as a challenge to petrified structures. For example, the Montanist movement of the second century can be interpreted as a spirit-inspired protest against the institutionalization and codification of the early church's tendency toward a catholic (i.e., unified) structure. Yet, protest and revival movements may equally happen with reference to the word, as several of the Reformation movements showed: It was in the name of the word of the Bible and reviving the word of God that Luther protested against the medieval church and its elaborate mediation of salvation. The Radical Reformation protested against the magisterial Reformers both by radical reference to the Bible and by claiming special revelations from the Holy Spirit. Some Pentecostal groups, on the other hand, appear as institutionalizations of the Holy Spirit—when, for instance, they define glossolalia as necessary manifestations of the Holy Spirit and as evidence of Spirit baptism. Both institutionalization and protest thus can happen with reference to the Spirit or with reference to the word of the Bible. The two emphases stand in a dialectic relationship. A one-sided stress on the word of God is dead and turns the letter into law, as Paul maintained (2 Cor 3:6), thus triggering a countermovement. Vice versa, a one-sided emphasis on the Spirit turns into idolatry of subjective religious feelings—a sense of being touched by God does not guarantee that it is God who has touched the individual, i.e., that it is not simply the person's own feeling. In short: the spirit without the letter is blind and equally triggers a countermovement.

Still another category of dialectic movement that shapes the history of the church is the one between *mission to* the world and *separation from* the world. Both mission and separation can be either institutionalizing or countercultural revivalist movements. The story is again simple: For Christians, the purpose of one's faith does not lie in one's own person or one's church, but in the world. Christ did not die for the church but for the world. Accordingly, Christian faith is fundamentally an incarnational movement always moving beyond its own boundaries in order to transform and serve the world. Theologically speaking, it is a *kenotic* movement, paralleling the movement of Jesus Christ becoming human, humbling himself, and self-emptying himself of divinity (Phil 2:6–8). However, in this kenotic movement of Christian faith entering the world, the specificity and difference of Christian faith can get lost. The most radical form of churches becoming fully worldly and giving up their distinctiveness is secularization. Some theological traditions like the "God is dead" tradition or some mission scholars have interpreted this movement of secularization as necessary and positive. Cox, in his early years, argued that "secularization represents an authentic sequence of biblical faith. Rather than oppose it, the task of Christians should be to support and nourish it."[15] As Christianity enters the world, it is always in danger of losing its purity and distinctiveness, and it ultimately risks adapting to the pattern of the world. Against such a faith movement that becomes too worldly, Christians emphasize the radical otherness of the Christian community. They stress that the best witness to the world is an alternative community that radically follows different values than those propagated by society. Christians are called not to conform to the pattern of this world (Rom 12:2) but to be pure, to separate from the corruption of the world. Using the typology of H. R. Niebuhr[16] we may call it the difference between a "Christ and culture" and a "Christ against culture" model of theology and Christian existence; in the typology of Stephen

---

15. Cox, *Secular City*, 18.
16. Niebuhr, *Christ and Culture*.

Bevans,[17] it corresponds to the anthropological and the countercultural models of contextualization, respectively.

Again, examples for both movements can be found throughout the history of the church. The missional movement of Christian faith entering the world may be seen in the fate of the churches in western Europe, where societies have absorbed many values of the Christian tradition; yet, in this process the churches struggle with maintaining their specific raison d'être and are in danger of appearing redundant. Likewise, the YMCA: though initially a revivalist mission movement that combined social care with preaching as it reached out to young people moving to the cities, many critics argue that it has lost its Christian identity. Or, more recently, when the World Council of Churches (WCC), driven by a strong missional concern for engagement with the world, participated in the struggle to overcome the apartheid system in South Africa, critics were quick to criticize the WCC for making common cause with political groups that would not disavow military violence.

On the other hand, various Christian movements have assumed a countercultural stance toward mainstream Christian life by stressing purity, distinctiveness, and separation from the world. Among these movements were the early church's monastic movement and later medieval monastic groups, Radical Reformers and separatist Puritans, and (more recently) parts of Evangelicalism and Fundamentalism. It should be noted, though, that some of these groups were indeed successful in balancing the two competing emphases—missionary involvement *in* the world and countercultural separation *from* the world. The best example of such successful combination is the monastic movement, which kept its distance from the world while maintaining its missional impact, transforming society by witnessing to and serving the world. Similarly, the Jesuits combined missionary zeal with a strict spiritual discipline that set them apart from the world. Some parts of the Protestant mission movement of the early nineteenth century also combined missionary practice with a separatist lifestyle and a rejection of the "pagan" culture of the mission field. One recent example of a theology that combines missional engagement in the world with an emphasis on the church as an alternative community can be found in the writings of Stanley Hauerwas.

The different dialectics that drive church history may be imagined in spatial form and summarized in the following graph:

---

17. Bevans, *Models of Contextual Theology*.

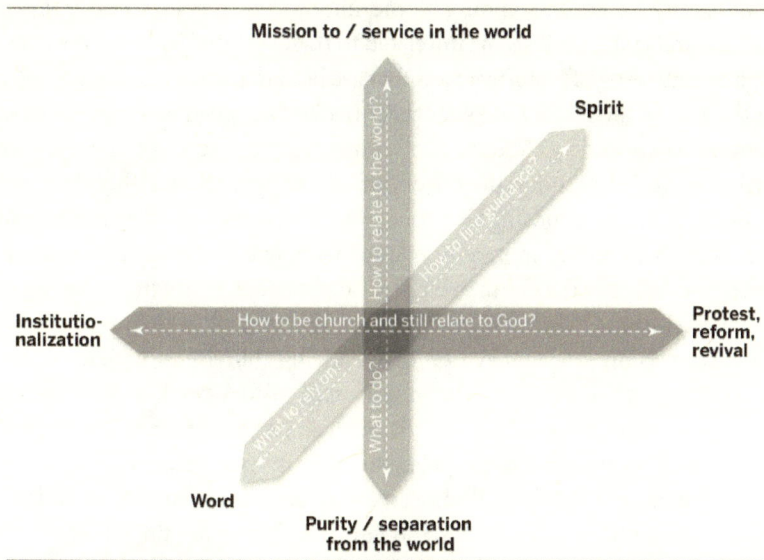

Core dialectics in Christianity's historical movement

Of course, there are further dialectic tensions driving the historical development of Christianity—for instance, the tension between sacramental and non-sacramental churches or, more importantly, the tension between social classes and their respective churches. In this regard, Niebuhr's classic discussion of different denominations and their social backgrounds[18] still offers inspiring reading even though it was written nearly a century ago. The significant dialectics of social classes are not included in the diagram above because those often appear in the form of the other dialectic tensions discussed.

BEYOND UNDERSTANDING: CHRISTIAN HISTORICAL STUDIES AND SPIRITUAL FORMATION

But the study of the history of Christianity is not concerned only with understanding. It has a deeply spiritual and pastoral dimension and contributes to a holistic spiritual formation. Within the world of theological training, it is often regarded as *propaedeutic*, a preparation for the more significant and important studies of theology proper. Many aspiring young theologians regard either biblical studies or systematic theology as the "real" focus. Students of theology are not usually drawn to the history of

18. See Niebuhr, *The Social Sources of Denominationalism*.

Christianity because—standing at the interface of theology and politics, society, and culture—it seems unrelated to their spiritual lives, simply a discipline consisting of historical facts that are hard to memorize. Additionally, in the case of the history of Western Christianity studied in a non-Western context, many students find the subject irrelevant and too far removed from their own reality. Besides, the history of Christianity tells a rather dark and not edifying story, exposing Christianity as no less corrupted by the human obsession with power, money, or status than any other human movement. Or, in the words of the German writer and philosopher Goethe, "The whole of church history is a mishmash of error and power."[19]

Yet, it is my deep conviction that studying church history contributes to spiritual formation. First, studying church history teaches *gratitude*: all that we have in our spiritual and theological life has come to us through tradition. Not only was the gospel handed down to us through generations of Christians; our theological understanding has also been shaped and enriched by centuries of theological thought, long before our time. History is a rich reservoir of knowledge and wisdom. Second, studying church history is a form of establishing *relationships*. Christians of past centuries—although temporally far away—are brothers and sisters to today's Christians, no different to contemporary but geographically far away Christians. Learning the history of Christianity establishes a relationship to our spiritual forefathers and foremothers. Learning from them, knowing them and trying to understand them is an expression of basic respect. Third, studying church history teaches us *humility*: we are not the first Christians. The history of Christianity puts our present-day theological debates into perspective. Many contentious issues have been discussed in earlier times, possibly more intelligently and faithfully than we have today. To see how again and again we stand in critical contrast to the teaching and life of Christ is a humbling process of learning. Related to this is a fourth point. By studying church history, *awareness of our own limitations and our contextual character grows*: we understand that our faith and our reading of the Bible are shaped by tradition, whether we like it or not. We should therefore know this history and tradition, and we should understand how our tradition-shaped perspective in turn shapes our reality. Yet, it is not only tradition that shapes us, but equally our context. Theology today is (possibly more than in earlier times) aware of its necessarily contextual character, and recent research in the history of Christianity has uncovered how this history is one of a continuous—and more or less successful—inculturation in a changing context. Studying the history of Christianity as a history of subsequent contextualization allows

---

19. Quoted in Ebeling, *Study of Theology*, 68.

us to learn from earlier successful forms of inculturation and equips us with sensitivity in our own contextualizing ministry. Further, learning about the history of Christianity may have a *liberating dimension* by freeing us from the constraints of earlier errors. What Freud described as repetition compulsion, a psychological phenomenon according to which a person repeatedly puts herself into a situation where a traumatic event happens again,[20] may also apply to our collective history of Christianity. And just as Freud suggests analytically working through the traumatic roots of such repetitive behavior to find liberation, so the community of Christians may overcome our own compulsion to repeat by analyzing and integrating the past through understanding. Sixth, studying the history of Christianity is an *eminently political act*. Critical historical research uncovers the politically or socially repressed elements of history against the dominant discourse of history. Political leaders manipulate history to underline their own legitimacy. Mainstream history is written from the perspective of the winner, as the Jewish-Marxist German philosopher Walter Benjamin famously pointed out: "Whoever has emerged victorious participates to this day in the triumphal procession in which the present rulers step over those who are lying prostrate."[21] In contrast to such official historiography, critical historical research uncovers the politically or socially repressed elements of history and asks, What about women, who are rarely mentioned in historical accounts? What about racial, ethnic, sexual, or other minority groups? What about religious groups that were labeled heretical? Seventh, history *contributes to our mental health*. In the words of Diarmaid MacCulloch, one of the great present-day church historians, "Putting it crudely, it is to stop you going mad. Those who have no history are always on the verge of insanity. When individual people lose their memory, they find it a very distressing experience.... When a nation forgets its history, or worse still, invents a history to take the place of the facts, the consequences are tragic."[22] Indeed, we need a history to remain mentally healthy; furthermore, history, the telling of stories, creates identity.[23] By repeatedly telling their children stories that merge together into the story of a family, parents create familial identity. Stories thus establish community. Finally, the study of the history of Christianity helps us *clarify our theology and our values* and *enhances our self-knowledge*.

---

20. Freud, "Remembering, Repeating and Working-Through," 145–56.
21. Benjamin, "On the Concept of History," 391.
22. MacCulloch, *Groundwork of Christian History*, 1.
23. Ritschl, *Logic of Theology*, 19–21.

HOW DOES THE HISTORY OF CHRISTIANITY UNFOLD?

The first book of the *Institutes* by John Calvin begins with this famous sentence: "Our wisdom, in so far as it ought to be deemed true and solid Wisdom, consists almost entirely of two parts: the knowledge of God and of ourselves" (I, 1.1). This connection between the knowledge of God and the knowledge of ourselves may be modified to equally apply to the knowledge of the history of Christianity. A deeper historical knowledge and its critical reflection indeed lead to a deeper understanding of ourselves. We discover that our theological thought has been shaped by subconscious and "pre-reflective intentionality,"[24] as well as unexamined assumptions, most importantly about what history actually is and how it develops. What is the history of Christianity and whose history is it? Is it God's history, a history of the continuous incarnation of Jesus Christ? And is it, as such, only apparently or superficially changing, while in its core maintaining continuity as simply the ongoing revelation of God? Such an approach is typically found in (though not restricted to) Roman Catholicism. Or is the history of Christianity the history of spiritual heroes, or of ecclesial leaders, or of ordinary believers? Is it the history of the disenfranchised, protesting against rulers who make use of religion in their oppressive regimes? Or is it, rather than a history of people and their institutions, a history of ideas unfolding through the centuries, as the Hegelian view of history has it?

And how does this history unfold? Is the history of Christianity a history of gradual improvement, of progress, and of triumphal victory? This is how the first great church theologian, Eusebius of Caesarea, saw it. He interpreted the history of Christianity as culminating in the conversion of the Emperor Constantine, an event that brought victory after centuries of persecution. Such a triumphal view of history has always been popular among historians and theologians who like to see their own era as the peak of history. Often, they write such histories on behalf of political rulers who present their own time as a time of glory and draw legitimacy from their claimed successes. Some periods of church history simply absorbed this optimistic view of history from their (worldly) context—for example, the Enlightenment and the postmillennial view that characterized the Evangelical Awakening in the late eighteenth and early nineteenth century. Similarly, the idealistic conception of Hegel, most clearly represented by Ferdinand Christian Baur, interprets the history of Christianity as a gradual unfolding of the idea of the church itself, which in turn is nothing else than the christological idea of the unity of God and humankind. In this conception,

---

24. Ibid., 48–50.

even the dark moments of history appear as necessary transitional stages, just as what seems true also needs to be understood as only a relative and transitional reflection of what is still to come. For both Eusebius and Baur, the present becomes the eschatological goal of church history.[25]

Or is the history of Christianity rather a history of decay, as many theologians of the Protestant tradition would see it? And if so, when did this decay start? Had it already started in the apostolic era? Or did it start only after the first ecumenical councils? Or once the popes started to assume worldly power? Various movements throughout the history of Christianity have agreed on a negative view of history, but with different answers regarding the beginning of the decay. Mainstream Protestantism often sees the fall of Christianity in the rise of the papacy. The Radical Reformers and a good number of revivalist groups see Christianity as having lost its purity right after the apostolic age. The different answers to the question of "the fall of Christianity" lead to different ways of "solving" the problems of Christianity, be it by restoring a church without the papacy or by attempting a return to original apostolic "purity." Negative views of history easily go together with pessimist views regarding the future: An example of such pessimism is the premillennialist view of history, which sees the present as a time of deepening darkness and turmoil, understood as signs of the time that point to Jesus' second coming. Followers of such a view of history see themselves as standing counterculturally against overall deterioration and as receiving the blessings of the imminent second coming of Christ. An example of such an approach is the Latter Rain movement of the late nineteenth century, or Pentecostal groups in the twentieth century.

While some see history in a dialectic development, as above, others see history in a dialectic tension that remains static. This is, in part, how Luther's historical view could be described. Although Luther also believed that Christianity took a wrong turn at some point in history and needed to be restored (as for instance expressed during the Leipzig Disputation in 1519), he maintains an overwhelming dialectic pattern that sees corporate Christianity in analogy to the individual Christian, that is, as both justified and corrupt at the same time. Similar to this static-dialectic view of history, some see the history of Christianity as a plurality of stories that are in conflict with each other, with some stories more visible and some more hidden. The German mystic Jakob Boehme (1575–1624) described the true church as the church of Abel hidden within the false church of Cain.[26] Influenced by him, the Pietist theologian Gottfried Arnold (1666–1714), in his book

---

25. Ebeling, *Study of Theology*, 73–74.
26. Grass, *Modern Church History*, 15.

An Impartial History of the Church and of Heresies (1699–1700), saw the true church preserved in some small groups that were often rejected as heretical by the mainstream church. An understanding of the story of Christianity as a multiplicity of simultaneous stories that are partly in harmony and partly in conflict, partly more visible at the surface and partly more hidden beneath, reflects well the postmodern context in which the diversity of Christians has become so obvious. The stories of Christian individuals and Christian groups reflect simultaneously an *emancipatory movement* and a *hegemonic movement*, where Christian faith pacifies and suppresses while at the same time moves people to liberating action and radical change.

A summary of the different views of history can be seen in the chart below.

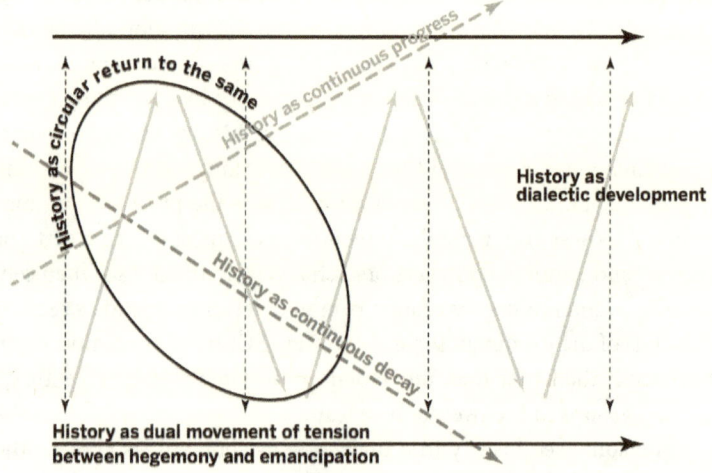

Basic views of historical development

To discover something of the multiplicity of stories causes ongoing fascination when studying the Christian movement. It is disillusioning to uncover fellow Christians' participation in repressive acts, yet it is comforting to recognize our irrepressible subversive and countercultural streak. Theological education equips Christians with both a spiritual humility that is aware of past failure as well as a sense of spiritual freedom that grasps the diversity of stories we are invited to join.

Bibliography

Augustine of Hippo, Saint. *Confessions and Enchiridion*. Edited and translated by Albert Cook Outler. Reprint, Louisville: Westminster John Knox, 2006.

———. *De Civitate Dei*. Edited and translated by P. G. Walsh. Oxford: Aris & Phillips, 2016.

———. *Of True Religion*. Translated by J. H. S. Burleigh. Chicago: Regnery, 1959.

Ayer, Joseph Cullen, Jr. *A Source Book for Ancient Church History: From the Apostolic Age to the Close of the Conciliar Period*. New York: Scribner's, 1941.

Barnes, Timothy David. *Athanasius and Constantius: Theology and Politics in the Constantinian Empire*. Cambridge, MA: Harvard University Press, 1993.

Barrett, C. K., editor. *The New Testament Background: Writings from Ancient Greece and the Roman Empire That Illuminate Christian Origins*. Rev. ed. San Francisco: Harper, 1995.

Barth, Karl. "The Word of God and the Task of the Ministry [1922]." In *The Word of God and the Word of Man*, translated by Douglas Horton, 183–217. New York: Harper, 1957.

Bede, Saint. *Ecclesiastical History of England*. Translated by A. M. Sellar. London: George Bell, 1907.

Benjamin, Walter. "On the Concept of History." In *Selected Writings*, vol. 4, *1938–1940*, translated by Edward Jephcott et al., edited by Howard Eiland and Michael W. Jennings, 389–400. Cambridge, MA: Harvard University Press, 2003.

Bercken, Wil van den. *Holy Russia and Christian Europe: East and West in the Religious Ideology of Russia*. Translated by John Bowden. London: SCM, 1999.

Berger, Peter L. *The Heretical Imperative: Contemporary Possibilities of Religious Affirmation*. Garden City, NY: Anchor, 1979.

Bettenson, Henry S., editor. *Documents of the Christian Church*. 2nd ed. Oxford: Oxford University Press, 1967.

Bevans, Stephen B. *Models of Contextual Theology*. Rev. and exp. ed. Maryknoll, NY: Orbis, 2002.

Bevans, Stephen B., and Roger P. Schroeder. *Constants in Context: A Theology of Mission for Today*. Maryknoll, NY: Orbis, 2004.

Blumenthal, Uta-Renate. *The Investiture Controversy: Church and Monarchy from the Ninth to the Twelfth Century*. Philadelphia: University of Pennsylvania Press, 1988.

Bonhoeffer, Dietrich. *Letters and Papers from Prison*. Edited by Eberhard Bethge. Enl. ed. New York: Macmillan, 1972.

Bosch, David Jacobus. *Transforming Mission: Paradigm Shifts in Theology of Mission.* Maryknoll, NY: Orbis, 1991.

Brown, Peter. *Augustine of Hippo: A Biography.* Berkeley: University of California Press, 1967.

———. *The Rise of Western Christendom: Triumph and Diversity, A.D. 200–1000.* 2nd ed. Malden, MA: Blackwell, 2003.

Brown, Schuyler. *The Origins of Christianity: A Historical Introduction to the New Testament.* Rev. ed. Oxford: Oxford University Press, 1984.

Brundage, James. *The Crusades: A Documentary Survey.* Milwaukee: Marquette University Press, 1962.

Burns, J. H., editor. *The Cambridge History of Medieval Political Thought c. 350–c. 1450.* Cambridge: Cambridge University Press, 1988.

Chadwick, Henry. *The Making of a Rift in the Church: From Apostolic Times until the Council of Florence.* Oxford: Oxford University Press, 2003.

Cohn, Norman. *The Pursuit of the Millennium: Revolutionary Messianism in Medieval and Reformation Europe and Its Bearing on Modern Totalitarian Movements.* New York: Harper & Row, 1961.

Cox, Harvey. *The Future of Faith.* New York: HarperOne, 2009.

———. *The Secular City: Secularization and Urbanization in Theological Perspective.* New York: Macmillan, 1965.

Cross, Frank L., editor. *The Oxford Dictionary of the Christian Church.* New York: Oxford University Press, 2005.

Denzinger, Henry. *The Sources of Catholic Dogma.* Translated by Roy J. Deferrari from the thirtieth ed. of Henry Denzinger's *Enchiridion Symbolorum.* Reprint, Fitzwilliam, NH: Loreto, 1955.

Dickson, Gary. "Medieval Revivalism." In *Medieval Christianity*, edited by Daniel E. Bornstein, 147–78. People's History of Christianity 4. Minneapolis: Fortress, 2010.

Digeser, Elizabeth Depalma. *The Making of a Christian Empire: Lactantius & Rome.* Ithaca: Cornell University Press, 2000.

Drake, Harold Allen. *Constantine and the Bishops: The Politics of Intolerance.* Baltimore: John Hopkins University Press, 2000.

Dunn, James D. G. *The Partings of the Ways: Between Christianity and Judaism and Their Significance for the Character of Christianity.* 2nd ed. London: SCM, 2006.

———. *Unity and Diversity in the New Testament: An Inquiry into the Character of Earliest Christianity.* 3rd ed. London: SCM, 1990.

Ebeling, Gerhard. *Luther: An Introduction to His Thought.* Translated by R. A. Wilson. London: Collins, 1970.

———. *The Study of Theology.* Translated by Duane A. Priebe. London: Collins, 1979.

Eco, Umberto. *The Name of the Rose.* Translated by William Weaver. London: Vintage, 2004.

Elliott, J. K., editor. *The Apocryphal New Testament: A Collection of Apocryphal Christian Literature in an English Translation.* Oxford: Clarendon, 1993.

Eusebius. *The Church History: A New Translation with Commentary.* Translated by Paul L. Maier. Grand Rapids: Kregel, 1999.

Evans, Gillian Rosemary. *The Church in the Early Middle Ages.* I. B. Tauris History of the Christian Church 2. London: I. B. Tauris, 2007.

Ferguson, Niall. *Civilization: The West and the Rest.* New York: Penguin, 2011.

Fremantle, Anne Jackson. *The Protestant Mystics.* 1st ed. Boston: Little, Brown, 1964.

Frend, William H. C. *Martyrdom and Persecution in the Early Church*. Garden City, NY: Doubleday, 1967.

———. "Persecutions: Genesis and Legacy." In *The Cambridge History of Christianity*, vol. 1, *Origins to Constantine*, edited by Margaret M. Mitchell and Frances M. Young, 503–23. Cambridge: Cambridge University Press, 2006.

———. *The Rise of Christianity*. Philadelphia: Fortress, 1984.

Freud, Sigmund. "Remembering, Repeating and Working-Through (Further Recommendations on the Technique of Psycho-Analysis II)." In *The Standard Edition of the Complete Psychological Works of Sigmund Freud*, edited by James Strachey, 12:145–56. London: Hogarth, 1958.

Grass, Tim. *Modern Church History*. SCM Core Text. London: SCM, 2008.

Gregg, Robert C., and Dennis E. Groh. *Early Arianism: A View of Salvation*. London: SCM, 1981.

Gregorios, Paulos, William H. Lazareth, and Nikos A. Nissiotis, editors. *Does Chalcedon Divide or Unite? Towards Convergence in Orthodox Christology*. Geneva: World Council of Churches, 1981.

Habig, Marion A., editor. *St. Francis of Assisi: Writings and Early Biographies; English Omnibus of the Sources for the Life of St. Francis*. 3rd ed. London: SPCK, 1973.

Harnack, Adolf von. *Marcion: The Gospel of the Alien God*. Translated by John E. Steely and Lyle D. Bierma. Durham, NC: Labyrinth, 1990.

Harrison, Carol. *Augustine: Christian Truth and Fractured Humanity*. Oxford: Oxford University Press, 2000.

Hen, Yitzhak. "Converting the Barbarian West." in *Medieval Christianity*, edited by Daniel E. Bornstein, 29–52. People's History of Christianity 4. Minneapolis: Fortress, 2010.

Holzherr, Georg. *The Rule of Benedict: An Invitation to the Christian Life*. Translated by Mark Thamert. Athens, OH: Cistercian Publications, 2016.

Horsley, Richard A., editor. *Christian Origins*. People's History of Christianity 1. Minneapolis: Fortress, 2005.

Horsley, Richard A., and Neil Asher Silberman. *The Message and the Kingdom: How Jesus and Paul Ignited a Revolution and Transformed the Ancient World*. Minneapolis: Fortress, 1997.

Hussey, Joan Mervyn. *The Orthodox Church in the Byzantine Empire*. Oxford: Oxford University Press, 2010.

Jenkins, Philip. *Jesus Wars: How Four Patriarchs, Three Queens, and Two Emperors Decided What Christians Would Believe for the Next 1,500 Years*. New York: HarperOne, 2010.

———. *The Lost History of Christianity: The Thousand-Year Golden Age of the Church in the Middle East, Africa, and Asia—and How It Died*. New York: HarperOne, 2008.

Justin Martyr, Saint. *The First and Second Apologies*. Translated and edited by Leslie William Barnard. Mahwah, NJ: Paulist, 1997.

King, Karen L. *What Is Gnosticism?* Cambridge, MA: Belknap Press of Harvard University Press, 2003.

Krausmüller, Dirk. "The Rise of Hesychasm." In *The Cambridge History of Christianity*, vol. 5, *Eastern Christianity*, edited by Michael Angold, 101–26. Cambridge: Cambridge University Press, 2008.

Kreider, Alan. "Changing Patterns of Conversion in the West." In *The Origins of Christendom in the West*, edited by Alan Kreider, 3-46. Edinburgh: T&T Clark, 2001.

Lai, Pin-chao. "Cong da cheng fo xue kan jiakedun jidulun." *Furen zongjiao yanjiu* 2 (2000.12) 231-62.

———. "Hong Kong Christians' Attitudes towards Chinese Religions." *Studies in World Christianity* 5.1 (1999) 18-31.

Lieu, Judith M. *Marcion and the Making of a Heretic: God and Scripture in the Second Century*. Cambridge: Cambridge University Press, 2015.

Lieu, Samuel N. C. *Manichaeism in the Later Roman Empire and Medieval China*. 2nd rev. and exp. ed. Tübingen: J. C. B. Mohr, 1992.

Limor, Ora. "Christians and Jews." In *The Cambridge History of Christianity*, vol. 4, *Christianity in Western Europe c. 1100-c. 1500*, edited by Miri Rubin and Walter Simons, 135-48. Cambridge: Cambridge University Press, 2009.

Lossky, Vladimir. *The Mystical Theology of the Eastern Church*. 1st ed. London: J. Clarke, 1957.

Louth, Andrew. *Greek East and Latin West: The Church, AD 681-1071*. Crestwood, NY: St. Vladimir's Seminary Press, 2007.

———. *The Origins of the Christian Mystical Tradition: From Plato to Denys*. Oxford: Clarendon, 1981.

Lüdemann, Gerd, and Martina Janssen. *Suppressed Prayers: Gnostic Spirituality in Early Christianity*. London: SCM, 1998.

MacCulloch, Diarmaid. *Christianity: The First Three Thousand Years*. New York: Penguin, 2009.

———. *Groundwork of Christian History*. London: Epworth, 1987.

MacMullen, Ramsay. *Christianity and Paganism in the Fourth to Eight Centuries*. New Haven: Yale University Press, 1997.

———. "Christianity Shaped through Its Mission." In *The Origins of Christendom in the West*, edited by Alan Kreider, 97-117. Edinburgh: T&T Clark, 2001.

———. *Christianizing the Roman Empire (A.D. 100-400)*. New Haven: Yale University Press, 1984.

Madigan, Kevin, and Carolyn Osiek, editors. *Ordained Women in the Early Church: A Documentary History*. Baltimore: John Hopkins University Press, 2005.

McGrath, Alister E. *Christian Theology: An Introduction*. Oxford: Blackwell, 1994.

———. *The Intellectual Origins of the European Reformation*. 2nd ed. Malden, MA: Blackwell, 2004.

Mechthild of Magdeburg. *The Flowing Light of the Godhead*. Translated and introduced by Frank Tobin. Mahwah, NJ: Paulist, 1998.

Merlo, Grado G. "Heresy and Dissent." In *Medieval Christianity*, edited by Daniel E. Bornstein, 229-64. People's History of Christianity 4. Minneapolis: Fortress, 2010.

Meyendorff, John. *Byzantine Theology: Historical Trends and Doctrinal Themes*. New York: Fordham University Press, 1979.

———. *Rome, Constantinople, Moscow: Historical and Theological Studies*. Crestwood, NY: St. Vladimir's Seminary Press 1996.

Moffett, Samuel Hugh. *A History of Christianity in Asia*. Vol. 1, *Beginnings to 1500*. Maryknoll, NY: Orbis, 1998.

Morris, Colin. *The Papal Monarchy: The Western Church from 1050-1250*. Oxford: Clarendon, 1989.

Musurillo, Herbert, editor. *The Acts of the Christian Martyrs*. Oxford: Clarendon, 1972.
Neuner, Joseph, and Jacques Dupuis, editors. *The Christian Faith in the Doctrinal Documents of the Catholic Church*. 6th rev. and enl. ed. New York: Alba House, 1996.
Niebuhr, Helmut Richard. *Christ and Culture*. New York: Harper, 1951.
———. *The Social Sources of Denominationalism*. Gloucester, MA: Peter Smith, 1987.
Niederwimmer, Kurt. *The Didache: A Commentary*. Translated by Linda M. Maloney. Edited by Harold W. Attridge. Minneapolis: Fortress, 1998.
Nirenberg, David. "Christendom and Islam." In *The Cambridge History of Christianity*, vol. 4, *Christianity in Western Europe c. 1100–c. 1500*, edited by Miri Rubin and Walter Simons, 149–69. Cambridge: Cambridge University Press, 2009.
Ogg, Frederic Austin, editor. *A Source Book of Medieval History: Documents Illustrative of European Life and Institutions from the German Invasions to the Renaissance*. New York: American Book Company, 1908.
Osborn, Eric Francis. *The Emergence of Christian Theology*. Cambridge: Cambridge University Press, 1993.
Pegg, Mark Gregory. *A Most Holy War: The Albigensian Crusade and the Battle for Christendom*. Oxford: Oxford University Press, 2008.
Peters, Edward, editor. *The First Crusade: The Chronicle of Fulcher of Chartres and Other Source Materials*. 2nd ed. Philadelphia: University of Pennsylvania Press, 1998.
Petry, Ray C. *A History of Christianity: Readings in the History of the Early and Medieval Church*. Englewood Cliffs, NJ: Prentice-Hall, 1962.
Plato. *The Dialogues of Plato: With Analyses and Introductions*. Translated by B. Jowett. Vol. 1. 3rd ed. New York: Oxford University Press, 1892.
Pliny the Younger. *Complete Letters*. Translation with an Introduction and Notes by P. G. Walsh. Oxford: Oxford University Press, 2006.
Poliakov, Léon. *The History of Anti-Semitism*. Vol. 1, *From Roman Times to the Court Jews*. London: Routledge & Kegan Paul, 1965.
Purinton, Carl E. *Christianity and Its Judaic Heritage: An Introduction with Selected Sources*. New York: Ronald Press, 1961.
Riley-Smith, Jonathan. *The Crusades: A History*. 2nd ed. New Haven: Yale University Press, 2005.
———. *The First Crusaders, 1095–1131*. Cambridge: Cambridge University Press, 1997.
Ritschl, Dietrich. *The Logic of Theology: A Brief Account of the Relationship between Basic Concepts in Theology*. London: SCM, 1986.
Robinson, George W., editor and translator. *The Life of Saint Boniface, by Willibald*. Cambridge: Harvard University Press, 1916.
Robinson, James Harvey, editor. *Readings in European History*. Vol. 1, *From the Breaking Up of the Roman Empire to the Protestant Revolt*. Boston: Ginn & Co., 1904.
Roldanus, Johannes. *The Church in the Age of Constantine: The Theological Challenges*. London: Routledge, 2006.
Rossing, Barbara R. "Prophets, Prophetic Movements, and the Voices of Women." In *Christian Origins*, edited by Richard A. Horsley, 261–86. People's History of Christianity 1. Minneapolis: Fortress, 2005.
Roukema, Riemer. *Gnosis and Faith in Early Christianity: An Introduction to Gnosticism*. Translated by John Bowden. Harrisburg, PA: Trinity Press International, 1999.

Runciman, Stephen. *The Byzantine Theocracy*. Cambridge: Cambridge University Press, 1977.
Smith, Andrew. *Philosophy in Late Antiquity*. London: Routledge, 2004.
Smith, Lesley. "The Theological Framework." In *The Cambridge History of Christianity*, vol. 4, *Christianity in Western Europe c. 1100-c. 1500*, edited by Miri Rubin and Walter Simons, 75–88. Cambridge: Cambridge University Press, 2009.
Stark, Rodney. *God's Battalions: The Case for the Crusades*. New York: HarperOne, 2009.
———. *The Rise of Christianity: A Sociologist Reconsiders History*. Princeton: Princeton University Press, 1996.
———. *The Victory of Reason: How Christianity Led to Freedom, Capitalism, and Western Success*. New York: Random House, 2005.
Stevenson, James, editor. *Creeds, Councils and Controversies: Documents Illustrating the History of the Church AD 337-461*. Revised with additional documents by W. H. C. Frend. London: SPCK, 1989.
Tacitus. *Annals of Tacitus; Tr. into English, with Notes and Maps*. Edited by Alfred John Church and William Jackson Brodribb. London: Macmillan, 1876.
Tanner, Norman P., editor. *Decrees of the Ecumenical Councils*. Vol. 1, *Nicaea I to Lateran V*. London: Sheed & Ward, 1990.
Theissen, Gerd. *Social Reality and the Early Christians: Theology, Ethics, and the World of the New Testament*. Translated by Margaret Kohl. Minneapolis: Fortress, 1992.
———. *Sociology of Early Palestinian Christianity*. Translated by John Bowden. Minneapolis: Fortress, 1982. (= *The First Followers of Jesus*. London: SCM, 1978.)
Thomas, Aquinas, Saint. *The "Summa Theologica" of St. Thomas Aquinas*. Pt. 1, vol. 1, QQ I.-XXVI. Literally translated by Fathers of the English Dominican Province. 2nd and rev. ed. London: Burns, Oates & Washbourne, 1920.
Thomsett, Michael C. *The Inquisition: A History*. Jefferson, NC: McFarland, 2010.
Tillich, Paul. "On the Boundary: An Autobiographical Sketch." In *The Interpretation of History*, 3–73. New York: Scribner's, 1936.
———. *The Protestant Era*. Edited by James Luther Adams. Chicago: University of Chicago Press, 1948.
Trevett, Christine. *Montanism: Gender, Authority, and the New Prophecy*. New York: Cambridge University Press, 1996.
Tuchman, Barbara. *Bible and Sword: England and Palestine from the Bronze Age to Balfour*. New York: Ballantine, 1984.
Ullmann, Walter. *A Short History of the Papacy in the Middle Ages*. 2nd ed. London: Routledge, 2003.
Van Nieuwenhove, Rik. *An Introduction to Medieval Theology*. Cambridge: Cambridge University Press, 2012.
Wakefield, Walter L., and Austin P. Evans. *Heresies of the High Middle Ages: Selected Sources, Translated and Annotated*. 2nd ed. New York: Columbia University Press, 1991.
Walls, Andrew F. *The Missionary Movement in Christian History: Studies in the Transmission of Faith*. Maryknoll, NY: Orbis, 1996.
Watt, W. Montgomery. "Muhammad." In *The Cambridge History of Islam*, edited by P. M. Holt, Ann K. S. Lambton, and Bernard Lewis, 1:30–56. Cambridge: Cambridge University Press, 1970.
Whalen, Brett Edward. *Dominion of God: Christendom and Apocalypse in the Middle Ages*. Cambridge, MA: Harvard University Press, 2009.

———. *The Medieval Papacy*. Basingstoke: Palgrave Macmillan, 2014.
Wilken, Robert Louis. *The Spirit of Early Christian Thought: Seeking the Face of God*. New Haven: Yale University Press, 2003.
Young, Frances M. "Monotheism and Christology." In *The Cambridge History of Christianity*, vol. 1, *Origins to Constantine*, edited by Margaret M. Mitchell and Frances M. Young, 452–69. Cambridge: Cambridge University Press, 2006.
———. "Prelude: Jesus Christ, Foundation of Christianity." In *The Cambridge History of Christianity*, vol. 1, *Origins to Constantine*, edited by Margaret M. Mitchell and Frances M. Young, 1–34. Cambridge: Cambridge University Press 2008.
Young, Frances M., Lewis Ayres, and Andrew Louth, editors. *The Cambridge History of Early Christian Literature*. Cambridge: Cambridge University Press, 2004.
Young, Robin Darling. "Martyrdom as Exaltation." In *Late Ancient Christianity*, edited by Virginia Burrus, 70–94. People's History of Christianity 2. Minneapolis: Fortress, 2005.

Index

Note: Page numbers in italic refer to words or names appearing in footnotes.

Abbasids, 229
Abelard, Peter, 245
Abraham, 17, 71
Acacian Schism, 189, 190
Acacius of Constantinople, bishop, 189
Acre, 212
Acts of the Martyrs, 34, 281
Adiabene, 38
Adoptionism (Dynamist Monarchianism), 78
Adversus Haereses, by Irenaeus, 46
Agatho of Rome, pope, 191
Age of the Spirit, 54, 221–22
Aistulf, 175
Al-Aqsa Mosque, 229
Alaric, 127
Albert the Great, 215, 246
Albigensian Crusade, 219, 240, 281
Albigensian Wars, 219
Albigensians, 219
Alexander of Alexandria, *104*, 105, 106
Alexander of Hales, 214
Alexandria, 44, 46, 58, 74, 105–8, 111, 114, 120–24, 152, 153, 170
Alexandrian School, 119
Alexandrine party, 106
Alexios I, emperor, 229
Alexius IV, emperor, 231
Ambrose of Milan, 69, 94, 128, 130

Amillennialism, 91
Anachoretism, 93
Anamnesis, 64
Anglo-Saxons, 159, 162
Anselm of Canterbury, 245, 251
Antioch, 6, 19, 34, 44, 58, 78, 107, 111, 114, 118–19, 121–22, 153, 170, 195, 229
Anti-Semitism, 16–17, 234, 281
Antonine Plague, 39
Apocalyptic Christianity, 44
Apocalypticism, 221
Apocatastasis, 75
Apollinaris of Laodicea, 111, 120
Apologetic theology, 62, 69, 70, 71, 75, 133
Apologists, 69, 70, 71, 72
Apostles' Creed, 56, 58, 61
Apostolic succession, 56, 58, 59, 168
Arian controversy, 90, 100, 103, 104, 107, 108, 111, 114
Arian soteriology, 104, 114
Arianism, 78, 103, 111, 113, 146, 147, 148, 279
Aristides, 69
Aristotle, 235, 242, 246, 251, 252, 254, 255
Arius, 103, 104, 105, 106, 112, 114
Armenian Orthodox Church, 124
Armenians, 188
Arnold, Gottfried, 275

286 *Index*

Arthur, king of England, 234
Asceticism, 48, 49, 51, 91, 92, 96, 97, 210, 213, 219
Assyrian Church of the East, 121, 126, 188, 190
Athanasians, 108, 109
Athanasius, 78, 93, 94, 96, 103, 104, 106, 108, 109, 113, 277
Atharaxia, 92
Attila, 144, 145, 171
Augustine, 47, 69, 94, 102–3, 116–17, 127–38, 144, 157–59, 242, 243, 246, 256, 259, 277, 278, 279
Augustus, emperor, 25, 85
Auto-cephalous churches, 200
Averroes, 246
Avicenna, 246
Avignon, 237, 239, 240

Babylonian Exile of the Church, 237
Baldwin of Flanders, 222
Bar Kochba, 18, 21
Barlaam, 202, 203, 209
Barnabas, 10, 17
Barnabas, Epistle of, 17
Barnes, Timothy D., 113, 277
Barth, Karl, 263, 277
Baruch, II, 15
Basil the Great, 69, 109
Basilides, 46
Basilidians, 46
Battle of Adrianople, 144
Battle of the Cattalaunian Fields, 144, 145
Battle of the Milvian Bridge, 32, 84, 86
Baur, Ferdinand Christian, 274
Bavaria, 160
Beghards, 222, 223, 235
Beguinage, 223
Beguine movement, 222–23, 235
Beguines, 222–23, 235, 248
Benedict of Nursia, 94–95
Benedictine monasticism, 94–95, 159, 210–211
Benedictine rule, 94, 95, 177, 210–211
Benedictines, 210
Benjamin, Walter, 273, 277
Berengar of Tours, 245, 253

Berger, Peter L., 277
Bernard of Clairvaux, 211, 231
Bevans, Stephen B., 40, 277
Biblia Pauperum, 199
Bierma, Lyle D., 60, 279
Birgitta of Sweden, 209, 237
Black Death, 222
Blandina, 34
Blumenthal, Uta-Renate, 187, 277
Bogomiles, 219
Bohemia, 156, 239
Bonaventura, 209, 214, 246
Bonhoeffer, Dietrich, 277
Boniface VIII, pope, 184, 237
Boniface, missionary to Germany, 161
Boris, king of Bulgarians, 156
Bosch, David, 80, *157*, 278
Bowden, John, 20, 60, 277, 281, 282
Britain, 38, 127, 131–32, 145, 150, 173
Brothers Karamazov, 236
Brown, Peter, 136, 187, 278
Brown, Schuyler, 20, 278
Bruno of Cologne, Saint 211
Bulgaria, 156, 200, 219
Burgundians, 144, 147, 148, 154
Burning of the Vanities, 224

Caecilian, 85, 101
Caecilian of Carthage, bishop, 85, 101
Calabria, 202
Caliphs, 151
Calixtus, 182
Calvinists, 268
Canons Regular of St Augustine, 211
Canossa, 181–82
Canticle of the Sun (Francis of Assisi), 214
Cardinals, 178, 180, 195
Carolingian Dynasty, 177
Carolingian Renaissance, 244
Carpocrates from Alexandria, 46
Carpocratians, 46
Carthusians, 211
Cassian, 132
Cathars, 183, 215, 219, 224, 235–36
Catherine of Siena, 209, 237
Celibacy, 109, 178, 199
Celsus, 70

Cessationism, 57
Chadwick, Henry, 203, 278
Chalcedonian Christology, 119
Charlemagne, 145, 151, 154–55, 157, 174, 176, 183, 198, 244
Charles Martel, 151, 174
Children's Crusade, 223, 230, 232
Christmas, 89, 174
Christotokos, 120, 125
Cistercians, 210, 211
City of God (Augustine), 128, 133, 134
Clare from Assisi, 213
Clement, First Letter of 168,
Clement V, pope, 237
Clement of Alexandria, 46, 69, 71–74, 91, 242
Clement of Rome, 69, 168
Clement V, pope, 237
Clotilde, Frankish queen, 148
Clovis, 148, 154
Cluny, 96, 177–78, 180, 210–211
Cluny reform movement, 96, 177–78
Cohn, Norman, 221, 224, 278
Columba, 159
Columbanus, 159
Columbus, 141, 233
Communicatio Idiomatum, 125
Compendium against all Heresies, 46
Conceptualism, 254
Conciliar movement, 195, 226–27, 238–40
Conciliarism, 195, 238–41
Concordat of Worms, 182
Confessions (Augustine), 127–29, 135, 277
Congregation of the Holy Office, 237
Constantia, sister of Constantine, 108
Constantine, 32, 34, 40, 41, 82–88, 90–91, 98–99, 100–102, 105, 108, 113, 133–34, 149, 170, 172, 187, 267, 274, 278, 279, 281, 283
Constantine V, emperor, 191
Constantinian Donation, 175
Constantinople (see also Ecumenical Council of Constantinople, Constantinople), 84, 105, 111, 114, 119, 120–21, 122, 124, 133, 142, 143, 146, 153, 155–56, 170, 172–75, 183, 188, 189, 190–93, 195–97, 200–201, 203, 229, 231, 280
Constantinople, fall of, 142, 200
Constantius (son of Constantine), 108–9, 113, 277
Comte, Auguste, 221
Coptic Orthodox Church, 124, 153
Copts, 188
Corinthian Church, 20
Corpus Mixtum, 135
Council of Basel, 239–40
Council of Constance, 239–40
Council of Constantinople, see Ecumenical Council, Constantinople (second or fifth or sixth)
Council of Ferrara/Florence, 195, 240
Council of Nicaea, see Ecumenical Council, Nicaea, (first or seventh)
Council of Pisa, 239
Council of Trent, 57
Council of Vienne, 223
Cox, Harvey, 278
Crosier, 182
Crusades, 194, 212, 223, 226–36, 240–241, 246 278, 281, 282
Cur Deus Homo, 245
Cyprian, 35, 37, 40, 41, 168, 184
Cyril of Alexandria, 119–23
Cyril, missionary to the Slavic world, 155

d'Ailly, Pierre, 238
Damascus, 9, 114, 152, 192, 202, 231
Daniel, prophet of the OT, 35
David, king of Israel, 176, 220, 230,
Decius, emperor, 31–32, 37, 40–41
Denmark, 156, 157
DePalma Digeser, Elizabeth, 98, 278
Descartes, 136
Deus Absconditus, 264
Deus Revelatus, 264
Dialogue with Trypho, 69
Dickson, Gary, 224, 278
Didache, 20, 69, 281

288 Index

Diocletian, emperor, 32, *34*, 40, 84, 101, 107
Diodore of Tarsus, 118
Dionysius the Areopagite, 209, 243–45
Dioscorus of Alexandria, patriarch, 122
Docetist Christology, 48, 50, 119
Dome of the Rock, 229
Dominic of Guzman, 215
Dominicans, 213, 215, 219, 246, 248
Domitian, emperor, 30
Donation of Pippin, 175
Donatism, 101–2, 114
Donatist controversy, 100–103
Donatist Schism, 37, 107
Donatus, 101, *103*
Dostoevsky, 236
Drake, Harold Allen, 98, 278
Dunn, James, 18, 20, 59, 278
Duns Scotus, 214, 247, 256
Dyophysite, 190
Dyotheletism, 191

Eastern Frankish Empire, 160
Eastern Frankish Kingdom, 151, 155
Eastern Orthodox Church, 69, 183, 189, 192, 193, 194, 196–200, 202, 203, 204, 279
Ebeling, Gerhard, 278
Ebionitism, 117
Eco, Umberto, 253, 259, 278
Ecumenical Council, Chalcedon (fourth), 119, 122, 172
Ecumenical Council, Constantinople (fifth), 190
Ecumenical Council, Constantinople (second), 109–11, 114, 116, 124
Ecumenical Council, Constantinople (sixth), 191
Ecumenical Council, Ephesus (third), 119, 121–24, 188, 190
Ecumenical Council, Nicaea (first), 68, 84, 90, 105–9, 114, 124, 192, 282
Ecumenical Council, Nicaea (seventh), 192
Edessa, 28, 114, 229

Edict of Milan, 84, 94
Elijah, 92
Ephesus, 114, 117
Ephesus Council, 'robber synod' (449), 122
Episcopalism, 168–69
Epistle to Diognetus, 25
Essenes, 5, 8, 15, 21, 92
Estonia, 156
Ethiopia, 124, 153
Ethiopian Orthodox Church, 124
Eusebius of Caesarea, 29, 32–34, 69, 85, 90–91, 105, 106, 134, 274–75, 278
Eusebius of Nicomedia, 105, 106, 108
Eutyches, 122
Eutychian Debate, 122
Eutychianism, 119, 124
Evangelical Awakening, 268
Evangelicalism, 270
Evans, Gillian Rosemary, 164, 278
Ex Opere Operato, 158
Exclusivism,
Extra Ecclesiam Nulla Salus, 184
Ezra, IV, 15

Fall of Rome, xvi, 133–34, 144, 146
Felicitas (martyr), 34
Felix III, pope, 189
Ferguson, Niall, *xx*, 278
Fides Quaerens Intellectum, 252
Filioque, 197–98, 204, 244
Filofei, 201
Finland, 156
Flagellants, 221–22
Flavian of Constantinople, patriarch, 122
Francis of Assisi, 213–14, 221, 279
Franciscans, 213–16, 221, 246
Franks, 144, 148, 154, 174, 183
Frederick I Barbarossa, emperor, 222, 231
Frederick II, emperor, 222, 231
Frederick II, king, 182, 222, 231
Frend, William H.C., 40, 279
Freud, Sigmund, 273, 279
Frisia, 155
Fulcher of Chartres, 229, 230, 281

Fulda, 155
Fundamentalism, 270

Galerius, emperor, 32, 84
Gelasius I, pope, 171
Gerson, Jean, 238
Gnosis, 43, 46, 60, 74, 76, 281
Gnostic movement, Gnosticism, 42–44, 46–52, 56–61, 65, 72, 117, 279, 281
God-fearers, 7, 10–12, 21
Gospel of Thomas, 48, 57
Granada, 233
Grass, Tim, 275, 279
Great Awakening, 268, 274
Great Cappadocians, 69
Great Hallelujah, 223
Great Schism (of 1054), 193–94, 204, 266, 268, 269
Great Western Schism, 237–39, 241
Gregg, Robert C., 113, 279
Gregorian reform movement, 178, 217, 226, 237
Gregorios, Paulos, 136, 279
Gregory II, pope, 191
Gregory III, pope, 191
Gregory IX, pope, 236
Gregory of Nazianzus, 69, 109
Gregory of Nyssa, 69, 109
Gregory Palamas, 202, 209
Gregory the Great, pope, 158, 159
Gregory VII, pope, 178–81
Gregory, bishop of Tours, 148
Groh, Dennis E., 113, 279

Hadrian, emperor, 31
Hagia Sophia, 193
Harald Bluetooth, king of Denmark, 156, 157
Harnack, Adolf von, 47, 60, 279
Harrison, Carol, 136, 279
Hauerwas, Stanley, 270
Hegesippus, 69
Hellenist Christians, 7, 10–12, 19, 21, 38, 44, 50, 75, 81, 87
Hen, Yitzhak, 164, 279
Henoticon, 189–90
Henry III, emperor, 178, 180

Henry IV, king, 178, 180–81
Henry V, king, 182
Henry VI, king, 182
Herodian family, 8
Hesse, 155, 160
Hesychasm, 202, 203, 279
Heterousians, 108
Hildebrand, 180
Hildegard of Bingen, 209
Hillel, 8
Hippolytus of Rome, 46, 69
Holiness Revival, 268
Homoiousians, 108
Homoiousios, 112
Homoousians, 108–9
Homoousios, 106, 107, 110
Honorius, pope, 190–91
Horsley, Richard A., 12, 19, 20, 60, 279, 281
Hugo of St Victor, 209
Hugo, abbot of Cluny, 178
Humbert, 193
Humiliati, 216–17
Hussey, Joan Mervyn, 203, 279
Hylics, 49
Hypostasis, 122
Hypostatical Union, 122

Iberian Peninsula, 144, 148, 151, 233
Iceland, 156
Iconoclasm, 192
Iconodules, 191
Ignatios, patriarch, 192
Ignatius of Antioch, 34, 69
Incarnate logos, 18
Indifferentism, 254
Indulgences, 215, 222
Infancy Gospel of Thomas, 48
Infralapsarianism, 73
Innocent III, pope, 182–84, 213, 236
Inquisition, 183, 215, 219, 226, 235–37, 240, 282
Institutes (Calvin), 274
Investiture controversy, 96, 150, 167, 177–78, 182, 185–86, 187, 259, 277
Ireland, 145, 150
Irenaeus of Lyon, 69, 73

Irene, empress, 192
Irish monks, 95, 147, 150–51, 159
Isaiah, 29, 35, 220
Ivan IV, of Moscow, 201

Jacobites, 188
Jakob Boehme, 275
James, brother of the Lord, 9
Janssen, Martina, 60, 280
Jean Gerson, 238
Jenkins, Philip, 113, 137, 164, 279
Jerome, 69, 94
Jerusalem, 4–7, 10–11, 13–14, 16, 25, 37, 44, 58, 72, 107, 114, 134, 152, 153, 170, 195, 212, 229, 231, 233–35
Jerusalem Council, 9–11, 13, 21
Jewish Passover, 107
Jewish-Roman War (first), 14–15, 18, 20, 21, 44
Jewish-Roman War (second), 18
Joachim of Fiore, 221, 222
John Calvin, 274
John Climacus, 202
John Huss, 224, 239
John of Antioch, 121
John of Damascus, 192, 202
John of England, king, 183
John Scotus Eriugena, 245
John Tauler, 209, 248
John the Baptist, 8, 92
John Wycliffe, 224
Josephus, 4, 5
Julian of Norwich, 209, 248
Julian the Apostate, 85
Justin I, emperor, 190
Justin Martyr, 2, 28, 31, 34, 46, 69, 72, 279
Justinian I, emperor, 144, 190

Kiev, 200
King, Karen L., 60, 279
Krausmüller, Dirk, 203, 279
Kreider, Alan, 164, 280
Kyrios, 18, 19

Lai, Pin-chao, 53, 133, 280
Lateran Council, fourth (1215), 183

Lateran Council, second (1139), 178
Latvia, 156
Lay investiture, 150, 178, 180, 187
Lazareth, William H., 279
Le Goff, Jacques, 141
Leipzig Disputation, 275
Leo I, pope, 122, 125, 170–73, 189
Leo III, emperor, 191
Leo III, pope, 154, 174–75
Leo IX, pope, 178, 180, 193–94
Leo V, emperor, 192
Letter of Clement, 168
Letter of James, 14
Licinius, 84
Lieu, Judith M., 60, 280
Lieu, Samuel N.C., 47, 280
Limor, Ora, 240, 280
Lithuania, 156
Logos, xx, 18, 28, 62, 66, 67, 71, 74–75, 77–78, 87, 118, 119, 209
Logos christology, 66, 77, 78, 119
Logos Spermatikos, 67
Lombards, 144, 173, 174, 175
Lossky, Vladimir, 280
Louis IX, king of France, 231
Louth, Andrew, 80, 98, 203, 280, 283
Lüdemann, Gerd, 60, 280
Lutheran Orthodoxy, 268
Lyon, 34, 73, 114, 215

MacCulloch, Diarmaid, 273, 280
MacMullen, Ramsay, 98, 164, 280
Macrina the Younger, 109
Madigan, Kevin, 58, 280
Magna Carta, 238
Majorinus, 101
Malankara Jacobite Syrian Orthodox Church (Thomas Christian Church), 124
Maltesian Order, 212
Manchus, 147
Manichaeism, 46, 47, 87, 92, 127, 280
Marcian, 122
Marcion, 42, 43, 51–53, 57, 60, 61, 68, 267, 279, 280
Marcionism, 51–53
Marcus Aurelius, 31, 67
Mark (gospel), 78, 279

Marsilius of Padua, 238
Martin I, pope, 191
Martin Luther, 264
Marx, Karl, 221
Masada, 15
Maxentius, 82, 84
Maximilla, 54
Maximinus, 32
Maximus the Confessor, 191, 202
McGrath, Alister E., 80, 259, 280
Mechthild of Magdeburg, 209, 248, 249, 280
Medieval investiture controversy, see Investiture controversy
Meister Eckhart, 209, 248
Meletian Schism, 107
Meletius, 107
Melito of Sardis, 69
Mellitus, abbot, 162
Merlo, Grado, 224, 280
Methodism, 268
Methodius, missionary to the Slavic world, 155
Meyendorff, John, 203, 280
Miaphysite Christianity, 153, 154, 190
Michael Cerularius, patriarch, 193
Miecislav, ruler of Poland, 156
Minucius Felix, 69
Mitchell, Margaret M., 40, 113, 279, 283
Mithras, 38, 87
Modalism (Modalist Monarchianism), 78
Moffett, Samuel, 40, 280
Monarchic Episcopate, 58, 168
Monasticism, 51, 69, 83, 91, 93-99, 130, 159, 165, 202, 210, 211, 235
Monasticism, communal (Pachomianism), 93-94
Monenergism, 190
Monophysite Churches, 119
Monophysites, 123, 153, 172, 188, 190
Monotheletism, 190, 191
Montanism, 42, 53-56, 60, 61, 282
Montanus, 43, 54-55, 60
Moravia, 155-56
Morris, Colin, 187, 280
Mosaic Law, 5, 7, 8, 10-12, 20, 53, 74

Moses, 10, 52, 71, 92, 176
Moses Maimonides, 246
Mother Mary, 89, 120, 126
Mount Athos, 202
Mount Tabor, 202
Muhammad, 151-52, *153*, 282
Muslims, 102, 223, 227, 229, 231, 233-36
Mysticism, 97, 203, 208, 209, 211, 224, 243, 248

Nag Hammadi, 46
Neo-Platonism, 62, 65-67, 76, 78, 80, 208, 242, 255
Nero, 28, 29, 40,
Nestorian Debate, 118, 119, 122, 197
Nestorianism, 122
Nestorius, 119-21, 125, 190
Nicene Creed, 107, 108, 110, 115, 192, 197, 198, 244
Nicene Party, 170
Niceno-Constantinopolitan Creed, 110, 115
Nicholas I, pope, 176, 192
Niebuhr, H.R., *267, 269, 271*, 281
Nirenberg, David, 240, 281
Nissiotis, Niko A., 136, 279
Nominalism, 252-55
Non-Chalcedonian Churches (Oriental Orthodox Churches), 119, 124, 126,
Non-Chalcedonians, 197
Norway, 156
Novatian, 35-37, 41, 101, 107
Novatian Schism, 36-37, 41, 101, 107

Odilo, abbot of Cluny, 178
Odoacer, 145
Ophites, 46
Order of Hospitallers, 212
Order of Knights Templar, 212
Order of Preachers, 215
Order of St Augustine, 212
Order of the Poor Clares (Clarisses), 213
Origen of Alexandria, 32, 34, 38, 51, 69, 73-75, 92, 105, 115, 208
Origenist theology, 106

Osborn, Eric Francis, 80, 281
Osiek, Carolyn, 58, 280
Ostrogoths, 144–47
Otto the Great, king, 145, 157, 176
Otto, Rudolf, 265
Ousia, 64, 106, 109

Pachomius, 93
Paideia, 74
Pantheism, 252
Pantocrator, 87
Papal absolutism, 184, 186
Paraclete, 54
Parousia, 25
Paschasius Radbertus, 245
Patres Ecclesiae, 68
Patrick, Saint, 150
Patristic theology, xx, 62–63, 68, 73, 75–77, 81, 203, 242, 255, 259
Paul, apostle, 3, 4, 9–13, 17–20, 22, 24, 29, 39, 50, 52, 68, 71, 130–31, 168, 243, 269
Paul of Samosata, 78
Paulicians, 219
Pegg, Mark Gregory, 240, 281
Pelagian Conflict, 133
Pelagianism, 120, 132, 137
Pelagius, 127, 131–33, 138, 157
Pentecostals, 211, 268, 275
Pepin, Frankish king, 148
Perpetua, martyr, 34
Peter, apostle, 10, 29, 162, 168, 170–73, 183, 194
Peter the Lombard, 245
Peter Abelard, see Abelard, Peter
Pharisees, 8, 15–16, 20, 21
Philip IV, king of France, 237
Philipp the Arabian, 38
Philo of Alexandria, 65–66, 74, 78
Photian Schism, 192
Photios of Constantinople, patriarch, 156, 192, 200
Phrygia, 54
Physis, 109, 122, 125
Pietism, 268
Pippin, king, 154, 174, 175
Pistis, 76
Pius X, pope, 237

Plato, 55, 63–66, 71, 98, 208, 246, 250, 253, 255, 280, 281
Platonism, platonist, 47, 62–63, 65–67, 74–76, 78, 80–81, 208, 242, 250
Pliny the Younger, 30, 281
Plotin, 66
Pneumatomachians, 110
Poland, 156
Poliakov, Léon, 234, 281
Polycarp of Smyrna, 34, 69
Ponticianus, 128
Ponticus (martyr), 34
Porphyrios, 66
Poseidonios, 67
Prayer of 18 Benedictions, 18
Premonstratensians, 212
Priscilla, 54
Prosopon, 78, 109
Pulcheria, 122
Purgatory, 215
Puritans, 270
Pythagoreans, 73

Quadratus, 69
Qumran, 8, 15

Rabbinic Judaism, 15, 17–18
Radical Reformation, 238, 258, 268
Rationalism, 243, 254, 256–57
Ravenna, 147, 170, 173, 175
Realism, 251–53, 260
Recared I, Visigoth king of Spain, 148
Refutation of all Heresies, by Hippolytus 46
Renaissance, 141, 244, 281
Richard the Lionhearted, 231
Riley-Smith, Jonathan, 240, 281
Ritschl, Dietrich, 273, 281
Robber Synod (449), 122
Roldanus, Johannes, 98, 281
Romulus Augustulus, 145
Roscellin, 253
Rossing, Barbara R., 60, 281
Roukema, Riemer, 60, 281
Russia, 154, 156, 200, 201, 203, 277
Russian Orthodox Christianity, 200

Sabellianism, 78, 110
Sabellius, 78
Sacking of Rome, 127, 171
Sadducees, 9, 21
Saladin, sultan, 231
Santiago de Compostela, 227
Saturnalia, 89
Scholasticism, 243, 245–46
School of Antioch, 118, 119
Schroeder, Roger P., 40, 277
Scotland, 145, 150, 159, 238
Second Temple, 14
Secular investiture, 150, 178
Secularization, 186, 269, 278
Seljuk Turks, 229
Semi-Pelagianism, 132, 137
Seneca, 67
Septimius Severus, emperor, 31
Sergius of Constantinople, 190
Severus Alexander, 38
Shammai, 8
Shepherd of Hermas, 69
Silberman, Neil A., 20, 279
Simony, 150, 178, 187
Sinai, 202
Smith, Andrew, 80, 282
Smith, Lesley, 259, 282
Socrates, 27, 28, 71, 256
Sol Invictus, 31, 89
Spiritual Franciscans, 221
St Catherine's Monastery, 202
Stark, Rodney, xx, 31, 35, 39, 40, 77, 205, 212, 234, 240, 259, 282
Steely, John E., 279
Stephen III, pope, 174
Stephen, of the seven deacons (NT), 6, 21
Stoa, 67, 92
Stoicism, 62, 67
Stylites, 93
Supersessionism, 16
Supralapsarianism, 73
Sweden, 156, 209, 237
Sylvester I, pope, 172
Symeon the New Theologian, 202
Symeon the Stylite, 93
Symmachus, 171, 172
Syncretism, 163

Synod of Clermont, 229
Synod of Orange (Southern France), 132
Syriac Orthodox Church, 124, 125

Taborites, 202
Tacitus, 4, 29, 40, 282
Tatian, 69, 72, 93
Tertullian, 26, 46, 51, 54, 55–56, 69, 72–74, 119, 122
Teutonic Knights, 212
The Imitation of Christ, 35, 104, 132, 248, 272
Theissen, Gerd, 20, 282
Theoderic the Great, Ostrogoth king, 145, 147
Theodora, empress, 192
Theodore of Mopsuestia, 118, 190
Theodore, abbot, 192
Theodosius II, emperor, 121–22
Theodosius I, the Great, emperor, 86, 110
Theosis, 74, 131
Theotokos, 120, 121, 125
Thessaloniki, 155
Thomas Aquinas, 215, 246, 282
Thomas de Torquemada, 236
Thomas of Kempen, 248
Thomas, apostle, 57
Thomism, 257
Thomsett, Michael C., 240, 282
Thor, 161
Thuringia, 160
Tillich, Paul, 263, 282
Tome, by Pope Leo I, 172, 189
Torah, 12, 13, 15, 16, 18
Trajan, emperor, 30, 31, 41
Transubstantiation, 193, 245, 253
Trevett, Christine, 53, 282
Trinitarian, Trinitarian Formula of God, 62, 74, 77, 79–81, 109–12, 116, 118, 147, 170, 197
Trinity, 78–81, 113, 116, 197, 257
Tripoli, 229
Tuchman, Barbara, 234, 240, 282

Ullmann, Walter, 187, 282
Umayyads, 151

Unam Sanctam, 184
University, 243, 246
University of Bologna, 246
Urban II, pope, 229

Valentinians, 46
Valerian, emperor, 31, 32, 41
Van Nieuwenhove, Rik, 259, 282
Vandals, 144–47, 171
Vasilij III, grand prince of Moscow, 201
Verbum Alienum, 264
Verbum Revelatum, 264
Via Antiqua, 247
Via Augustiniana Moderna, 247
Via Moderna, 247
Vicarius Christi, 183
Visigoths, 144, 147
Vladimir of Kiev, 200
Vladimir the Great, Czar, 156
Voluntarism, 243, 254, 257

Wailing Wall, 14
Waldensians, 215, 216, 219, 223–24
Waldes, 215–16
Walls, Andrew F., xvii, 282

Weaver, William, 259, 278
Whalen, Brett Edward, 187, 224, 282
Wilken, Robert Louis, 80, 283
William I, Duke of Aquitaine, 177
William of Champeaux, 245
William of Ockham, 238, 247, 253
Willibald, missionary to Germany, 161
Willibrord, missionary to Frisia, 155
World Council of Churches, 126, 136, 270, 279
Wulfila, Apostle to the Goths, 147

Xie Fuya, 53
Xunzi, 133

Yavneh, 15
Young Robin Darling, 40, 283
Young, Frances M., 40, 113, 279, 283

Zealots, 8, 14, 15, 21
Zeno (Stoa), 67
Zeno, emperor, 67, 189
Zoroastrianism, 46
Zwinglians, 268

www.ingramcontent.com/pod-product-compliance
Lightning Source LLC
Chambersburg PA
CBHW021650230426
43668CB00008B/574